A SHAMBHALA THRESHOLD BOOK

# SIGNS OF THE UNSEEN

*The Discourses of*

# JALALUDDIN RUMI

Introduction & Translation by
W. M. Thackston, Jr.

SHAMBHALA

*Boston & London*

1999

SHAMBHALA PUBLICATIONS, INC.
Horticultural Hall
300 Massachusetts Avenue
Boston, Massachusetts 02115
www.shambhala.com

9  8  7  6  5  4  3  2  1
Printed in the United States of America
♾ This edition is printed on acid-free paper
that meets the American National Standards Institute Z39.48 Standard.
Distributed in the United States by Random House, Inc.,
and in Canada by Random House of Canada Ltd

Library of Congress Cataloging-in -Publications Data

Jalāl al-Dīn Rūmī, Maulana, 1207–1273.
[Fīhi mā fīh. English]
Signs of the unseen: the discourses of Jalaluddin Rumi /
introduction & translation by W. M. Thackston, Jr.
p. cm.
Originally published: Putney, VT. : Threshold Books, 1994.
Includes bibliographical references.
ISBN 1–57062–532–8 (pbk.)
I. Sufism—Early works to 1800. I. Thackston, W. M. (Wheeler
McIntosh), 1994– . II. Title.
BP189.7.M42A323  1999
297.4—dc21                                                    99–31398
                                                                          CIP

# CONTENTS

# INTRODUCTION

## Biographical Sketch[1]

Mawlana Jalaluddin Muhammad, known as Rumi,[2] was born in 1207 in the metropolis of Balkh, today in northern Afghanistan, long one of the greatest centers for the study, practice, and inculcation of Islamic mysticism. Jalaluddin's father, Baha'uddin Muhammad, known as Baha Valad, was one of the leading theologians, preachers, and masters of Sufism in Balkh. Through his influence the young Jalaluddin received a thorough education in the then current Arabic and Persian classical and religious studies. Special attention was given as a matter of course to Koranic reading, exegesis, and interpretation, to Islamic jurisprudence, and to *hadith*—the study of the words and acts of the Prophet Muhammad and his companions, with which Rumi shows an intimate familiarity in his works.

---

[1]The primary sources for Rumi's biography are (1) the *Ibtidanama* of his son Sultan Valad, (2) a biography by a disciple of Rumi, Faridun ibn Ahmad Sipahsalar, *Risala dar ahval-i Mawlana Jalaluddin Mawlavi*, and (3) the *Manaqib al-'arifin* by Shamsuddin Ahmad al-Arifi. A full bibliography of printed material on Rumi may be found in Mehmet Önder et al., *Mevlana Bibliyografyasi*.

[2]He is known by the Turks as Mevlâna, the Turkish pronunciation of the Arabic *mawlânâ* ("our lord," a title accorded to masters of Sufism and other learned persons). It is from this same epithet that the order of dervishes of which he was the founder, the Mevlevi, takes its name. From this same derivation comes Mawlavi, the name by which he is generally known in the Persian-speaking world. Because of his long residence in Anatolia (see below), called by the Muslims *Rûm* after its Byzantine designation of "East Rome," he is known in the West as Rumi. By birth he was Balkhi.

Balkh was a flourishing seat of learning and a commercial center during the early years of the thirteenth century, but the political climate was growing ever more threatening as the Mongol onslaught from Inner Asia began to make itself felt in the region. The imprudent execution of some Mongol merchants by the Khwarazmshah,[3] in whose realm Balkh lay, was to have catastrophic effects: in 1220 Balkh was overrun, sacked, and reduced to rubble by the Mongols. Mawlana Baha'uddin and his family, however, had migrated from Balkh a year or two prior to this devastation, probably, like many others, influenced by tales of horror borne by those whose lands had already been destroyed by the Mongolian horde. The wanderings of the family took them through Baghdad to Mecca, then to Syria and finally to Central Anatolia, where they settled in Laranda (present-day Karaman, Turkey). There Jalaluddin was married to Jawhar Khatun, a young woman originally from Samarkand.

In 1228, at the invitation of Prince Ala'uddin Kay-Qubad, Baha Valad took his family to Konya, the thriving capital of the Rum Seljuq sultans and, at that time, still far from the reach of the Mongols, and there he taught and preached as he had done in Balkh. In January 1231 Baha'uddin Valad, the "Sultan of the Learned," died, leaving his son Jalaluddin as his successor.

Shortly after Baha'uddin's death, one of his former pupils, Sayyid Burhanuddin Muhaqqiq of Termez, arrived in Konya. It was he who initiated the young Jalaluddin into the mysteries of the spiritual life. Up to that time he seems not to have taken more than a passing interest in mysticism, but he had been an eager student of the intricate Arabic poetry of al-Mutanabbi, lines of whose corpus he often quotes in his discourses. After his discipleship with Burhanuddin, Jalaluddin was sent to Aleppo and Damascus to complement his formal spiritual training by meeting with other Sufi masters. He remained nominally under Burhanuddin's tutelage until

---

[3]This event is mentioned in the text, section 15.

the latter's death in nearby Kayseri in 1240. For several years thereafter Rumi was alone, teaching and ministering to his pupils and disciples. In October 1244, however, an enigmatic figure, a wandering dervish named Shamsuddin Muhammad of Tabriz, arrived in Konya and stopped at the hostel of the sugar merchants.

At that time Mawlana was engaged in teaching. One day he rode out of the school with a group of learned men and chanced to pass the sugar merchants' hostel. Shamsuddin came up, took Mawlana's horse by the bridle, and asked, "Leader of Muslims, was Bayazid greater, or the Prophet?"[4]

Mawlana later said, "Due to the tremendousness of that question, it was as though the seven heavens were ripped apart and came crashing down to earth. A great conflagration arose from within me and set fire to my brain, whence I saw a column of smoke rising to the pillars of God's Throne. I replied, 'The Prophet is the greatest of all human beings. Why speak of Bayazid?'

"He asked, 'Then how can the Prophet have said, "We have not known Thee as Thou ought to be known," while Bayazid said, "Glory be to Me! How great am I!" and, "I am the power of Powers!"?'

"I answered, 'Bayazid's thirst was slaked with one gulp. He spoke of being full, and the jug of his comprehension was filled. His illumination was only as much as came through the skylight of his house. The Prophet, on the other hand, sought to be given much to drink and thirsted after thirst. . . . He spoke of thirst and was ever beseeching to be drawn closer.'"

Shamsuddin uttered a cry and fell unconscious. Mawlana got down from his horse and told his pupils to take Shamsuddin to the school. When he came to himself again, he placed his blessed head on Mawlana's knees.

---

[4]For Bayazid of Bistam see Glossary of Persons.

Afterward Mawlana took him by the hand and departed. For three months they were in isolation, day and night in the feast of union, and never once did they emerge. No one cared to interrupt their privacy.[5]

Rumi's friends and students were scandalized to see their sober master so completely absorbed in this bizarre dervish, but in him Jalaluddin had found the ideal "beloved," the one in whom the Divine was most perfectly mirrored. If it were not enough for Rumi to have become infatuated with Shams, his preoccupation with his "prince of the beloveds" took him away from his disciples, who became jealous and angry to the point of threatening Shams' life. Shortly after their meeting, Shams suddenly disappeared, and Mawlana was left disconsolate.

The loss of Shams and the longing engendered in his soul for his spiritual beloved moved Mawlana to sing his passionate yearning in lyric Persian poetry. Eventually, it was discovered that Shamsuddin had gone to Damascus; and Rumi's eldest son, Sultan Valad, was dispatched to bring him back. Shams was installed in Mawlana's home and married to a young woman of the household. There he remained until 1248, when he disappeared once more and was never found again. The accusation of murder leveled by Aflaki, one of the early biographers, against Rumi's second son is now generally accepted as valid."

Mawlana was profoundly shocked by this second separation and went himself to Syria once, perhaps twice, to search for his friend. In the end, however, he realized that the physical, or "metaphoric" Shams was not to be found and that he should rather seek out the "real" Shams within himself. The process of complete identification between lover and beloved had been completed: Jalaluddin and Shamsuddin were no longer two separate entities; they were one forever.[6]

---

[5]Narrated by Jami, *Nafahât al-uns*, p. 465f. Translation mine.

[6]Annemarie Schimmel, *The Triumphal Sun*, p. 23.

Not long thereafter, Mawlana Jalaluddin discovered a new "mirror" to reflect perfect love, this time in the person of Salahuddin Faridun Zarkub, a goldsmith who had been a disciple of Sayyid Burhanuddin Muhaqqiq. If Rumi's attachment to Shamsuddin—who was, for all his peculiarity, a highly educated and learned person—was difficult for Mawlana's disciples to tolerate, this new spiritual union with an uncultivated craftsman was more than they could bear. Rumi ignored the gossip and slander, however, and continued his association with Salahuddin in quiet friendship, a marked contrast with the fiery ardor that had characterized his attachment to Shams. During Salahuddin's protracted illness that led to his death in 1258, the need for a "mirror" onto which the lover could cast his image once again manifested itself, and Rumi emerged as an inspired master and teacher against the reflection of Husamuddin Chelebi, an ascetically-minded man Mawlana had long known. It was Husamuddin's request that inspired Rumi to compose the *Masnavi*,[7] and for years Husamuddin was at his master's side to record every verse he uttered.

After an active life of teaching, counseling, and ministering to the needs of his disciples and friends, Mawlana Jalaluddin died on December 17, 1273. During his final illness he said to his friends, "In this world I have two attachments, one to the body and one to you. When, of God's grace, I shall be disembodied in the world of solitude and abstraction, my attachment to you will still exist."[8]

---

[7] It had been assumed that Husamuddin's inspiration to compose the *Masnavi* came only after Salahuddin's death, but Professors Schimmel and Gölpïnarli have shown from internal evidence in the *Masnavi* and *Divan* that Husamuddin was already close to Rumi before Salahuddin died and that the first book of the *Masnavi* was dictated between 1256 and 1258. See Schimmel, *The Triumphal Sun*, p. 34.

[8] Jami, *Nafahat al-uns*, p. 463. Translation mine.

## Rumi's Written Legacy[9]

Rumi "wrote" no books in the conventional manner. What we possess today of his prose and poetry was either taken down by his disciples from oral recitation or dictation and checked by him, as is the case with the *Masnavi* and the *Divan*, or written down by his followers from memory or notes after his death, as is most likely the case with *Signs of the Unseen* (Fihi ma fihi).

Mawlana Rumi's major work is the monumental *Masnavi-i ma'navi*, or *Masnavi of Intrinsic Meaning*.[10] Divided into six books and containing about 25,000 couplets, the *Masnavi* was composed at the request of and dedicated to Rumi's third inspirer, Husamuddin Chelebi. Through the rambling medium of story, anecdote, and tale, many layered one inside another and interspersed with interpretation and parallel digression, the *Masnavi* touches upon every aspect of spiritual learning and thought. Like his father before him, Rumi excels in the elevation of the mundane to the sublime and can see a profoundly mystical reality manifested in a pot of chickpeas boiling on a stove. From a pious anecdote drawn from the Prophet's career to a vulgar story, he runs the

---

[9]Rumi composed in his native tongue, Persian, the learned language of the Seljuqs and the Ottoman Turks after them. There are occasional lines in the *Masnavi*, whole poems in the *Divan*, and entire sections in *Fihi ma fih* in Arabic, not at all unusual in a society that used Persian for polite discourse but was educated from childhood in Arabic. There are a few stray lines in the *Masnavi* and *Divan* in Turkish and even in the colloquial Greek of Anatolia, which are of some philological interest. See Mecdut Mansuroglu, "Celâleddîn Rûmî's türkische Verse," and "Mevlâna Celâleddin Rûmî'de türkçe beyit ve ibareler," and P. Burguière and R. Mantran, "Quelques vers grecs du XIIIe siècle en caractères arabes."

[10]*Masnavî* is a Persian poetic form consisting of rhymed couplets. It is used for long didactic, epic, or historical narrative poems. The *Masnavî-i ma'navî* was edited, translated into English, and commented upon by Reynold A. Nicholson in eight volumes and published in the E.J.W. Gibb Memorial Series. For other translations see the bibliography.

gamut of human experience, ties it in to the mystical realization of the divine purpose and compacts it into the terse poetic form. It is probably safe to say that from the time of its completion, no book within the realm of Islam, with the exception of the Koran, has been so venerated and revered as Rumi's *Masnavi*, which to this day is called "the Koran in the Persian tongue"—so all-embracing, authoritative and inspired are its contents felt to be.

Rumi's other major work is the enormous collection of his short poems, the *Divan-i Shams-i Tabriz*,[11] which comprises his *ghazals*, quatrains and other, less common forms. Rumi's identity has so completely merged with his alter ego that in the last line of his *ghazals*—where by convention in persian poetry the poet inserts his own pen name—Rumi placed the name of his beloved Shams of Tabriz. In contrast to the highly artificial, controlled, and refined style that characterizes the typical Persian *ghazal*, Rumi's poems—often recited extemporaneously while in an ecstatic state—are spontaneous outpourings of a soul elated with mystical joy and enraptured with divine love. His poetic style is so idiosyncratic and his *ghazals* so spontaneous that, although it has always been reckoned among the best of the genre, they are seen as too alien to the Persian poetic tradition—with its emphasis on elegance and polish—to attract imitation. The highly rhythmic quality of many of his poems confirms the observation made by his biographers that he often composed while dancing or whirling around a pole. In his enthusiasm he even on occasion violated the most sacrosanct of the canons of Persian poetry, the meter. In fact, Rumi disclaimed being a poet, which he equated with a profession that not only dealt with the intricacies of rhyme, metrics, and poetic artifice but also involved sycophancy and dependence upon the favor and whim of patronage. In one of

---

[11]The *Divan* was edited by Badi'uzzaman Furuzanfar in ten volumes and published by the University of Tehran as, *Kulliyyat-i Shams, ya divan-i kabir*. For selections and translations see the bibliography.

his discourses he says that he is annoyed and vexed by poetry and only "spouts rhymes" to keep his audience amused: it is like having to put one's hands into tripe, he says, because one's guest has an appetite for it.

In addition to the *Masnavi* and *Divan*, we possess 144 of Mawlana Jalaluddin's letters, which were collected and preserved by his followers.[12] The majority of the letters are addressed to the Parvana Mu'inuddin or other officials and grandees of Konya and were written on behalf of those in need of assistance.

In addition to Rumi's recorded sermons and sessions, in *Signs of the Unseen*, there are the homilies preserved in the *Majalis-i sab'a-i Mawlana* (Sermons from Seven of Mawlana's Sessions).[13]

*Signs of the Unseen* (Fihi ma fihi)[14] is a collection of Rumi's lectures, discourses, conversations, and comments on

---

[12]For editions and translations see the bibliography.

[13]For editions and translations see the bibliography.

[14]The Arabic title of the book means literally "in it what is in it" and implies a miscellaneous collection of disparate pieces. The phrase appears to have been adopted from an Arabic occasional piece that occurs in Muhyiddin Ibn-Arabi's *al-Futûhât al-makkiyya* (Bulaq edition, II, 777): *Kitâbun fîhi mâ fîhi / badî'un fî ma'ânîhi // idhâ 'âyanta mâ fîhi / ra'ayta 'l-durra yahwîhi* ("This is a book that contains what it contains, novel in its meanings. If you look closely at what is in it, you will see that it contains pearls of wisdom.") This title occurs on the cover of the manuscript used as the basis for editing up to section 45 (Fâtih Library, Istanbul, No. 2760), dated A.H. 716 (A.D. 1317) it is also mentioned by Faridun b. Ahmad Sipahsalar in his *Ahval-i Mawlana* (p. 68), which was composed ca. 1320-30. On the other hand, manuscript H (Fâtih Library, Istanbul, No. 5408), dated A.H. 751 (A.D. 1350) and used as basis from the middle of section 45 to the end, calls the book *al-Asrâr al-jalâliyya* ("Tremendous Mysteries," or, punning on Rumi's name Jalaluddin, "Jalalian Mysteries"). Rumi was not fond of Ibn-Arabi's theosophical philosophizing and almost certainly would not have borrowed from his work; however, from the end of the thirteenth century on, Ibn-Arabi's theories dominated Sufistic thinking to such an extent that it is not at all surprising to see this literary reference attached to Mawlana's sessions. *Kitâb-i Fîhi mâ fîhi* was edited by

various topics. Most of the seventy-one sections contained in the book are representative of the loose, associative nature of a master Sufi's "session" *(majlis)*, or informal gathering with his pupils and disciples, during which the master expounds on one or more subjects. The topic may be introduced by a question or comment from one of those present; such sections often begin with the phrase, "So-and-So said," or "Someone said." In other sections we are given only the substance of Mawlana's discourse. If some sections appear to contain many different topics without clear demarcation or transition from one topic to the next, this is due either to the informal nature of the session or to the original collators' artificial assembling of various bits and pieces of Mawlana's discourses in one section.

Although many, or even all, of the sections may have been written down during Rumi's lifetime, it is fairly certain that the collection as a whole was not made until after his death. The form of the book is reminiscent of his father's collection of discourses,[15] which generally tend more toward the visionary (like section 34 of *Signs of the Unseen*).

Because Mawlana's major works are in poetry and his ideas are often loosely developed or alluded to through the symbolic imagery of that genre, in many cases the discussion with his disciples preserved in *Signs of the Unseen* provides us with the most sustained exposition available of his thought on a given topic. Nonetheless, Rumi was everywhere poetic and laced his prose with much the same associative allusion

---

Badî'uzzamân Furûzânfar. For translations see the bibliography. The discourses, like all of Rumi's other works, are in Persian, with the exception of sections 22, 29, 34 (except the first phrase), 43, 47, 48 (except middle section), and 71, which are in Arabic, as are the numerous quotations from prophetic *hadith*, sayings of various Sufis, and Arabic poetry.

[15]The *Ma'arif* of Baha'uddin Valad have been edited by Badi'uzzaman Furuzanfar in two volumes. Twenty sections of the *Ma'arif* have been translated by A. J. Arberry in his *Aspects of Islamic Civilization as Depicted in the Original Texts*, pp. 227–55.

that characterizes his emotive and imaginative didactic poetry. Not a systematic thinker himself, and even hostile by and large to methodical philosophers and rationalist theologians, Rumi nowhere organizes his ideas in a structured fashion. This is not to say that he was unacquainted with the technique of philosophical or theological argument, in which he had been well trained as a youth, for he does exhibit his facility with the style in more than one section of the discussion. However, ever chary of being forced into doctrinal terms, he generally prefers parable and symbol, not only for their elusiveness but more importantly because the symbolic is the only means available to the mystic to express realities beyong the intellect he wants to awaken within his audience. Most, if not all, writers of the mystical experience have been forced into the same position. Since their perception is beyond reason they are unable to communicate the experience in a rationally structured manner and must perforce resort to a symbolic treatment.

## Rumi's Spirituality and the Tradition of Sufism

Rumi's works fall within the realm of Islamic thought and practice known as Sufism. Sufism had begun around the ninth century as a strictly ascetic movement, but by the thirteenth century it had become an institutionalized alternative expression of piety within the broad Islamic social and religious fabric. Often called "Islamic mysticism," Sufism is mystical in the original sense of the word, that is, an initiation into the mysteries or inner workings of the faith. At no time has Sufism been at odds with the essential tenets of Islam, which it indeed takes as its basis,[16] although

---

[16]The sources of authority for Sufism, like any other branch of Islamic learning, derive directly from the Koran, considered to be God's word revealed to the Prophet Muhammad, and *sunna*, the practice of the Prophet as recorded in the *hadith*. To these two, however, the Sufis add an important third source of authority: inner, or gnostic revelation, the locus of which is the hearts of God's saints: "There is no knowledge known or

individual Sufis often incurred the wrath of theologians, not so much for doctrinal lapses as for their bizarre lifestyles or for incautious, ambiguous public statements of esoteric belief. The only real distinction between non-Sufistic Islam and Sufism is the one made by the Sufis themselves: Sufism is not content with the outer, external manifestations of religion but internalizes or interiorizes them for a spiritual awareness of the esoteric significance of exoteric doctrine. That is, Sufism looks beyond the manifest form of religion into the spiritual reality, a practice that necessitated the development of an idiom that often appeared blasphemous to the uninitiated.

Islam, which sees itself as the final and full revelation of Abrahamic monotheism and the Mosaic law, stresses God's utter transcendence from his creation. With this Sufism is in full agreement: "Whatever you imagine God to be, he is different from that," as an early Sufi expressed the concept.[17] While maintaining that nothing is like God and that he has no equal imaginable, the Sufis also see in the very transcendence of the deity that he is immanent in his creation. "Whatever notion you have of God," says Rumi, "He must be something like that because he is the creator of all your

---

anything understood that is not found in God's book, or traceable back to the Prophet, or in what is revealed to the hearts of God's friends" (Sarraj, *Kitab al-luma' fi'l-tasawwuf*, p. 1f.). Rumi discusses gnostic revelation on p. *7. Intuitive inspiration persists in the world—unlike prophetic inspiration, or the revelation of God's law through a prophet-spokesman—which was ended by Muhammad, the last revelatory prophet.

[17] Attributed to Dhu'l-Nun of Egypt (d. 859) in Qushayri, *al-Risala al-Qushayriyya*, I, 29. The saying was expanded by Abu-Ali Ahmad al-Rudhbari (d. 934): "Whatever in ignorance you imagine Him to be, reason indicates that He is otherwise" (Qushayri, p. 39). See also Sana'i, *Hadiqat*, p. 386: "Whatever comes to your mind that I am that, I am not that."

notions."[18] God's creatures are not like Him in any way; yet they cannot be other than Him either.

The ontological view of the Sufis is based, as is all of Islamic doctrine practically speaking, on *tawhid,* the affirmation of God's uncompromising unity and oneness, a concept that allows for nothing to be worshiped or adored but God, for the likening of anything to God in any respect whatsoever would constitute another "divinity." As a necessary corollary, *tawhid* posits existence to God alone, so that anything perceived to exist can possess no reality of its own but must be nothing more than a reflection of the one divine Reality.[19]

Symbolically stated, and based on a Koranic passage (7:172), before the creation of serial time and space, before God's fiat that brought the cosmos into being, the undifferentiated souls of potential mankind slumbered as an idea within God in the unfathomable recess of infinity. Since there was no created being to adore the deity, God said, in a divine *hadith* often quoted by the Sufis, "I was a hidden treasure and wanted to be known, and so I created creation that I might be known." Humankind, therefore, along with the rest of creation, was made to know God; but, according to an epistemological premise put forward many times by Rumi, one can know a thing only through its opposite. Because it is unthinkable, in terms of *tawhid,* for God to have an opposite in substance, he remains substantially unknowable. As the Sufis put it paradoxically, the only way one has to know God is one's own inability to know him. However, in form or attribute, it is possible to imagine an

---

[18]So also Fakhruddin Iraqi: "Every image that appears on the slate of existence is a picture of the one who drew the image" (Iraqi, *Lama'at,* p. 380).

[19]This is summed up in the Muslim profession of faith: the first, or negative half of which (*la ilah,* "no god") strips everything of objective existence; the second, or positive half (*illa 'llah,* "but God") then posits essential reality to God alone.

opposite to God. For instance, the opposite in attribute to God's light is the nothingness of darkness created to reflect his light: the reflection of that light is this created world, in which all things are manifestations of God, and their end is to know him.

All things manifest God, whether they are aware of it or not. The believer manifests the attributes of faith and positive testimony to God's existence; the unbeliever also manifests God by his denial of God's existence, which provides the opposite against which faith becomes knowable. God manifests Himself in His beautiful and beneficent attributes, through the good things of the earth; He manifests Himself through the opposites to good, ugliness and evil, and thus provides the means to know good and beauty. In relation to God, as Rumi says, all things are good because God is good and beautiful, and it is a logical absurdity to think that He would create His opposite. What appears to man to be ugly or evil is only so in relation to man—that is, evil provides the opposite whereby man can know truth and beauty, but it has no real existence as evil in relation to God. What we perceive through our senses in this world is only form, a coincidental shell that has temporarily adhered to an aspect of the essences that exist in Rumi's "other world." For Mawlana the distinction between "this world" and the other, or "that world," is crucial. They are not two separate, distinct worlds so much as they are two aspects of a continuum, the back and front of a mirror, as he often puts it. This world, which is inhabited by corporeal creatures, is the dense, gross end of the spectrum of matter and exists within time and space. The "other world" is the subtle, incorporeal end of the same spectrum, wherein are contained the universal archetypes, or essences of everything that is manifest here. According to Rumi that world is the realm of intrinsic concepts, which have a higher status of reality than the "metaphorical" phantasmagoria of this world. However, these concepts or essences are not apprehensible to the physical eye, which is limited in its sphere of operation to the sensibles of this world. In Rumi's image, all things that are manifested in this world are like the leaves on a tree: the tree's root lies buried in the invisible world, but its branches spread over the dividing wall into this world, where they bear fruit.

If that world is the realm of the substance, this world is the realm of form. Although the substance is naturally of more importance in Rumi's eyes, it cannot be reached without regard for the form itself. Far from denigrating the value of this-worldly form, Rumi acknowledges that it has its proper function and purpose, although to cultivate it for its own sake is to concern oneself with the "leaves of the tree" or the "back of the mirror" and thereby neglect the principal thing. Form and substance are for Mawlana like the shell and kernel of a seed. If the seed is stripped of its shell before being planted, it will never grow. In contrast to the so-called *bêshar‘*, or antinomian dervishes, who abandoned the formal dictates of Islamic praxis and claimed that they were distracted by formalized practice from the reality that lay beyond, Mawlana insists on the importance of maintaining form, without which the underlying concept cannot be achieved. He maintains that only through its visible form can the intrinsic concept of a thing be discerned by the "eye of insight"—a sense innate in every person and potentially perfectible but cultivated and honed to an exquisite sharpness among a singular elevated class of humans—the prophets and saints.

God purposefully created this world as a training ground for man to grow spiritually. This view, which was elaborated on the theoretical level by many a Sufi thinker, is also responsible for the social context of Sufism and the much greater involvement of Muslim Sufis in society than their counterparts in the Christian West. For Rumi, man's physical attributes represent an evolutionary stage in his theory of cyclic being. The microcosm of the universe, man contains within him inorganic, organic, and animal characteristics, all of which states evolve both outside and inside of man to help him in his upward development from the nadir of pure matter, the lowest rung in the hierarchy of being. Only man is capable of this development. Beasts, being totally earthly and material with no trace of rationality or discernment, respond only to their natural animal instincts. Man, on the other hand, as the last and ultimate creature of God's universe, was endowed with two natures. Physically shaped from the earth itself,[20] he shares animality with the beasts and materiality with inorganic things; nonetheless, man's spirit was breathed into him by God,[21] thus imparting something of the Divine to him. In addition he was given intellect and discernment to know good from evil. Man then contains within himself a fish that pulls him toward the water of eternal life and a serpent that tugs on him toward the dust, a bird that tries to lift its cage upward and a rat that wants to hold it down. He is the donkey "onto to which angels' feathers were stuck in hopes of his becoming angelic." Man must struggle against his animal part and subdue it in order to release the ray of eternality that desires to reunite itself with the source of all light whence it emanated. Man must abandon the false data based upon the phantom, unreal world that are fed to him by his senses and, having perfected his reason,[22] make the leap beyond the rational into the spiritual realm.

When man's spiritual awareness is perfected, he is ready to shed his material aspect and evolve into the angelic state,

---

[20]As Koran 15:33 ("a mortal whom Thou hast created out of potter's clay of dark mud altered") and also 18:37.

[21]As Koran 15:29 ("when I have made him and have breathed into him of My spirit") and also 38:72, 32:9.

[22]When Rumi speaks of a "rational" or "intelligent" person he means someone who exercises his gift of human reason (*'aql*), as opposed to the bestial type who is buffeted about by his passions and instincts. Rumi most emphatically does not mean "intelligent" or "intellectual" in the modern sense: the intelligentsia is included among those he blames for squandering their time on acquiring worldly accomplishments, among which are erudition and intellectual pursuits.

that is, to ascend to the next plane of being. To maintain this world as the realm of spiritual development, it is necessary for each person to perform his allotted function, and this necessitates the spiritual unawareness of the generality of mankind, for if all men were spiritually aware, then they would cease to tend to the affairs of this world, and it would fall into ruination. Above all else, this world must be maintained for the sake of the saint, the perfect man of the age, who has reached such a stage of development that he stands in relation to the rest of mankind as the Universal Intellect, the first cause and prime mover of the heavens, stands in relation to all that emanates from it.

As man was fashioned from the stuff of the earth but has been elevated among his fellow creatures to the special rank of vicegerency of the earth, so too are there among humanity certain individuals who enjoy special favor and elevation of rank—and these are the prophets and saints, those rare humans who have reached spiritual perfection. They have passed through Rumi's three stages of development.

In his primitive condition man first serves "other than God," that is, he sees only the "now" of time and, mistaking the proper object of adoration, allows himself to be held in bondage to things of this world such as money, power, learning, and intellectual accomplishments. Such people, deluded by their concupiscent animal souls into believing that they have independent existence, proclaim their ego-identity by thinking of God as a remote "He," or something other than themselves. By affirming their own existence they necessarily postulate an existence other than God and thus deny basic *tawhid*.

The second, or ascetic stage of development is represented by one who determines not to serve other than God. The ascetic rejects worldly things by denying their importance and looks to the "end" of time, that is, he labors to reap a heavenly reward instead of this-worldly grati-fication. He moves from a third-person objectivity in his relationship to God into a second-person relativity: "You are

God, and I worship You," a second-stage man might say. Nonetheless, by positing his own existence, he "others" himself from God and is still off the mark of *tawhid*.

The final stage is reached by realizing that all things, including one's own subjective ego, are but impermanent pseudo-determinations of the only reality, which is God. The goal has now become to recognize that God is the sole reality. That is, one must die to the self; one must abandon the ego and be "born again to the spirit" by being subsumed in the reality of God's unity and oneness. Such a person can say neither "He" nor "You" of God but is engulfed in the total "I" of the Divinity and falls to silence within this world. This is the saint, who, having attained existential union with God, becomes an instrument in God's hand, devoid of all subjective will. As the famous divine *hadith* says, for such a person God becomes the "eye through which he sees, the ear through which he hears, the arm through which he grasps." Rumi often compares such a disindividuated person to a drowned person floating on water, whose every movement is actualized by the water, not by the person.

The saint has regard neither for the "now" nor for the "end" of time: he has gazed upon the beginning and thus removed himself from the strictures of time and space by having completed the process of *anamnesis*, or recollection of his origin, a potentiality that lies dormant in most people. Because he knows the beginning, he knows what the infinite end is and is thus unconcerned with the "now." The saint is then the interior-seeing guide for the rest of exterior-seeing mankind who have not reached his level. Having already traversed the way, the saint knows the path and its pitfalls and stands ready to guide others if they will only follow.

Rumi rejects the notion of grace by merit in no uncertain terms. The elevation to sainthood and the election to prophecy are not merited by any amount of extraordinary pious works; they are free gifts of God bestowed upon whomsoever He chooses, although it is assumed that by means of works one may motivate the gift. Anyone who has been elected to this grace is no longer subject to ordinary behavioral criteria. What may appear to be a sin is not sinful; such a person cannot commit a crime because it is not he who acts but God. Of certain of his saints God is so jealous that they are concealed from the vulgar gaze and never recognized by the world for what they are—yet they are the cause of the maintenance and stability of the world.

A natural element of sympathy for the saint lies dormant within every human, but unless that sympathetic chord is struck, the saint's words have no effect. When, however, the sympathetic element is stirred, one's yearning for his origin will be set in motion. When a person breaks free of false perceptions, the falcon of his soul will spread its "wing of aspiration" to take flight out of the dimensional world back to the arm of the Eternal King who calls him incessantly.

In an allegory to which Rumi refers in the *Fihi ma fihi* (section 50) and which is given in more detail in the *Masnavi* (I, 3157ff.), Joseph, the son of Jacob, receives an old friend who has just returned from a long journey. When asked what gift he has brought from his travels, the friend replies that he searched far and wide for a present to bring to Joseph but was unable to find anything suitable since there was nothing Joseph did not already possess in abundance. Finally he realized that the only worthy gift would be a mirror in which Joseph's beauty could be reflected.[23] Similarly, man will be asked by God what gift he has brought from his sojourn in this world, and the only answer he will be able to make without humiliation is to present God with a perfectly polished mirror in which God's awesome beauty can be reflected. This mirror is the human heart, and when the verdigris of material attachment and the corrosion of selfish desires are eliminated from the surface of the heart-mirror, it can then reflect the beauty of divinity. The mirror of man's

---

[23]Joseph is known in Islamic legend as the ideal beauty, the most perfect manifestation of divine beauty in human form. Because of his beauty Zulaykha, the wife of Potiphar, fell hopelessly in love with him.

existence can then be held up against the emanating rays of the godhead, and God's purpose in creation will have been accomplished, for God will then be able to see His own reflection and know Himself.

## The Translation

The present work is a translation of Professor Badi'-uzzaman Furuzanfar's edition of *Fihi ma fihi* published by the Majlis Press in Tehran, 1330 (1952 A.D.). The edited version maintains the traditional division into sections *(fasl)*, which represent what appeared to the collators as breaks in subject matter, the end of a particular *majlis*, or session, or perhaps even the end of a foliation. Subdivision within sections was done to a limited extent by the editor, but most of the divisions marked by asterisks in the translation have been made by the translator to facilitate reading. Often the Persian text indicates no break, even when an obvious transition from one topic to another occurs. Unfortunately, the sections were not numbered by the editor so that the only means of reference is to page number. In the translation each section has been numbered, and the page number of the edited text is given on page 250 to facilitate reference to the Persian.

Given the divergent paths of evolution followed over the centuries by Islam and the West, we cannot expect the technical terms of Sufism and Islamic jurisprudence to have absolute equivalents in English, and even where equivalents may once have existed, in most cases modern usage has rendered them useless. Such terms have been translated with their nearest or most commonly accepted equivalents. Since the singularly undogmatic and unsystematic Rumi rarely attaches hard and fast meanings to his terms, there is little use in obscuring the text with transliterated Persian and Arabic terminology. The few terms that have been left untranslated are defined in the glossary. Names of persons occurring in the text have also been identified in the glossary.

In the notes to the text, quotations from other poets, quotations from Rumi's own words, and prophetic and divine *hadith* are identified with reference to editions and/or standard compilations. Most of these identifications were made in the copious notes to the edition by Professor Furuzanfar; all references made by him have been verified, however, and more precise locations given.

Koranic quotations within the text are printed in italics for easy identification; numbers following in brackets give chapter and verse reference. In the original text all Koranic and *hadith* quotation is of course in Arabic and contrasts immediately with Rumi's Persian. It is hoped that George Sale's eighteenth-century English translation of the Koran is remote enough from modern English to capture something of the contrast between the two languages of the original. Quotations from prophetic and divine *hadith* are identified in the notes along with the first two words of the original.

*The Discourses*

# ONE

The Prophet (peace be with him) said, "The worst scholar is one who visits princes, but the best prince is one who visits scholars. Happy the prince at a poor man's door; wretched the poor man at a prince's gate."[60]

People have taken this saying at its face value to mean that it is not fitting for a scholar to visit a prince lest he become a bad scholar. It does not, however, mean what people imagine. Its true meaning is that the worst scholar is one who receives support from princes, whom he must fear in order to gain his livelihood. Such a man's primary aim in the pursuit of learning is for princes to bestow gifts upon him, to hold him in high esteem, and to grant him official positions. Therefore, it is on their account that he betters himself and exchanges his ignorance for learning. When he becomes a scholar, he learns proper etiquette out of fear of them and their power to punish. So, willy-nilly, he conducts himself as they would have him do. Therefore, whether outwardly it be the prince who visits the scholar or the scholar who visits the prince, such a scholar must conduct himself as a guest while the prince acts as host. On the other hand, when a scholar dons the robe of learning, not for the sake of princes but rather first and foremost for God's sake, and when his conduct and comportment are along the path of rectitude, as his natural inclination should be, and for no other reason—like a fish, which can live only in water—then such a scholar is so ruled by reason that during his time all men stand in awe of his presence and are illuminated by his reflected radiance, whether they are aware of it or not. If such a scholar goes to a prince, it is he who acts as the host and the prince the guest, because the prince will be receiving assistance and will be dependent upon the scholar. The scholar is quite independent of the prince; he will shed light like the sun,

---

[60]The prophetic hadith *(shirâru 'l-'ulamâ')* is given in Ghazâlî, *Ihyâ' 'ulûm al-dîn*, I, 116 *(juz' i, bâb vi)*. A similar hadith *(abghadu 'l-khalq)* is given in Suyûtî, *Jâmi' al-saghîr*, I, 85.

whose only property is to give and bestow. The sun turns ordinary stones into rubies and carnelians and earthen mountains into mines of copper, gold, silver, and lead;[61] the sun makes the earth green and fresh and produces various fruits on the trees. Its only function is to give and bestow; it does not take anything, as the Arabs say proverbially, "We have learned to give, not to take." Such scholars are therefore hosts in any situation, and princes are their guests.

It occurs to me to interpret a verse of the Koran, even if it is not pertinent to this discussion. Anyway, since it occurs to me now, I may as well say it out. God said: *O prophet, say unto the captives who are in your hands, If God hath known any good to be in your hearts, He will give you better than what hath been taken from you; and He will forgive you, for God is gracious and merciful* [8:70]. The reason for the revelation of this verse is as follows. The blessed Prophet had defeated the infidels. Having slain and plundered, he took many prisoners and had them bound hand and foot. Among these prisoners was his uncle Abbas. All night long the prisoners wailed in their fetters and bemoaned their miserable, wretched condition. Having given up all hope, they were waiting for the sword to end their lives when the Prophet saw them and laughed.

"You see," they said, "he does have humanity in him. The claim that he is not human is untrue, for here, seeing us in these bonds and fetters as his prisoners, he rejoices exactly as a carnal man would rejoice in glee if he had conquered his enemy and seen him vanquished."

The Prophet, however, read their thoughts and said, "Oh, no, I am not laughing because I see my enemies vanquished or because I am rejoicing at seeing you at a loss. I am laughing because with my inner eye I see myself forced to drag with chains and fetters a group of people out of hell's fiery furnace

---

[61]According to the physical theories of antiquity adopted by Islamic science, precious stones were thought to be produced by the effect of sunlight on ordinary rocks, which, after exposure to the sun, sink into the mountains, where they are incubated into gems.

and black smoke into the eternal garden of heavenly paradise.[62] They are bewailing and lamenting, saying, 'Why are you taking us away from this place of perdition into that asylum and rose-bower?' That is why I am laughing. Since you still do not have the power of vision to comprehend and see clearly what I am saying, God commands me to say this to you: 'First you gathered many hosts and much might and, relying totally upon your own strength, valour, and might, you told yourselves that you would do thus and so and would utterly vanquish the Muslims. You thought no one was stronger than you. You could not imagine anyone mightier than yourselves. Now that all you had planned has turned out otherwise, and now that you lie trembling in fear, you have not repented of your malady and are in desperate straits. You still cannot conceive that anyone could be more powerful than you are. It is therefore necessary for you to see me in my might and power and yourselves as subject to my wrath in order that things may be made easy for you. Do not despair of me in your fear, for I am able to deliver you from this fear and lead you to safety. He who can bring forth a black cow from a white one can bring forth a white cow from a black one. *He causeth the night to succeed the day, and He causeth the day to succeed the night* [35:13]. *He bringeth forth the living out of the dead, and He bringeth forth the dead out of the living* [30:19]. Now in your present state as prisoners, despair not of my presence in order that I may take you by the hand, for *none despaireth of God's mercy, except the unbelieving people* [12:87].'"

Then the Prophet continued, saying, "Now God says, 'O prisoners, if you turn away from your former belief and perceive Me in both states of fear and hope[63] and realize that

---

62 Cf. the prophetic hadith *('ajiba rabbunâ)*, "Our Lord is amazed at people who must be led into paradise in chains," given in Badi'uzzaman Furuzanfar, *Ahâdîth al-mathnawî*, p. 103, #305. Where possible, all prophetic and divine *hadith* quoted by Rumi in this book will be referred to Prof. Furuzanfar's work, hereafter abbreviated as *FAM*.

63 The stages of fear *(khawf)* and hope *(rajâ)* are integral to the mystic "path" and are technical terms of Sufism. "Fear" represents the stage wherein

you are subject to My will in all conditions, I shall release you from this state of fear. I shall restore to you all your property that has been plundered and lost, nay I shall restore it to you many times over. I shall pardon you, and to your wealth in this world I shall join the wealth of the next world also.'"

"I repent," said Abbas. "I have turned away from what I was."

"God requires a token of this claim you make," said the Prophet.

It is easy to lay claim to love,
But the proof of it remains otherwise.

"In God's name," asked Abbas, "what token do you require?"

"Give to the armies of Islam," said the Prophet, "all the wealth you have left. If you have truly become a Muslim and wish well to the religion and community of Islam, give in order that the army of Islam may be strengthened."

"O Apostle of God," he said, "what have I left? Everything has been plundered. I have not so much as an old straw mat left to my name!"

"See," said the Prophet, "you still have not become righteous. You have not turned away from what you were. Let me tell you how much wealth you have, where you have hidden it, to whom you have entrusted it, and in what spot you have buried it."

"Oh, no!" cried Abbas.

---

the mystic's heart is severed from the calm of security by the expectation of a possible evil emanating from the carnal self. When the mystic fears all that is other than God and puts his hope in God alone, God guarantees his faith. According to Junayd, "hope," the complement of "fear," means to be confident that good will come from God's grace and generosity. See Sajjadi, *Farhang*, pp. 252-54, 228. What Rumi stresses here is that the believer should not be so preoccupied with fearing what is other than God—or with hope of security—that God is forgotten in the process.

"Did you not entrust a certain amount to your mother? Did you not bury it under a wall and stipulate that if you came back she was to give it to you, and if you did not return alive she was to spend it on a certain thing, give so much to a certain person, and keep a certain amount for herself?"

When Abbas raised his finger and professed the faith sincerely, saying, "O Prophet, in truth I used to think that you had good luck through the machinations of fortune, as did many ancient kings like Haman, Shaddad, and Nimrod. However, when you told me what you said, I knew for certain that this good fortune is mysterious and divine in origin."

"You speak the truth," said the Prophet. "This time I heard that girdle of doubt you wore inwardly snap. The sound of its breaking reached that ear of mine that is hidden in the depths of my soul. Whenever anyone's girdle of doubt, polytheism, or infidelity snaps, I can hear the sound of it breaking with my inner ear, my soul's ear.[64] Now you have truly become righteous and professed the faith."

٭

All this I said to the Parvana. I told him, "You, who have become the head of Islamdom, have said, 'I sacrifice myself and my intellect and all my power of deliberation and judgment for the continued existence and spread of Islam.' But since you have relied upon yourself and not looked to God to realize that everything is from Him, God has caused that very endeavor of yours to be the cause for the diminution of Islam. You have united yourself with the Tatar, whom you aid to annihilate the Syrians and Egyptians and thus to lay waste the realm of Islam.[65] The very thing that was to be a cause for the

---

64 Cf. the two "cries for protection" attributed to the Prophet in Ayn al-Qudat al-Hamadhani, *Tamhidat*, p. 214: "O God, I seek refuge in Thee from polytheism *(shirk)* and doubt *(shakk)*" (p. 76) and, "O God, I seek refuge in Thee from infidelity *(kufr)*."

65 Rumi alludes to the diplomatic posturing of the Parvana vis-a-vis the Mamluk sultans of Egypt and Syria and the Mongol Ilkhanids of Iran. He may well have invited the Mamluk Baybars to invade Seljuq Anatolia in

expansion of Islam has become the cause for its diminishment. Therefore, in this state, which is a fearful one, turn to God. Give alms that He may deliver you from this evil condition, which is fear. Do not despair of Him, even if He has cast you down from a state of obedience into disobedience. Because you thought your obedience was in and of yourself, you have fallen into disobedience. Even now in this disobedience, despair not but turn humbly to God, for He is almighty. If He turned that obedience into disobedience, He can turn this disobedience into obedience and give you repentance. He can provide you the means to strive anew on behalf of the propagation of Islam and to be a strength for Islam. Despair not, for *none despaireth of God's mercy, except the unbelieving people* [12:87]."

My purpose was to make him understand, give alms and humble himself before God, for from a most exalted position he had come to a low state, even in which he should be hopeful.

God works in mysterious ways. Things may look good outwardly, but there may be evil contained inside. Let no one be deluded by pride that he himself has conceived good ideas or done good deeds. If everything were as it seemed, the Prophet would not have cried out with such illuminated and illuminating perspicacity, "Show me things as they are!⁶⁶ You make things appear beautiful when in reality they are ugly; You make things appear ugly when in reality they are beautiful. Show us therefore each thing as it is lest we fall into a snare and be ever errant." Now your judgment, however good and clear it may be, is not better than his, and he spoke as

---

1276. In the spring of 1277 the Mamluk did invade, inflicted a crushing defeat on the Mongol army of occupation at Abulustan, and immediately withdrew. The Mongol defeat brought the Ilkhan Abaqa himself to Asia Minor, and the Parvana was summoned, tried, and heinously executed in 1277. See Boyle, ed., *The Cambridge History of Iran*, V, 361.

66 The prophetic hadith *(arinâ 'l-ashyâ)* may be found in *FAM* 45 (116).

he did. Don't rely on your every thought and opinion, but humble yourself before God and fear Him.

Such was my purpose in speaking to the Parvana. However, he applied this verse and this interpretation to his own strategy, saying, "At this time, when we are moving our troops, we must not rely on them. Even defeated, we must not despair of Him in time of fear and helplessness." He applied my words to his own design, whereas my purpose was as I have said.

## TWO

Someone said, "Our master is not saying anything."

"Well," I replied, "this person has been projected up to my presence by a mental image of mine. This image of mine did not ask him, 'How are you?' or 'How do you do?' My mental image attracted him here without the use of words. If my reality attracts him without words and can remove him hence to another place, what is so strange about that?"

Words are but "shadows" of reality. They are, as it were, a branch of reality. If the "shadow" can attract, how much more so can the reality attract!

Words are just pretexts. It is the element of sympathy that attracts one man to another, not words. If a man should see a thousand prophetic or saintly miracles, it will profit him nothing if he does not have sympathy with the prophet or saint. It is that sympathetic element that unsettles and disquiets. Were there no element of sympathy to amber in straw, then straw could never be attracted by amber. The sympathy between them is hidden, however; it cannot be seen.

The mental image of anything brings man to that thing: the image of "garden" leads him to a garden, the image of "shop" to a shop. There is, however, a deception hidden in these images. Don't you see that often, when you go to a place, you are disappointed and say, "I thought it would be better. It wasn't what it was supposed to be"? These images are like shrouds, and one can hide beneath a shroud. When the images are dispelled and the realities appear without the shroud of the mental image, there is a "reawakening." When the case is thus, there is no occasion for disappointment. The reality that attracts you is nothing other than itself. *The day whereon all secret thoughts and actions shall be examined into* [86:9].

What is this of which we are speaking? In reality the "attractor" is one, but it appears to be many. Don't you see how a person often has a hundred different wants? "I want vermicelli. I want pastry. I want sweets. I want fritters. I want fruit. I want dates." These appear to be many different wants that have been expressed verbally. The origin of them all, however, is one—and that is hunger. Don't you see that when this same person has had his fill of any one of these things he will say, "I don't need any of the rest"? It is obvious therefore that there were not ten things or a hundred, but only one. *We have expressed the number of them only for an occasion of discord* [74:31]. This multiplicity among people is deceiving, for they say, "This is one," and, "These are a hundred"—that is, they say that a saint is unique while the many they call "a hundred" or "a thousand." This is a great deception. This way of thinking you have that calls the many multiples and the one unique is extremely deceptive. *We have expressed the number of them only for an occasion of discord* [74:31]. Which hundred? Which fifty? Which sixty? People, lost and uncontrolled, without reason, mindless, like a talisman they quiver like mercury and quicksilver. Will you call them sixty? a hundred? a thousand? and yet call this one one? You might as well call them nothing and him a thousand, or a hundred thousand, or a thousand thousand. "Few if counted, many in force."[67]

A king once gave a single soldier enough rations for a hundred men. The army objected, but the king said to himself, "The day will come when I will show you why I do this." On the day of battle all fled except for that one man, who stood and fought. "Here is my reason for what I did," said the king.

Man must strip secondary motives from his power of discerning and look to religion for assistance, for it is religion

---

67 The line is quoted from Mutanabbi. See al-Mutanabbi, *Diwan*, p. 183.

that is capable of discovering whence comes aid. If, however, a man spends his life with the undiscerning, his own discernment will grow weak and he will be unable to recognize the power of religion. You cultivate this physical existence, in which there is no discernment. Discernment is merely one of its attributes. Don't you see that a madman has physicality but no discernment? Discernment is that subtle concept that is inside you, but night and day you are occupied with nourishing that physical being indiscriminately: you labor under the false pretext that the subtle concept subsists through the physical being, when it is actually the other way around. How is it that you expend all your energies caring for the physical and totally neglect the subtle, when it is the physical that subsists through the subtle and not the other way around? That light escapes through the apertures of the eyes and ears, and so forth. If you did not have these apertures, it would escape through others. It is as though you were to bring a lamp outside in order to see the sun. Even if you were to bring no lamp, the sun would still show itself. What do you need a lamp for?

One must not despair of God, for hope is the first step on the road to salvation. Even if you do not travel the road, at least keep the road open. Do not say that you have gone astray. Take the straight way, and there will be no crookedness. Straightness is the quality of Moses' staff; the kinks are in the staves of the sorcerers: when straightness comes it devours all the others.[68] If you have done evil you have done it to yourself. How could the evil you have done ever reach Him? When a bird perches on a mountaintop and

---

68 In the Moses-Pharaoh episode in the Koran (20:65–70, 10:80ff.), based on Exodus 4:3 and 7:15, Moses engaged in a duel with Pharaoh's magicians. The magicians cast down their staves, which became serpents; Moses then cast down his staff, which turned into a great serpent that devoured all the others. See Thackston, *Tales of the Prophets*, p. 228f.

then flies away, what has the mountain gained or lost?[69] When you straighten yourself out, nothing else remains. Do not abandon hope.

The danger in associating with kings is not that you may lose your life, for in the end you must lose it sooner or later. The danger lies in the fact that when these "kings" and their carnal souls gain strength, they become dragons; and the person who converses with them, claims their friendship, or accepts wealth from them must in the end speak as they would have him speak and accept their evil opinions in order to preserve himself. He is unable to speak in opposition to them. Therein lies the danger, for his religion suffers. The further you go in the direction of kings, the more the other direction, which is the principal one, becomes strange to you. The further you go in that direction, this direction, which should be beloved to you, turns its face away from you. The more you accommodate yourself to worldly people, the more the proper object of love grows estranged from you. "Whosoever rendereth aid to the unjust is subjugated to them by God." When you have fully inclined toward the one to whom you are inclining, he will be made master over you.

It is a pity to reach the sea and be satisfied with only a cupful of water. When pearls and hundreds of thousands of beneficial things can be extracted from the sea, what is the use of taking water? What pride does a rational man have in doing such a thing? This world is but foam, while the oceanful of water is the knowledge of the saints. Where then lies the pearl? This world is foam, full of flotsam and jetsam; however, from the turning of the waves and the accord between the churning of the sea and the quaking of the waves, that foam takes on a beauty, for *the love and eager desire of wives, and children, and sums heaped up of gold and silver, and excellent horses, and cattle, and land, is made beautiful for men: this is the provision of the present life* [3:14]. Now, since God said that it "is made

---

69 From a *ruba'i* attributed to Rumi in Muhammad ibn al-Munawwar, *Asrar al-tawhid*, p. 122.

beautiful," it is not really beautiful: its beauty is vicarious, of another place. It is a gilded counterfeit coin. That is to say, this world, which is foam, is counterfeit, without worth, without value. We have gilded it, for it "is made beautiful."

The human being is an astrolabe of God, but one needs an astronomer to know how to use the astrolabe. If a seller of leeks or a greengrocer were to possess an astrolabe, what use could he make of it? How could he fathom the conditions of the celestial spheres, the turning of the zodiacal signs or their influences? In the hands of an astronomer the astrolabe is beneficial, for whoso knoweth him or herself knoweth his/her Lord.[70] Just as this brass astrolabe is a mirror of the heavens, the human being—*and We have honoured the children of Adam* [17:70]—is an astrolabe of God. When God makes a person to know himself, through the astrolabe of that person's own being he can witness the manifestation of God and His unqualified beauty moment by moment and glimmer by glimmer. That beauty is never absent from this "mirror." God has servants who cover themselves with wisdom, mystical knowledge, and miracles even though people do not have the perspicacity to see them. They cover themselves out of their extraordinary zeal, as Mutanabbi says:

> They put on brocades, not to beautify themselves,
> But that they may protect thereby their beauty.[71]

## THREE

The Parvana sent a message in which he said, "Night and day my heart and soul have been at your service, but I have not been able to attend you because of my preoccupation with Mongol affairs."

---

70 For this favorite hadith *(man 'arafa)* of the mystics, see *FAM* 167 #529. The saying is classed as fictitious *(mawdu')* by the *muhaddith*s. Cf. the Delphic maxim, *gnothi seauton*.

71 From Mutanabbi, *Diwan*, p. 129.

[The Master responded:] "These also are works of God inasmuch as they have to do with the safety and security of Islamdom. You have sacrificed your all, both materially and physically, to give a few Muslims the inner tranquility to occupy themselves with acts of devotion in security. Therefore, this too is a good work. Inasmuch as God has inclined you to such good works, your excessive zeal is a sign of His favor. Conversely, when there is a slackening off in this inclination it is a sign of disfavor. God would not wish such a critical good work to be executed by means of a person unless that person is worthy of reward and exalted station. It is like a warm bathhouse, the heat of which comes from a stove. God provides the means for heating, like straw, kindling, dung, and so forth. In external form these things may appear mean and ugly, but they are nonetheless divine favors with regard to their purpose. When the bath is heated by these things people benefit from it."

At this point some friends arrived, but the master apologized, saying, "If I do not rise for you or speak to you to inquire after your condition, it is out of respect for you. The measure of respect for a thing is determined by the propriety of the occasion. During prayer it is not fitting to inquire after one's father or brother or to bow to them. Not to acknowledge one's friends and relatives while one is at prayer is the essence of courtesy and respect because, if one does not disjoin oneself from total absorption in an act of devotion and does not become distracted by them, they will not deserve reproach or punishment. This, then, is the essence of attentiveness and courtesy, since one will have been on guard against something on account of which they would have to suffer."

Someone asked, "Is there any way to approach God other than prayer?"

The answer is more prayer. However, prayer does not exist only in outward form: that is just the "shell" of prayer because it has a beginning and an end. Anything that has a beginning and an end is a "shell." The proclamation of God's greatness is the beginning of the prayer and the greeting of peace is its end. Likewise, there is more to the pronouncement of faith than what is said with the tongue because it too has a beginning and an end. Anything that can be vocalized and has a beginning and an end is a "form," a "shell"; its "soul," however, is unqualifiable and infinite, without beginning and without end. Anyway, prayer as we know it was formulated by the prophets. Now the Prophet, who formalized prayer, says, "I have a 'time' with God during which there is room for neither message-bearing prophet nor angel near in station to God to share with me.[72] We know then that the "soul" of prayer is not only its external form but also a state of total absorption and unconsciousness during which all these external forms, for which there is no room, remain outside. In that state there is not room even for Gabriel, who is purely conceptual.

*

A story is told of Mawlana Baha'uddin. One day his companions found him totally absorbed in contemplation. When the hour for prayer came, some of his disciples cried out to the Mawlana that it was time to pray. The Mawlana paid no attention to what they said. They rose and began their prayers. Two disciples, however, remained in attendance on their master and did not rise to pray. One of the disciples who were at prayer, a man named Khwajagi, saw clearly with his inner eye that all those who were at prayer, including the prayer-leader, had their backs to the kiblah, while those two who had remained in the master's company were facing the kiblah.

Since the master had passed beyond the state of ego-consciousness and become lost to himself, consumed in the light of God, as is the meaning of the prophetic saying, "Die

---

72 For the prophetic hadith *(li ma'a 'llah)* see *FAM* 39 #100. The word "time" *(waqt)* in this *hadith* has generally been taken to mean "state," and indeed the word *hâlat* ("state") replaces *waqt* in the ignorant disciple's recasting of this *hadith* in section 63.

13

before you die,"[73] he had then become the Light of God, and whoever turns his back on the Light of God to face a wall has assuredly turned his back to the kiblah because the light is the soul of the kiblah. Now if people face the Kaaba because the Prophet designated it as the direction of prayer for the whole world, it is more fitting for Him to be the direction of prayer since it was for His sake that the Kaaba became the kiblah.

The Prophet once admonished one of his friends, saying, "I summoned you. Why did you not come?"

"Because I was at prayer."

"Was it not I who summoned you?"

"I am helpless," he said.

"It is good," said the Prophet, "for you to acknowledge yourself to be helpless at all times, to see yourself helpless in times of strength even as in times of weakness because over your strength lies another.

At all times and in all conditions you are subject to God's will. You are not two halves such that at times you are in control and at other times not. Keep His strength in view and always realize that you yourself are helpless, not in control, impotent, wretched. If even lions, tigers, and crocodiles are helpless and quake before Him, what then of puny mankind? The heavens and earth are all helpless and dominated by His law; He is a mighty king. His light is not like the light of the sun and moon, in spite of whose existence things remain as they are. No, when His light shines without being screened, neither the heavens remain nor the earth, neither the sun nor the moon—save that King, no one remains.

A king once said to a dervish, "When you enjoy glory and proximity at God's court, make mention of me."

"When I am in that Presence," said the dervish, "and am exposed to the radiance of that Sun of Beauty, I am unable to make mention of myself, much less of you!"

Nonetheless, when God has chosen one of His servants and caused him to be absorbed into himself, if anyone should

---

73 For this prophetic hadith *(mûtû qabl)* see *FAM* 116 #352.

grab hold of his skirt and make a request of God, God will grant that request without the mystic so much as mentioning it to God.

The story is told of a king who had a subject he held in the highest esteem. When that man was about to set out for the king's palace, all those who had requests to make would give him letters to present to the king, and he would put them in a pouch. When he came into the king's presence and the king's radiant beauty shone over him, he would fall unconscious at the king's feet. The king would put his hand lovingly into the man's pouch, saying, "What does this subject of mine, who is absorbed by my beauty, have?" He would draw out the letters and note approval on the backs and then replace them in the pouch. Thus, without being presented, all the requests were granted. Not one was ever denied. In fact, the petitioners were given more than they asked. However, out of the hundreds of requests made by other subjects who retained consciousness and were able to present petitions to the king on behalf of others, only rarely were any granted.

## FOUR

Someone said, "There is something I have forgotten."

There is one thing in the world that should not be forgotten. You may forget everything except that one thing, without there being any cause for concern. If you remember everything else but forget that one thing, you will have accomplished nothing. It would be like a king who sends you to a village on a specific mission. You go and perform a hundred other tasks. If you neglect to accomplish the task for which you were sent, it is as though you did nothing. Man therefore has come into the world for a specific purpose and aim. If he does not fulfill that purpose, he does nothing. *We proposed the faith unto the heavens, and the earth, and the mountains: and they refused to undertake the same, and were afraid thereof; but man undertook it: verily he was unjust to himself, and foolish* [33:72].

"We offered the faith to the heavens; they were not able to accept it." Consider how many mind-boggling feats they perform: they turn rocks into rubies and emeralds; they turn mountains into mines of gold and silver; they cause the plants of the earth to burst forth; they give life; and they create a Garden of Eden. The earth too receives seed and gives forth fruit; it covers up blemishes and does innumerable miraculous things. The mountains also produce various minerals. All these things they do, but that one thing they cannot do: that one thing is for mankind to do. *And We have honoured the children of Adam* [17:70]. Since God did not say, "We have honored the heavens and earth," it is therefore for mankind to do that which the heavens, the earth, and the mountains cannot do. If man accomplishes his task, his injustice to himself and folly are cancelled out. You may object and claim that, although you do not accomplish that task, you do nonetheless perform many other deeds. But I say to you that man was not created for those other deeds. It is as though you were to use a priceless blade of Indian steel, of the sort found in kings' treasuries, as a cleaver for rotten meat and then justify your act by saying, "I am not letting this blade stand idle. I am putting it to good use." It is as though you were to use a golden bowl to cook turnips in. One fraction of that bowl could buy a hundred pots. It is as though you were to use a gem-encrusted dagger to hang a broken gourd on and say, "I'm putting it to use by hanging the gourd from it. I'm not letting the dagger stand idle." Is it not both pitiful and ludicrous? When the gourd could be as well served by a wooden peg or an iron nail, the worth of which can be measured in pence, what is the logic in using a dagger worth a hundred dinars to such a purpose? God has fixed a high price on you, as He has said: *Verily God hath purchased of the true believers their souls, and their substance, promising them the enjoyment of paradise* [9:111].

You surpass this world and the next in value.

> What am I to do if you do not know your own worth?[74]
> Do not sell yourself short, for you are extremely valuable.[75]

God says, "I have bought you, every breath you take, your substance and your life span. If they are spent on Me and given to Me, the price is eternal paradise. This is what you are worth to Me. If you sell yourself to hell, you will have done injustice to yourself, like the man who sticks a blade worth a hundred dinars in the wall and hangs a pot or a gourd on it."

You use the pretext of busying yourself with a hundred "exalted works": you say that you are learning jurisprudence, wisdom, logic, astronomy, medicine, and so forth. These are all for yourself. You learn jurisprudence so that no one will be able to rob you of a loaf of bread, or tear your clothing, or kill you. This is all in order for you to live in well-being. What you learn in astronomy, such as the phases of the celestial spheres and the influences they have on the earth, the gravity or levity of security or fear, is all connected with your own condition. All these are for yourself. In astrology, the lucky or unlucky portents are connected with your own ascendant. It is still for your own ends. If you ponder the matter, you will realize that you are the "principal" and these things are subordinate to you. Now, if those things that are subordinate to you have so many miraculous subdivisions, consider what you, who are the "principal," must be like. If your subordinates have "apogees" and "nadirs," lucky and unlucky "portents," consider what "apogees" and "nadirs" you must have in the world of spirits. Consider what lucky and unlucky portents, indications, and counterindications you, who are the "principal," must have that such a spirit possesses this property, is capable of this, and is fitting for such a job.

Over and above the food you eat to maintain yourself physically, there is another food, as the Prophet said, "I spend

---

74 The line of poetry is quoted from Sana'i, *Hadiqat,* p. 500, line 2.

75 The hemistich may be from Rumi's *Divan-i kabir;* exact location not traced.

the night with my Lord, and He feeds me and gives me drink."[76] In this world you have forgotten that other food and occupied yourself with the food of this world. Day and night you cater to your body. Now this body is your steed, and this world is its stable. A horse's food is not fit for its rider; a horse maintains itself after its own fashion. Since you have been overwhelmed by your bestial and animal nature, you have remained in the stable with the horses and have no place among the ranks of the kings and princes of the world where your heart is. Since your body is dominant you must obey the body's orders. You are held prisoner by it, like Majnun when he set out for Layla's country. So long as he was conscious, he drove his camel in the right direction, but once he became absorbed in Layla he forgot both himself and the camel. The camel, which had a child back in the village, turned around toward the village at the first opportunity. When Majnun came to, he saw that he had been going the wrong way for two days. Thus he kept going to and fro for three months, when at last he cried, "This camel is a curse to me!" So saying, he jumped from the camel and set off on his own.

> My camel's desire is behind me,
> while my own desire lies ahead:
> Truly she and I are at odds.[77]

Someone came to Sayyid Burhanuddin Muhaqqiq and said, "I have heard praise of you from a certain person."

"Let me see," he replied, "what sort of person he is, whether he has reached such a degree that he can know me and praise me. If he knows me by what I have said, he does not know me because words are impermanent, sounds are

---

76 The prophetic hadith *(abîtu 'inda rabbî)* is given in *FAM* 36 #89. The *hadith* in full is: "I am not like any of you, for I spend the night. Which of you is like me?"

77 The line is attributed to the Arab poet 'Urwa ibn Hizâm and quoted by Rumi in the *Mathnavi*, IV, 1533.

impermanent, lips and mouths are impermanent. They are all incidental. If he knows me by what I have done, the case is likewise. If, however, he knows my essence, then I know that he is capable of praising me and that the praise belongs to me."

This is like a story they tell of a king who entrusted his son to a group of skilled men, with whom the boy remained until they had taught him total mastery of astronomy, geomancy, and other sciences, despite his utter stupidity and ineptitude. One day the king took a ring in his fist and, by way of testing his son, said, "Come, tell me what I am holding in my fist."

"What you are holding," he answered, "is round, yellow, and has a hole in the middle."

"Since you have described it correctly," said the king, "tell me what it is."

"It must be a millstone,"[78] he said.

"You have given its characteristics so precisely that the mind is boggled. With all the education and knowledge you have acquired, how has it escaped you that a millstone cannot be held in the fist?"

So it is now that the learned of our time miraculously fathom the sciences! They have learned perfectly to comprehend all sorts of extraneous things that do not concern them. What is truly important and closest of all to a man is his own self, but that our learned do not know. They pass judgment on the legality or illegality of everything, saying, "This is permissible, and that is not," or, "This is lawful, and that is not." However, the hollowness, yellowness, design, and roundness of the king's ring are coincidental, for if you cast it into the fire none of those things remains. It becomes its essence, free of any of these characteristics. All the sciences, acts, and words that they put forward are likewise: they have no connection with the substance of the thing, which will abide after all these others. Likewise are all these attributes of which they speak and upon which they expound. In the end they will render a judgment that the king is holding a millstone

78 Text has *ghirbîl*, "sieve."

in his fist, since they know nothing of that which is the principal thing.

I am a bird, a nightingale, or a parrot. Because my voice is fixed and cannot make any other sound, even if I am told to produce a different sort of sound, I cannot. Contrary to this is the case of someone who has learned to imitate birds. He is no bird at all; in fact, he is an enemy of birds, a hunter, but he can make bird calls in order to be taken as a bird. Since the sounds he makes are assumed and not properly his, he can, if asked, make different calls. He is able to make different calls because he has learned to "pilfer people's goods and show you a different piece of linen from every house."

## FIVE

The Atabeg[79] said, "What graciousness is this with which Mawlana has honored me? I never expected it. The thought never crossed my mind, since I am only worthy to stand humbly, night and day, among the ranks of those ready to serve him. I am not yet worthy of even that. What graciousness is this?"

The Master said, "This man is one of you who have lofty aspirations. No matter how high the degree you reach, no matter how grave and exalted the matters with which you are concerned, because of your sublime aspiration you consider yourselves imperfect; you are dissatisfied with yourselves and think that you still have a long way to go. Although our hearts are ever at God's service, nonetheless we desire formal honor because form too, being inseparable from substance, has great significance."

Just as a thing without substance cannot be effected, it cannot be effected without form either. It is like a seed: if you sow it without its shell it will not sprout, but when you plant it in the ground along with its shell it will sprout into a great tree. On this basis, the body too is of importance in principle,

---

79 "Atabeg" supplied from manuscript. H.

for without it neither can works be effected nor can the goal be reached. Yes, by God, in the eyes of those who know the intrinsic meaning and who have "become" the intrinsic meaning, the principal thing is the intrinsic meaning.

In this connection it is said that two *rak'as* of prayer are better than the world and all it contains.[80] This does not apply to every person. The person to whom this applies is one who considers it more serious to miss two *rak'as* than to lose the world and all it contains, that is, one for whom it would be harder to miss those two *rak'as* than to lose possession of the whole world.

A dervish went before a king. The king addressed him, beginning, "O ascetic. . . ."

"You are the ascetic," replied the dervish.

"How can I be an ascetic?" asked the king. "I possess the whole world."

"No," he said, "you are looking at it the wrong way. This world and the next, along with all your kingdom, belong to me. I have taken possession of the universe. It is you who are content with a morsel and a rag."

*Whithersoever ye turn, there is the face of God* [2:109]. That Face is ever current, uninterrupted, and abiding, never ceasing. True lovers sacrifice themselves to this Face and seek nothing in return. The rest are like cattle; yet although they are mere cattle, they are deserving of favor. Though they are only in the stable, they are acceptable to the stablemaster. If he wishes, he can move them from this stable to his private pen, just as in the beginning He brought them from nonexistence into being, then from the "pen" of being into the state of minerality, and from the pen of minerality into the state of vegetation, and from the state of vegetation into the state of animality, and from animality into the state of humanity, and from humanity into the state of angelicity, and so forth ad infinitum. He made all this manifest in order for you to know that He has many

---

80 The prophetic hadith *(rak'atâni khafîfatân)* is given in al-Munawi, *Kunuz al-haqa'iq,* I, 138.

"pens" of this sort, each more sublime than the other: *from state to state; what aileth them, therefore, that they believe not?* [84:19-20]. He made all this manifest that you might know that there are other states that lie ahead, not that you might deny them and say, "This is all there is." A master craftsman displays his mastery and craft in order for others to believe and have faith in him and in his other crafts, which he has not yet revealed. Likewise, a king bestows robes of honor and grants boons in order that other favors and grants may be expected of him, not in order for people to say, "This is all there is; the king will not grant any more favors," and content themselves with what they have been given. If a king knew that that was what people would say and think, he would never grant them favors in the first place.

An ascetic is someone who sees the hereafter; a worldly person sees only the stable of this world,[81] while those who are the mystic elite see neither the hereafter nor the stable. Since their gaze has fallen upon the beginning, they know what the end of everything will be, just as an expert who plants wheat knows that wheat will grow. He knows the outcome from the beginning. So also with barley, rice, and so forth: when an expert looks at the beginning, although his view is not toward the end, he knows what the end will be from the beginning. Such people are rare; those who look toward the end are mediocre, while those who are in the stable are cattle.

Man has a guide at hand for every endeavor. Nothing can be undertaken until a pain—a yearning and love for a thing—is awakened inside man. Without pain one's endeavor will not be easy, no matter whether it be this-worldly, other-worldly, commercial, regal, scholarly, astrological or anything else. Mary did not go to the blessed tree until she experienced birthpangs: *and the pains of childbirth came upon her near the trunk of a palm tree* [19:23]. Pain brought her to the tree, and the dry tree bore fruit. Our body is like Mary, and each of us

---

81 There is a "script" pun involved here between *âkhir* ("the hereafter") and *âkhur* ("stable"); the two are spelled identically in Persian.

bears a Jesus. If we experience birth pains, our Jesus will be born; but if there is no pain, our Jesus will return to his origin by that hidden road whence he came, and we will remain deprived.

> The soul within is in poverty;
> the body without is in the flush.
> The demon gorges itself to nausea;
> Jamshid has nothing to eat.
> Heal yourself now while your Jesus is on earth,
> For when Jesus has risen to heaven
> your cure will have departed.[82]

## SIX

These words are for those who need them in order to comprehend. What need of words has he who can comprehend without the medium of words? Heaven and earth are all words to him who comprehends and is born of the word *Be and it was* [36:82]. What need of shouting has he who can hear a whisper?

An Arabic-speaking poet appeared before a king who not only was a Turk but did not even know Persian. The poet had composed an extremely ornate poem for him in Arabic. When the king mounted his throne with all his courtiers, princes, and ministers in their places, the poet rose and began to recite his poem. In the part of the poem that was to evoke admiration, the king nodded his head; in the part that was to evoke astonishment, he stared wildly; and in the part that was to evoke humility, he paid rapt attention.

The courtiers, bewildered, said: "Our king never knew a word of Arabic. How can it be that he nods his head at the proper place, unless he can actually understand Arabic and has concealed it from us all these years? If we have said impolite things in Arabic, woe unto us!"

---

82 Quoted from Khaqani, *Divan*, p. 10, lines 7 and 16.

Now the king had a slave boy who was highly privileged. The courtiers went to him and gave him a horse, a camel, and some money and promised him as much again if he would find out whether or not the king knew Arabic or, if he didn't, how he came to nod his head at the proper place. Was it a miracle or inspiration? One day the slave found an opportune moment: while the king was on a hunt and, having bagged much game, and was in good spirits, he asked.

The king laughed and said: "By God, I don't know Arabic. As for my nodding my head and expressing approval, it was obvious what his intent was in that poem. Therefore I nodded and expressed approval. It was obvious that the 'principal thing' was intended. That poem was just a 'branch' of the 'principal.' If there had been no purpose, he wouldn't have composed the poem."

If then one looks at the purpose, no duality remains. Duality lies in the branches; the root principle is one. So it is with spiritual masters: if outwardly they seem to differ one from another, and there appears to be divergence in their conditions, acts, and words, with regard to purpose they are one thing, and that is the search for God. It is like a breeze blowing through the house: it lifts a corner of the carpet and ruffles the mats, causes the dust to fly into the air, ripples the water in the pool, and causes the branches and leaves of the trees to dance. All these things appear to be quite different; yet from the point of view of intent, principle, and reality they are all one thing, since their movement is all from one breeze.

*

Someone said, "We are imperfect."

The very fact that someone thinks this and reproaches himself, saying, "Alas, what am I about? Why do I act like this?" is a proof of God's love and favor. "Love persists as long as reproach persists," because one rebukes those one loves, not strangers. Now there are different kinds of reproof. To suffer pain while aware of it is a proof of God's love and favor. On the other hand, when a type of reproof is inflicted and the reproved does not experience pain, there is no proof of love (as when one beats a carpet to get the dust out), and such is not called rebuke by the intelligent. If, on the other hand, one rebukes one's child or beloved, a proof of love does arise in such a case. Therefore, so long as you experience pain and regret within yourself, it is proof of God's love and favor.

When you see a fault in your brother, the fault really lies in yourself but you see it reflected in him. Likewise, the world is a mirror in which you see your own image. "The believer is a mirror to the believer."[83] Rid yourself of your own fault because what distresses you in another is really in yourself.

You are not offended by any bad qualities you have in yourself such as injustice, rancor, greed, envy, insensitivity, or pride. Yet when you see them in another, you shy away, offended. No one is revolted by a scab or abscess of his own; anyone will put his own sore finger into the stew, lick that finger, and not feel squeamish in the least. If, however, there is a minor abscess or cut on someone else's hand, you would never be able to stomach the stew that hand had been in. Bad moral qualities are just like those scabs and abscesses: no one is offended by his own; yet everyone suffers distress and is horrified at seeing only a bit in another. Just as you shy away from another, you must excuse him for shying away when offended by you. Your distress is his excuse because your distress comes from seeing something he also sees. The believer is a mirror to the believer. The Prophet did not say that the infidel is mirror to the infidel—not because the infidel does not have the quality to be a mirror, but because he is unaware of the mirror of his own soul.

A king was sitting by a brook, dejected. The princes were terrified of him while he was in such a state, and no matter what they did they couldn't cheer him up. The king had a jester who was extremely privileged. The princes undertook to reward him if he would make the king laugh. The jester went to the king, but try as he might, the king would not even look up at him so that he could make a face and cause the king to

83 The prophetic hadith *(al-mu'minu mir'ât)* is given in *FAM* 41 #104.

laugh. All the king did was stare at the brook with his head down.

"What does the king see in the water?" asked the jester.

"I see a cuckold," said the king.

"Sire," the jester replied, "your servant is not blind either."

So it is when you see in another something that distresses you. That person is not blind. He sees the same thing you do.

With God there is no room for two egos. You say "I," and He says "I." In order for this duality to disappear, either you must die for Him or He for you. It is not possible, however, for Him to die—either phenomenally or conceptually—because "He is the Ever-living who dieth not." He is so gracious, however, that if it were possible He would die for you in order that the duality might disappear. Since it is not possible for Him to die, you must die that He may be manifested to you, thus eliminating the duality.

You can tie two birds together; but, although they may be of the same species and their two wings have become four, they will not be able to fly because duality still pertains. If, however, you tie a dead bird to a live one, it will be able to fly since there is no duality.

The sun is so gracious that it would die for a bat if it were possible. "My dear bat," the sun would say, my grace touches everything. I would like to do something of beneficence for you too. Since it is possible for you to die, die that you may enjoy the light of my splendor and, shedding your 'bat-ness,' become the phoenix of the Mount Qaf of proximity to me."[84]

One of God's servants was capable of annihilating himself for the sake of a beloved. He asked God to give him such a beloved, but this was not acceptable to Him. A voice came, saying, "I do not desire that you should see such a one."

---

84 Mount Qâf, in Islamic cosmology is the mountain that surrounds the earth. In mystical terms it is the extreme limit of this world and is where "no-place" begins. The "phoenix of Mount Qâf" is the mythical *'anqâ*, a bird that, having never been seen, is said to be totally abstracted from the world, existing in name only.

The servant of God, however, insisted and would not cease his entreaty, saying, "O Lord, you have placed the desire for such a one within me, and it will not go away!"

Finally a voice came, saying: "If you want this to come about, then sacrifice yourself and become nought. Tarry not in departing from the world."

"O Lord," he said, "I am content." And thus he did, sacrificing his life for the sake of that beloved so that his desire was fulfilled.

If a servant of God can possess the grace to sacrifice his life, one day of which is worth more than the life of the whole world from beginning to end, could the Author of Grace be less gracious? That would be ludicrous. Since, however, His annihilation is not possible, you must be annihilated.

*

A dullard came and sat himself above a saint. The saint said: "What difference does it make whether one is above or below a lamp? If the lamp is inclined to be above, it does not do so for its own sake. Its only purpose is to benefit others so that they may enjoy its light. Otherwise, wherever the lamp may be, high or low, it is still a lamp. It is the eternal sun."

If the saints seek status and exalted position in this world, they do so because people are unable to perceive their exaltedness. They want to ensnare worldly people with the trap of this world so that they may find their way to that other exaltedness and fall into the snare of the next world. Similarly, the Prophet conquered Mecca and the surrounding countries, not because he needed them but in order to bestow life and light on all. "This hand is accustomed to give; it is not accustomed to take." The saints deceive men in order to give to them, not in order to take anything from them.

When someone traps little birds by means of trickery in order to eat them or sell them, that is called deception. When, however, a king lays a trap to catch a rough, worthless falcon that does not know its own essence and then trains it to his arm so that it becomes noble, tutored, and polished, that is not called deception. Although outwardly it appears to be fraudulent, it is considered the essence of straightforwardness and munificence. It is like reviving the dead, turning base stone into ruby, turning inanimate sperm into a living human being, and more. If the falcon knew why he was being captured, he would not need grain as an enticement but would search for the snare with all his heart and soul and fly to the arm of the king.

People look only at the literal meaning of the saints' words and say, "We've heard all this talk many times before. We've had enough of such words. *Our hearts are uncircumcised: but God hath cursed them with their infidelity* [2:88]. The infidels say, "Our hearts are full of such talk." God answers them thus: "Woe betide them that they be full of these words. They are full of the temptations of the devil and vain imaginings. They are full of hypocrisy and doubt—nay, they are full of damnation." *God hath cursed them with their infidelity.* Would that they were free of those ravings, for then they would be capable of receiving these words. But they are not even capable of that. God has plugged up their ears and eyes and hearts so that they see the wrong color. They perceive Joseph as a wolf. Their ears hear the wrong sound. They hear wisdom as nonsense and raving. And their hearts, having become repositories for temptation and vain imaginings, perceive falsely. Having been knotted up with compounded imaginings, their hearts have frozen solid like ice in winter. *God hath sealed up their hearts and their hearing; a dimness covereth their sight* [2:7]. How then can they be full? In their whole lives neither they nor those on whom they pride themselves have ever sensed or perceived. They are not blessed by the jug that God gives to some full in order that they may drink to their fill. He gives it to some empty, and then why should they render thanks? The person who receives a full jug renders thanks.

When God made Adam of clay and water, "He kneaded the clay of Adam for forty days."[85] He completed Adam's shell and left it for a period of time on the earth. Iblis came down

---

85 For the prophetic hadith *(khammara tînat)* see *FAM* 198 #233.

and went into Adam's shell. Going through and inspecting every vein, he saw that it was full of blood and humors. Adam said: "Ugh! It is a wonder if this be not that very Iblis who, at the foot of God's Throne, I saw would appear. If that Iblis exists, this must be he."

Peace be with you!

## SEVEN

The Atabeg's son came in.

"Your father is always mindful of God, and his devotion is dominant," the master said. "It is apparent from what he says."

One day the Atabeg said, "The Greek infidels have suggested that we marry our daughter to the Tatar so that religion may be one and this latter-day religion of Islam disappear."

"When has religion ever been one?" I said. "It has always been two or three, and war has always raged among coreligionists. How are you going to unify religion? On the Day of Resurrection it will be unified, but here in this world that is impossible because everybody has a different desire and want. Unification is not possible here. At the Resurrection, however, when all will be united, everyone will look to one thing, everyone will hear and speak one thing."

There are many things in man. He is a rat, and he is a bird. Sometimes the bird lifts his cage up, but then the rat pulls it back down. There are thousands of other beasts in man—until he progresses to the point where the rat sheds its "ratness" and the bird its "birdness" and all are unified. Because the object sought is not up or down, when the object is found, neither "up" nor "down" exists. When someone loses something, he looks for it all over—left and right, hither, thither, and yon. However, when the lost thing is found, he ceases to search for it and is still. At the Resurrection, therefore, everyone will look with one eye, speak with one tongue, hear with one ear, and perceive with one sense. It is like ten men who own a garden or a shop in partnership. They speak of the same thing, worry about the same thing, and are preoccupied with the same thing. When the sought object is found (on the Day of Resurrection when all will be faced with God), all will be unified in this same way.

In this world everyone is preoccupied with something. Some are preoccupied with love for women, some with possessions, some with making money, some with learning— and each one believes that his well-being and happiness depend on that. And that also is God's mercy. When a man goes after it in search and does not find it, he turns his back on it. After pausing a while he says: "That joy and mercy must be sought. Maybe I did not look enough. Let me search again." When he seeks again he still does not find it, but he continues until the mercy manifests itself unveiled. Only then does he realize that he was on the wrong track before. God, however, has some servants who see clearly even before the Resurrection. Ali said, "If the veil were lifted I would not be more certain." By this he meant that if the shell were taken away and Doomsday were to appear, his certitude would not increase. His perception was like a group of people who go into a dark room at night and pray, each facing a different direction. When day breaks they all turn themselves around, all except the one man who had been facing Mecca all night long. Since the others now turn to face his direction, why should he turn around? Those servants of God face Him even during the night: they have turned away from all that is other than Him. For them the Resurrection is immediate and present.

There is an infinity of words, but they are revealed in accordance with the capacity of the seeker. *There is no one thing, but the storehouses thereof are in Our hands; and We distribute not the same otherwise than in determinate measure* [15:21]. Wisdom is like the rain: at the source there is no end to it, but it comes down in accord with what is best, more or less according to the season. Druggists put sugar or medicine in a piece of paper, but there is more sugar than what is in the paper. The sources of sugar and medicine are limitless, but how could they fit into a piece of paper?

Some people taunted the Prophet, saying, "Why does the Koran come down to Muhammad word by word and not chapter by chapter?"

The Prophet replied, "What are these fools saying? If it were all revealed to me at once I would melt and cease to exist."

One who is apprised of a matter understands much from a little; from one thing he understands many things; from a line, a whole book. It is like a group of people who are seated listening to a story. One of them knows the whole story, having been present when the event took place. From one allusion he comprehends it only as much as they hear since they are not aware of the whole situation. The one who knows it all, however, understands much more from the bit that is told.

Let us return to the druggist. When you go to the druggist's shop there is a lot of sugar there, but he looks to see how much money you have and gives to you accordingly. In this case your "money" means your "aspiration" and "devotion." So words are revealed according to your aspiration and devotion. When you go to get sugar, the druggist looks into your sack to see how much it will hold and measures out accordingly, one measure or two. If someone brings trains of camels and many sacks, they call for the weighing-men. In a like manner there are some men for whom oceans are not enough, while for others a few drops suffice and more would be injurious. This applies not only to the realms of meaning, learning, and wisdom, but to everything, possessions—wealth and mines—they are all limitless but are given in proportion to the individual who could not bear more and would be driven mad. Don't you see that Majnun and Farhad—and other lovers too, who took to the desert out of love for a woman—were overburdened with passion beyond their capacity? Don't you see that Pharaoh claimed divinity when he was given too much wealth and kingdom? *There is no one thing but the storehouses thereof are in Our hands* [15:21]. God indicates, "There is nothing, good or evil, that We do not have in limitless supply in Our storehouses, but We send it in accord with capacity, for that is the best way."

Yes, one may be a "believer" and yet not know what one believes in, as a child "believes" in bread without knowing what it is he believes in. Similarly, the fruits of a tree dry up and wither from thirst; yet they do not know what "thirst" is. Man's existence is like a banner raised in the air. Then soldiers are sent to rally round that banner from every direction known to God, from the directions of reason, understanding, anger, ire, clemency, magnanimity, fear, and hope, and endless states and limitless qualities. Anyone who looks from afar sees only the banner, but one who looks from nearby realizes what substances and intrinsic meanings are there.

❖

Someone came. "Where have you been?" he was asked.

"We have missed you. Why have you stayed away so long?"

"It was necessary due to circumstances." he replied.

"We have been praying that these circumstances would change. Circumstances that bring about separation are unseemly."

Yes, by God, even such circumstances are from God, but they are good in God's eyes. It is said truly that everything is good and perfect in relation to God, if not in relation to us. Impurity and purity, neglect and attention to prayer, infidelity and faith, polytheism and monotheism—all these things are good in relation to God. But for us fornication, stealing, infidelity, and polytheism are bad—while monotheism, ritual prayer, and charity are good. Everything is good in relation to God: a king may have in his possession gallows, prisons, robes of honor, wealth and property, retinue, celebrations and proclamations of joy, drums and standards. In relation to the king, all these things are good. Just as his kingship is complemented by robes of honor, so also is it complemented by the gallows, executions, and prisons. All these things are complemental to his kingdom, although to the people robes of honor and the gallows are scarcely the same.

## EIGHT

Someone asked what is more excellent than prayer. The answer is, as we have already said, that the soul of prayer is better than prayer, as has been explained. Another answer is that faith is better than prayer, for prayer is obligatory at five specific times a day whereas faith is uninterrupted. One can be excused from prayer for a valid reason, and it is also allowable to postpone prayer. Faith without prayer merits reward, whereas prayer without faith, such as the prayer of hypocrites, does not. Prayer differs according to religion, but faith does not change by religion. Its states, its focus, and so forth, are immutable. There are other differences too. One hears the Word in accordance with the degree to which one has been "attracted." The hearer of the Word is like flour in the hands of a kneader; the Word is like water, and the "right amount of water must be mixed into the flour."

✤

My eye looks at another. What am I to do?
Make your complaint of yourself,
for you are the light of my eye.

"My eye looks at another" means that it searches for a focus of satisfaction[86] other than you. "What am I to do? You are the light" means that you are with yourself. You have not escaped from yourself since your light would be a hundred thousand you's.

✤

There was once a man as puny, weak, and contemptible as a wretched little bird. Even the ill-favored looked upon him with contempt and thanked God they were not so ugly, though before seeing him they had complained of their own

---

86 Reading, at the editor's suggestion, *mustamtaʿ* for the text's *mustamiʿ*.

ill-favored faces. If this were not enough, he was also rough-spoken and an enormous braggart. A member of the king's court, he constantly vexed the vizier, who exercised forbearance until one day he lost his temper and shouted: "O men of court, we picked this nobody from the gutter and educated him. Thanks to our own wealth and bounty and that of our ancestors, he became a somebody. Now he has come to the point of speaking thus to me!"

The fellow stood up to the vizier and said: "Men of court, grandees of the realm, what he says is true. I was elevated by his favor and nourished from the crumbs of his and his ancestors' table. Therefore I am as wretched and contemptible as you see me now. Had I been brought up by someone else, my standing and worth might have been more than they are now. He raised me from the dust, and for that reason I say, *Would to God I were dust* [78:40] Had someone else raised me from the dust, I would not have been such a laughing stock."

A disciple who is cared for by a man of God will have purity in his soul. Anyone educated and taught by an impostor or a hypocrite will be as miserable, weak, impotent, sorry, hesitant, and confused as the one who taught him. As *to those who believe not, their patrons are Tagut; they shall lead them from the light into the darkness* [2:257].

All knowledge was originally kneaded into Adam so that hidden things might show forth through his spirit just as clear water reveals the stones and clay beneath as well as reflecting on its surface what is above. This is in the nature of water: it requires no special treatment or training to do so. However, when it is mixed with dirt or other discolorations it loses that quality. It "forgets" how God has sent prophets and saints, like great clear waters, in order that the dark and murky waters touched by the clear waters might free themselves of their coincidental murkiness and discoloration. The murky water then "remembers." When it sees itself clear, it realizes that it was originally clear and that its murkiness and discoloration are coincidental. It recalls how it was before the advent of these coincidentals and says, *"This is what we were formerly sustained by"* [2:25]. Prophets and saints, therefore, are "reminders" of one's past condition. They do not put anything new into one's substance. Now every murky water that recognizes that great water and says, "I am from and of this," mingles with it. But murky waters, that do not recognize that water and think they are different or of another type, withdraw so into their murkiness and discoloration that they are unable to mingle in with the sea. They become ever more estranged from the sea.

> Those who recognize their common bond
> are bound together;
> Those who deny their common bond
> are split asunder.[87]

Hence it is said, Now *hath an apostle come unto you of yourselves* [9:128], that is to say, the great water is of the same type as the small water. They share the same soul and the same substance. When the small one does not recognize the great as being of the same soul, the nonrecognition stems not from the water itself but from its evil adherent, which casts its reflection over the water so that the water does not know whether its flight from the great water and the sea comes from itself or from the reflection of its evil adherent, so closely are the two mixed together. In a like manner, humble clay does not know whether its inclination to mud comes from its own self or from some other cause that has been admixed to its nature. Realize then that every line, every report, and every verse brought as proof by the prophets and saints are like two witnesses and their two testimonies: capable of acting as witness to many different cases, they testify in every regard according to the matter at hand. For instance, the same two persons may be witnesses to the disposition of a house, the sale of a shop, and to a marriage. In whichever case they are present they confine their testimony to the case at hand. The "form" of the witnessing is always the same but the "substance" is

---

87 Part of a prophetic hadith *(al-arwâhu junûd);* see *FAM* 52 #132.

different. "May God be beneficent to us and you! The color is that of blood, but the odor is that of musk."[88]

# NINE

We said, "Some with a desire to see you kept saying, 'I wish I could have seen the Master'."

That person will not see the Master in reality just now because the desire he has to see the Master is itself a veil over the Master. At this time he will not see the Master without a veil.

All desires, affections, loves, and fondnesses people have for all sorts of things, such as fathers, mothers, friends, the heavens and earth, gardens, pavilions, works, knowledge, food, and drink—one should realize that every desire is a desire for food, and such things are all "veils." When one passes beyond this world and sees that King without these "veils," then one will realize that all those things were "veils" and "coverings" and that what they were seeking was in reality that one thing. All problems will then be solved. All the heart's questions and difficulties will be answered, and everything will become clear. God's reply is not such that He must answer each and every problem individually. With one answer all problems are solved. In winter everyone bundles himself up and huddles in a warm place to escape the cold. All plants and trees drop their leaves and fruit because of the biting cold, and they conceal their raiment within themselves lest they suffer from the chill. When spring "answers" them by manifesting itself, all their different "questions" with regards to living, growing things and dead things are answered at one blow: the secondary causes disappear. Everything sticks its head out and knows what has caused that calamity.

God has created these "veils" for a good purpose. If He showed His beauty without a veil, we would not be able to bear it or benefit from it because we are benefitted and

---

88 The hadith is given in Suyuti, *Jami'*, II, 27.

strengthened indirectly. You see the sun? In its light we come and go; we see, and we are able to distinguish good from bad. In it we warm ourselves. Because of it, trees and gardens bear fruit. In its heat, bitter and sour unripe fruit becomes ripe and sweet. Under its influence, mines of gold, silver, ruby, and sapphire come to be. If this same sun, which is so beneficial indirectly, were to come closer, not only would it give no benefit but it would cause the whole world and everything in it to burn up and perish. When God manifests himself through a veil to a mountain, the mountain becomes full of trees and flowers, bedecked with greenery. But if He were to manifest himself without a veil, the mountain would be crushed and crumble to dust. But *when his Lord appeared with glory in the mount, He reduced it to dust* [7:143].

Here someone said, "But the sun in winter is the same sun as in spring."

"Our intent here," replied the Master, "is to make a comparison. A consistent parallel is one thing, comparison another."

Even if the intellect, striving with all its might, does not comprehend something, how can it cease to strive? If the intellect ceases its endeavor, then it is not the intellect, because the intellect is by definition that thing which night and day is restless and in a state of commotion with thought and endeavor to comprehend the Creator—even if He is incomprehensible and inconceivable. The intellect is like a moth and the divine beloved a candle. When the moth hurls himself at the candle, it is inevitable that it burn and perish. A moth is that thing that cannot resist the candle, no matter how much it suffers and burns in agony. Any animal that, like the moth, is unable to resist the candle's light and hurls itself at that light is a "moth." A candle into the light of which the moth throws itself but which does not burn the moth is not a "candle." Therefore, a man who can resist God and not strive with all his might to comprehend Him is not a man. A god one can comprehend is not God. "Man" then is that which is never free of striving; he is that which hovers restlessly around the "light" of God's Awesomeness. "God" is that which "burns" man and renders him nought but which no intellect can comprehend.

## TEN

The Parvana said, "Before the master appeared, Mawlana Baha'uddin was apologizing to me and saying that our lord had said, 'The Prince should not trouble himself in coming to see us because we are subject to various states. In one state we speak; in another we do not. In one state we can deal with people; in another we prefer to withdraw in solitude. And sometimes we are completely absorbed and bewildered. God forbid the prince come while we are unable to commiserate with him or have not the leisure to converse with him and counsel him. It would be better therefore for us to go to visit our friends when we are at leisure so that we may pay attention and be of benefit to them.'

"I told Mawlana Baha'uddin in reply," said the prince, "that I do not come in order for our lord to pay attention to me and converse with me but rather in order that I may have the honor of being among the ranks of his servants. Now it happened at that time that our lord was preoccupied and did not make an appearance. He kept me waiting for a long time that I might realize how difficult it was for the Muslims and good people I kept waiting at my door. Our lord made me taste the bitterness of that experience, thereby teaching me better than to do the same to others."

"No," our master said to him, "I kept you waiting purely out of favoritism. It is told that God says, 'O servant of mine, I could grant the wishes you express in your prayer immediately, but your plaintive cries are dear to me. Response comes late in order that you plead more, so much do I enjoy the sound of your pleading.'"

For instance, two beggars come to someone's door. One is agreeable and dear to the master of the house, but the other is repulsive. The master tells his servant, "Quickly, without delay, give that repulsive man a piece of bread so that he will go away from our door as soon as possible. Tell the other one, who is dear to us, that the bread is not baked yet and that he should wait until it is ready."

I would rather see my friends and gaze upon them to my fill—and they upon me—because when friends here in this life have seen each other's substance thoroughly, their friendship will gain in intensity in the next world. They will recognize each other immediately. Knowing how they were together in this world, they will cling fast together because one quickly loses one's friends. Don't you see how in this world you become fast friends with someone? In your opinion that person is a paragon of virtue, like Joseph. Yet, with one untoward act he is severed from your sight and lost to you forever. That "Joseph" is turned into a wolf. The same person you used to consider a "Joseph" you now see as a wolf. Even though his form is unchanged and he is the same person you used to see, by virtue of this one incident you have lost him. Tomorrow when the Resurrection comes and this essence is changed into another essence, if you have not come to know a person well and not penetrated thoroughly into his essence, how then will you recognize him? The gist of this is that we must see each other deeply and go beyond those good and bad qualities that adhere to every human being. We must penetrate and see each other's essences because those qualities that distinguish men one from another are not their true characteristics.

They tell of a man who said, "I know so-and-so very well. I can tell you what he is like." When asked to describe him he said, "He was my herdsman and had two black cows. He is to this day the same."

Now people say that they have seen their friends and know them well; yet however they may describe them, in truth their description is no more than if they were to tell the story of the two black cows, which was no description of the man at all. One must go beyond a man's good and bad qualities and penetrate into his essence to see what he is like substantially, for that is really "seeing" and "knowing."

It is strange that people can ask how the saints and prophets are enamoured of, derive strength from, and are affected by the unqualifiable world, seeing that it has neither place nor form and is indescribable. They are always in that world. When a person loves another and derives strength from him, he derives grace and beneficence, knowledge, thought and contemplation, joy and sorrow from him. This all takes place in the "placeless" world. One derives sustenance from abstractions and is affected by them. This is not so surprising, and yet people are amazed that saints can be lovers of the "placeless" world and that they receive assistance from there.

There was a metaphysician who denied the existence of this concept. One day he fell ill and was in pain for a long time. A theologian went to visit him and asked, "What are you seeking?"

"Health," replied the metaphysician.

"Describe for me this 'health' so that I may bring it about," said the theologian.

"Health has no form," he answered.

"If health cannot be qualified, how can you be looking for it?" he asked. "Tell me what 'health' is."

"This much I know," he replied. "When health comes I am robust. I get plump; my color is ruddy and clear, and I feel fresh and in bloom."

"I am asking you for health itself," he said. "What is the essence of health?"

"I do not know," answered the other. "It cannot be qualified."

"If you become a Muslim and repent of your former ways," said the theologian, "I will treat you, make you whole, and help you regain your health."

The Prophet was asked whether or not one in human form could derive benefit from unqualifiable concepts. He replied, "Here are the sky and the earth; as you see their form you derive benefit through it from the universal concept." As you can see, the dominance of the celestial spheres, the rain that comes from the clouds as it should in summer and winter, and the seasonal changes are all for the best and in accordance with Providence. Now, how does an inanimate cloud know when it is time to rain? How does the earth which you see here take in plants and turn one into ten? Someone does this. Through this world you can see "someone" and be helped. Just as the "shell" helps you to perceive the intrinsic meaning of humanity, you can be helped to perceive the intrinsic meaning of the world through its form.

When the Prophet became "intoxicated" and spoke while beside himself, he said, "God spoke." Now, although from the point of view of form it was his own tongue that spoke; he himself was not there at all: the "speaker" was God. Since the Prophet knew from the very beginning that he was ignorant of such words, when he saw those words issuing forth from himself, he realized that he was not the same person he had been. This is known as the "domination" of God. The Prophet told not only about men and prophets who antedated his lifetime by thousands of years but also about what would happen until the end of the world; he could also speak of God's Throne and the cosmos. Yet his being belonged to "yesterday"; temporally-created beings cannot speak of these things.[89] How can the temporal tell about the eternal? It is obvious, therefore, that it was not he who was speaking but God. *He doth not speak of his own will; it is not other than a revelation which hath been revealed unto him* [53:3-4]. God transcends form and letters. His speech is outside of letters and voices, but He implements His speech through whatever words, voices, or languages He wills.

In caravans along the road there are stone figurines and stone birds set around the edges of pools. Water flows from their mouths and spills into the pools, but any intelligent person knows that the water does not come from the figurine's mouth but from some other place.

---

89 "Yesterday" in the language of the Sufis refers to a "time" in pre-eternity *(azal)* prior to the creation of serial time, when the uncreated souls of mankind slumbered within God's bosom.

If you want to "know" someone, make him speak. Then you can "know" him for what he is from his speech. What if he is an imposter and, having been told that a man may be known by his speech, intentionally refrains from speaking in order not to be found out? This is like the story they tell of a child in the wilderness who said to his mother, "At night when it's dark a bogeyman appears to me. I'm afraid of him."

"Don't be afraid," said the mother. "When you see that form, be brave and attack it. You'll see it's just a figment of your imagination."

"But, mother," said the child, "what should I do if the bogeyman's mother has told him to do the same thing?"

Now, if this fellow has been advised not to speak in order not to be found out, how am I to know him for what he is? The answer is to be silent in his presence. Give yourself over to him and be patient. Perhaps a word may escape from his lips. If not, a word may inadvertently escape from your lips, or a thought or idea may occur to you. From that thought or idea you may "know" him because you will have been "influenced" by him. It is his "reflection" and his "state" that will have showed up within you.

Shaykh Sarrazi was seated among his disciples, one of whom suddenly had a craving for roasted lamb's head. The shaykh indicated that some roasted lamb's head should be brought for him. "Shaykh," they said, "how did you know he wanted that?"

"Because," he replied, "for thirty years I have had no 'cravings.' I have purified myself and transcended all 'cravings.' I have become as plain as a mirror with no image upon it. When I had a desire for roasted lamb's head, and when it became a 'craving,' I knew that it was from that fellow. A mirror has no image: if an image appears in a mirror it must come from something else."

A saint went on a retreat to seek a sublime goal. A voice came to him, saying: "Such a sublime goal cannot be attained by means of retreat. Leave your retreat so that a great man's gaze may fall upon you and cause you to reach your goal."

"Where am I to find this great man?" he asked.

"In the congregational mosque," he was told.

"How am I to recognize him among so many people?"

"Go!" said the voice. "He will recognize you and gaze upon you. And the sign of his gaze shall be this, that a ewer shall fall from your hand and you shall fall unconscious, whence you shall know that he has gazed upon you." And so he filled a ewer with water and, going from row to row, gave drink to the assembly at the mosque. Suddenly he had a strange sensation and, uttering a loud shriek, dropped the ewer. While he was lying unconscious in a corner, the congregation departed. When he came to, he saw that he was alone. He never saw that "king" who had cast his glance upon him, but he did attain his goal.

God has men who never show themselves because of God's excessive jealousy of them, but they do bestow gifts and exalted goals upon those who seek them. Such great kings are rare and precious indeed.

We said, "Great men come into your presence."

"We have no 'presence' any more," he said. "It has been a long time since we have had 'presence.' If they come, they come into the presence of an image they themselves have shaped by belief. Some people once said to Jesus, 'We will come to your house.' 'Where and when in this world,' he said, 'have we ever had a house?' "

A tale is told of Jesus wandering in the desert. A heavy rainstorm began, so he took momentary shelter in a jackal's den in a cave until the rain should stop. While there he received an inspiration to this effect: leave the jackal's den for its young cannot rest with you here.

"O Lord," he cried, "there is refuge for the jackal's young but none for the son of Mary!"

"If the jackal's young has shelter," God replied," it has no beloved to drive it from its home. You do have such a motivator. If you have no home, what cause for concern is it?

The grace and honor done specially to you by such a motivator to drive you on is a thousand thousand times more valuable than the sky, the earth, this world, the next world, and the Divine Throne all together."

*

"Therefore," said the Master, "if the prince comes and we do not appear immediately, he should not be hurt or concerned. Does he come to honor us or himself? If he comes in order to honor us, then the longer he sits waiting for us, the more honor accrues to us. If he means to honor himself and be recompensed in heaven, then when he waits and suffers the waiting, his recompense will be all the greater. On both counts he gets double what he comes for. He should therefore be glad and rejoice."

## ELEVEN

The saying "hearts bear mutual testimony" refers to a communication that is not said openly. When hearts communicate directly one with another, what need is there for words or tongues?

"Yes," said the viceroy, "the heart does give testimony, but its function is separate from that of the ear, the eye or the tongue. There is a need for each of them so that the benefits may increase."

If the heart is totally absorbed, then everything else is obliterated by it, and there is no need for the tongue. Layla was not pure spirit; she was flesh and blood. Loving her exerted such a power of absorption on Majnun that he did not need to see her with his eyes or hear her voice because he did not consider her separate from himself.

> Your image is in my eye; your name upon my lips;
> The thought of you is in my heart.

To where should I write?[90]

A corporeal being has such power that love for it can put a
man into a state wherein he does not consider himself as
separate from that being: all his senses, seeing, hearing, smell,
and so forth are so absorbed in that corporeal being that no
member of his body seeks any other sensible stimulation. This
is because he sees everything "collected" and considers
everything "present." If any one of the members we have
mentioned finds total pleasure, then all the others will be
absorbed in the rapture of that one and will seek no other
stimulation. When a sensory organ seeks separate stimulation,
it indicates that it has not been entirely taken over—as can
happen—but has found partial fulfillment only. When one
sense has not become totally absorbed, the other senses seek
their own separate satisfactions. In substance the sensory
organs are a whole, but in form they are separate units. When
one organ is absorbed, all the others become absorbed in that
one. It is like a fly: when it flies, its wings move, its head
moves, all of its parts move. When it is immersed in honey, all
its parts alike cease to move: its "absorption" is such that it is
not aware of itself and no longer makes any exertion, motion,
or movement. Whatever motion comes from a drowned
person is not really from him but from the water. If he is still
thrashing about in the water, then he cannot be called
drowned. If he can cry out, "Help! I'm drowning!" then he
cannot be said to have drowned yet. People think that to say "I
am God"[91] is a claim of greatness, but it is actually extreme
humility. Anyone who says "I am God's servant" predicates
two existences, his own and God's, while the one who says "I
am God" nullifies himself—that is, he gives up his own

---

90 The line of poetry was attributed to Hallaj (see Glossary of Persons)
by Louis Massignon, *Le Diwan d'al-Hallaj*, p. 106. It has been excluded as
spurious from the *Diwan al-Hallaj*, edited by Kamil al-Shaybi.

91 *Ana 'l-haqq* ("I am God," or "I am Reality") is the famous theopathic
locution of the martyr-mystic Husayn ibn Mansur al-Hallaj (q.v.).

existence as naught. It is said that "I am God" means: "I do not exist; everything is He. Existence is God's alone; I am utter, pure nonexistence; I am nothing." There is more humility in this than any claim to greatness, but people do not comprehend. When a man acknowledges his servitude to God, he is aware of his act of being a servant. It may be for God, but he still sees himself and his own act along with seeing God. He is not "drowned"; drowned is he in whom there is no motion or action but whose movement is the movement of the water.

A lion chases a gazelle. The gazelle flees from the lion. There are two existences, the lion's and the gazelle's. When the lion catches the gazelle and the gazelle faints in fear under the lion's wrathful paw, then there remains only the lion's existence: the gazelle's being is obliterated.

The saints' "absorption" is such that God causes them to fear Him with a fear different from the fear humans have of lions, tigers, and tyrants. He reveals to them that fear is from God, security is from God, pleasure and ease are from God, and the necessities of day-to-day life are from God. To the saints God appears in a particular, sensible form that can be seen with the eye, like that of a lion, a tiger, or fire. It is apparent to the saint that the lion or tiger's form he is seeing is not of this world but rather an "ideal" form, one that has been given shape: it is God revealing himself in a form of exquisite beauty. Gardens, camels, houris, mansions, food and drink, robes of honor, cities, houses, and various wonders are the same: the saint knows that none of these is of this world, but God has made them visible by garbing them in form. He knows for certain that fear is from God, security is from God, and all serenity and beautiful things are from God. Now, although the saint's "fear" does not resemble ordinary fear, it can be glimpsed through ordinary fear. It cannot be proven logically. The concept of everything's being from God is bestowed by God. The philosopher knows this, but he knows it through logical proof, and logical proof does not last. The pleasure that is derived from logical proof has no eternality. If you expound a logical argument to someone, he will be happy and rejoice in it; but when the memory of it fades, so do his happiness and joy. For instance, one may know through logical proof that this house had a maker, that the maker had eyes and was not blind, that he was strong and not weak, that he existed and was not non-existent, that he was alive and not dead, and that he had had previous experience in making houses. All these things one can know through logical proof, but the proof does not last. It can be soon forgotten. When "lovers" on the other hand, do servitude, know the Maker, see with the Eye of Certitude, break bread and mingle together, then the Maker is never absent from their imagination and sight. Such men have "passed away" into God; with regard to these men sin is not sin and crime is not crime. These men are dominated and consumed.

A king once commanded each of his slaves to hold a golden goblet for a guest who was coming. Even his favorite slave he ordered to hold a goblet, but when the king himself appeared, that slave, intoxicated at the sight of the king, swooned and dropped the goblet, shattering it to pieces. Seeing this, the others said, "Perhaps this is what we are supposed to do." And they all threw down their goblets intentionally. The king rebuked them and asked why they had done what they did.

"Because your favorite did so," they answered.

"You fools," said the king, "he didn't do it, I did it!"

Considered externally, all those "forms" were transgressions—except for that one particular transgression, which was not only the soul of obedience but beyond the pale of obedience and transgression. The "goal" was that one slave: the rest were followers of the king and hence followers of that slave inasmuch as he was the essence of the king. Slavery was no more than a form over him; he was filled with the king's beauty.

God says, "Were it not for thee, I would not have created the firmament."[92] What "I-am-Reality" *(ana 'l-haqq)* means is,

---

92 For the divine hadith *(lawlâka lamâ)* see *FAM* 172.

"for myself have I created the firmament"—it is "I-am-Reality" expressed another way, by another symbol. The mystics' words appear in a hundred different forms, but if God is one and the Way is one, how can their words be other than one? They do appear in different guises, but in substance they are one. Variety occurs in form; in substance all is unified. When a prince orders a tent, one person twists rope, one makes stakes, one weaves cloth, one stitches, one cuts, one wields a needle. Although externally all these forms appear different and various, from the point of view of intrinsic meaning they are all unified in that they are all doing one thing. The conditions of this world are like this, when you think about it. Everyone, sinner and saint, obedient and disobedient, demon and angel alike, is performing servitude to God. For instance, a king desires to test his slaves in order to separate the constant from the inconstant, the trustworthy from the untrustworthy, the faithful from the treacherous. There must be a "devil's advocate," an agent provocateur, in order to discover constancy toward the king. How otherwise could it be ascertained? The advocate provocateur, therefore, acts as a slave of the king, for such is the king's desire that he should do. A wind is sent to distinguish the stable from the unstable, to dislodge the gnats from the trees in the garden. The gnats will leave, while the sparrow hawks will remain.[93]

A king once ordered his slave girl to bedeck herself and show herself to his slaves in order to discover their trustworthiness or treachery. Although the girl's action may have appeared outwardly to be a transgression of modesty, in reality it was an act of servitude to the king.

All these "slaves" then, good and bad, seeing themselves in this world, perform servitude and obedience to God, not by logical proof or blind adherence to authoritative tradition but by "veilless" witnessing, since all, good and evil, are slaves of God and do obedience to Him. *There is nothing that does not*

---

93 The construction depends on a word-play: *pashah* ("gnat") and *bâshah* ("sparrow hawk"), itself a homonym to pun with *bâ shah* ("with the king").

*exalt in His praise* [17:44]. For these people this world is the "reawakening" since "resurrection" consists of serving God and doing nothing other than serving Him. This concept they perceive here. "Were the covering to be removed, I would not be more certain."

Annotatively the word *âlim* should designate one who is more exalted than an *ârif* because God is called *âlim* but not *ârif*. *Ârif* means one who formerly did not know something and then came to know, and this cannot be said of God. Connotatively, on the other hand, an *ârif* is greater because he is someone who knows something outside of logical reasoning. What the mystics mean by *ârif* is someone who perceives the world by revelation and apocalypse. It is said that one *âlim* is better than a hundred ascetics. That is so because an ascetic must perform asceticism with knowledge. Asceticism without knowledge is absurd. What is asceticism? It means to turn away from this world and to attend to acts of piety and the next world. It is also necessary to know this world with all its ugliness and impermanence and likewise to know the grace, permanence, and eternality of the next world. To exert effort in pious acts means to know not only *how* to perform those acts but also *what* acts one should perform, and this means knowledge. Asceticism is thus impossible without knowledge, and an ascetic is of necessity a "knower" also.

The saying that an *âlim* is better than a hundred ascetics is true, though its meaning has not been properly understood. The knowledge that is meant is a "secondary knowledge" God gives after one possesses the primary asceticism and knowledge. The secondary knowledge is the fruit of the former knowledge and asceticism. Such a "knower" is absolutely better than a hundred thousand ascetics. It is like a man who planted a tree that then bore fruit. A tree that has already borne fruit is absolutely better than a hundred trees that have not yet yielded because it is possible that none of them may ever yield, given the many blights that may befall them. A pilgrim who has reached the Kaaba is better than one who is still making his way through the desert, since there is a chance that he may not make it, while the former has actually arrived. One actuality is better than a thousand chances.

"But the one who hasn't arrived yet still has hope," said the Viceroy.

"Where is the hopeful in comparison to the one who has made it?" said the Master. "There is a big difference between chance and surety. Why do we need to discuss the difference? It is readily apparent to all. We are discussing surety, and there are grave differences between one kind of surety and another. Muhammad's superiority over all the other prophets stems from surety. Otherwise, all prophets are in the state of surety in that they have passed beyond the state of fear, but there are different states of surety. *And We raise some of them several degrees above the others* [43:32]. The world of fear and the stages of fear can be described, but the stages of surety cannot. If one looks into the world of fear, one can see how each person exerts himself: one physically, another monetarily, another psychically. One fasts; another prays; one does ten *rak'as*, another a hundred. Their stages have form and determination, that is, they can be described, just as the stages from Konya to Caesarea are determinate. They are Qaymaz, Uprukh, Sultan, and so forth. On the other hand, the stages on the sea between Antalya and Alexandria cannot be described. A ship's captain may know them, but he won't tell them to 'landlubbers' because they would not understand."

"But the mere telling of them is beneficial," said the Prince. "Even if they do not know everything, they can learn a little and then guess the rest."

"Yes, indeed," said the Master. "A person who stays awake in the dark at night is determined to reach daybreak. Even if he does not know how he is going, he is still approaching daybreak while waiting. Again, a man traveling with a caravan on a dark, overcast night does not know where he is, how far he has gone, or what he has passed. At daybreak, however, he sees the results of having traveled, that is, he will have come to some place. Whoever labors for the glory of God is never lost, though he shut both his eyes. *Whoso doeth a particle of good shall see it* [99:7]. Here you are in darkness; you are 'veiled' so that you cannot see how far you have progressed. In the end, however, you will perceive that 'this world is the "seedbed" of the hereafter.'⁹⁴ Whatever you sow here you will reap there."

Jesus laughed a lot. John the Baptist wept a lot. John said to Jesus, "You have become mighty secure from God's subtle deceits to laugh so much."

"You," replied Jesus, "are mighty heedless of God's subtle and mysterious favor and grace to weep so much!"

One of God's saints, who was present at this exchange, asked God which of the two was the more exalted in station. God answered, "The one who thinks better of me," that is, "Wherever my servant thinks of me, I am there.⁹⁵ I have a form and image for each of My servants. Whatever each of them imagines Me to be, that I am. I am bound to images where God is; I am annoyed by any reality where God is not. O my servants, cleanse your thoughts, for they are my dwelling places. Now try yourself and see what is more beneficial to you—weeping, laughter, fasting, prayer, or retreat. Adopt whichever of these suits you best and causes you to advance more."

"Consult your heart even if the legalist has issued you an opinion."⁹⁶ You have a concept within you. Show the legalists' opinion to that concept so that it can choose what suits it best. When a physician comes to a sick person he makes inquiries of the "internal physician" you have within you, that is, your temperament, or that which accepts what is good for you and rejects what is bad. Therefore, the external physician inquires of the internal physician as to the quality of what you have eaten, whether it was heavy or light, and how you have been sleeping. The external physician makes his diagnosis based on what the internal physician tells him. The internal physician, the temperament, is then the principal one; and when he "falls

---

94 The prophetic hadith *(al-dunyâ mazra'at)* is given in *FAM* 112 #338.

95 The divine hadith *(ana 'ind)* is given in Suyuti, *Jami'*, II, 82.

96 For the prophetic hadith *(istafti qalbaka)* see *FAM* 188 #597.

ill," meaning that the temperament becomes corrupt, the result is that he sees things "backwards" and describes his symptoms "crooked." He calls sugar sour and vinegar sweet. In this case he is in need of the external physician to help him return to his normal condition, whereupon the external physician can once again take counsel from the internal. Now, man also has a temperament for concepts; and when it falls ill, whatever his internal senses see or say is contrary to actuality. In this case, the saints are the physicians who help his temperament to straighten out and his heart and religion to be strengthened. "Show me things as they are!"[97]

A human being is a great thing: everything is inscribed within him, but "veils" and "obfuscations" prevent him from reading the knowledge he has within himself. The "veils" and "obfuscations" are various preoccupations, worldly stratagems, and desires. Yet, despite all these things that lie hidden in the "darkness" behind the "veils," man does manage to read something and to be aware of what he reads. Consider how "aware" he becomes and what knowledge of himself he discovers when the veils are lifted and the darkness is dissipated. All manner of trades, like tailoring, building, harvesting, goldsmithery, astronomy, medicine—ad infinitum—have been discovered from within man, not from under rocks and mud clumps. It is said that a raven taught man to bury the dead,[98] but it actually came from a reflection of man cast onto the raven. It was man's own urge that caused him to do it, for, after all, animals are part of man. How can a part teach the whole? Similarly, if man wants to write with his left hand, he may pick up the pen but, no matter how firm his

---

97 For the prophetic hadith *(arinâ 'l-ashyâ')* see *FAM* 45 #116.

98 According to Islamic legend, when Cain killed Abel he did not know what to do with the corpse until two ravens appeared and fought to the death. The victor scratched the earth and dug a hole to bury that dead raven, thereby teaching mankind how to inter the dead. See Koran 5:34 and Thackston, *Tales of the Prophets*, p. 78. Rumi also summarizes this legend in section 38 below.

resolve may be, his hand will still shake as it writes. Nonetheless, the hand does write something because of the command from the heart.

When the Prince comes, Mawlana utters great words. Since speech cannot be interrupted when one is a master of words, words always come to him. Words are in communication with him. If trees do not put forth leaves or fruit in winter, one must not think that they are idle. They are always at work. Winter is their time for "input"; summer their time for "output." Their "output" can be seen by all, but their "input" is not visible. It is like someone who gives a banquet: he makes an elaborate "output," which all can see; but his "input," that is his saving little by little for the banquet, nobody sees or knows about. The principal thing is the "input," for it is that from which our "outputs" are made.

We are always and ever in communication with that person with whom we are in union—in silence, in his presence, and in his absence. Even in war we are together, mingled together. Even when we are striking each other with our fists we are in communication, in touch, in union. That is no fist, for in it are raisins. If you don't believe it, open your fist and see whether there are raisins or precious pearls in it!

Other men speak subtle and learned things in prose and poetry, but here the Prince is inclined towards us and is here with us. And it is not because of our great knowledge, subtle wit, or sage counsel. Those things can be found anywhere. They are in no short supply. He loves me and inclined to me for another reason, which is that he sees something else; he sees another illumination that transcends what he has seen in others.

It is said that a king summoned Majnun and asked, "What is wrong with you? What has happened to you that you have disgraced yourself, forsaken your kith and kin, and gone to wrack and ruin? What is this Layla? What beauty does she possess? Come, let me show you some real beauties. I shall give them to you."

When the beauties came in and were shown to Majnun, he lowered his head and gazed at the ground.

"Raise your head," said the king, "and behold!"

"I am afraid," said Majnun, "that my love for Layla is a drawn sword. If I raise my head it will be cut off." Such was his absorption in his love for Layla. The others too had eyes, lips and noses. What had he seen in Layla that had made him the way he was?

## TWELVE

"We have been longing to see you," the Master said, "but since we knew that you were preoccupied with the welfare of the people, we have not troubled you."

"The obligation was ours," said the Prince. "Now that the emergency is over, henceforth we shall attend you."

"It makes no difference," the Master said. "It is all the same. You are so gracious that all things are the same to you. How can one speak of troubling? Yet, since we know that today you are engaged in good deeds and charitable works, we of course have recourse to you."

We were just deliberating whether one should take from a man who has a family and give to a man who has none. The literalists say that one should take from a family man and give to one who has no dependents. Yet, upon close inspection, the latter is actually burdened. If a spiritual person possessed of substance strikes another and breaks his head and nose, everyone will say that the latter is the injured party, even though in reality the injured party is the one who has struck the blow. A wrongdoer is one who does not act in his own best interests. The one who was hit and got his head broken is the wrongdoer, while the one who struck the blow is assuredly the injured party. Since he is possessed of substance and is absorbed in God, his actions are God's actions, and God cannot be called a wrongdoer. Similarly, the Prophet slew, shed blood, and raided; yet those who were slain and raided were the wrongdoers: the Prophet was the injured party.

For example, a westerner dwells in the west and an easterner comes to the west. The "stranger" is the westerner.[99] What sort of stranger is he who comes from the east? Since the whole world is no more than one house, he has simply gone from one room to another, from one corner to another. Is he not still in the very same house? Nonetheless, the westerner who is possessed of substance has left the house. After all, the Prophet said, "Islam began as a stranger."[100] He did not say that the easterner began as a stranger. So, when the Prophet was defeated he was the injured party. When he was victorious he was still the injured party. In both cases he was in the right, and he who is in the right is the injured party.

The Prophet had pity on his captives. God sent an inspiration into the Apostle's heart, saying, "Tell them that if, in this state in which they are held in chains, they intend to do good, God will deliver them, restore to them manifold what they have lost, and grant them forgiveness and pardon in the next life—two treasures, one that has gone from them and one in the world to come."

The Prince asked, "If a man does a deed, do success and good come from the deed itself, or are they gifts from God?"

"Both good and success are God's gifts," the Master said, "but God is so extremely gracious that He attributes both to man, saying, 'Both are yours,' *as a reward for that which they have wrought.*" [32:17].

"If God is so gracious," said the Prince, "then anyone who truly seeks will find."

But without a leader it does not happen that way. When the Israelites were obedient to Moses, a dry way was opened in the sea for them to pass through; but as soon as they began to show opposition they wandered in the wilderness for many years. A leader must always attend to the best interests of those who are perceived to be obedient to him. For example, many

---

99 This argument depends on an etymological similarity between the word *maghrib* "west" and *gharîb* "stranger."

100 For the prophetic hadith *(al-islâmu bada'a)* see *FAM* 158 #489.

soldiers serve under a general. As long as they remain obedient to him, he will expend his intellect on their behalf and will be bound to their best interests. On the other hand, if they are insubordinate, why should he worry about managing their affairs? The intellect in man's body is like a prince: as long as the subjects of the body are in obedience all is well, but when they become rebellious, all falls to corruption. Don't you see what corruptions arise from a man's hand, feet, and tongue, the subjects of his body, when he has drunk too much wine? When he sobers up the next day, he says, "Oh, what have I done? Why did I get in a fight? Why did I curse?" So, matters are fine as long as there is a leader in the city and the inhabitants are in obedience to him. Now, as long as everyone is obedient, the intellect is thinking of the subjects' best interests. If, for example, the mind thinks, "I will go," it can only go if the feet are in obedience; otherwise it cannot have such a thought. Just as the intellect is the prince of the body, the saint is the intellect in the midst of these other entities, the people. In relation to the saint the people, despite their having their own intellects, knowledge, speculative ability, and learning, are nothing but a "body." Now, when the body of the people is not obedient to the intellect,[101] everything is in disarray. When they are obedient, they should follow whatever he does. Because they are incapable of understanding through their own intellects, they must not have recourse to their own minds but must obey that one. When a lad is apprenticed to a master tailor, he must be obedient. If he is given a patch to sew, he must sew the patch; if he is given a seam, he must stitch the seam. If he wants to learn, he must abandon his own initiative and be totally under his master's rule.

We hope that God will bring about a state, namely his providence, that is above and beyond a hundred thousand strivings and efforts, for *the night of Al Kadr is better than a thousand months* [97:3]. This statement is the same as the saying, "One tug from God is better than the worship of all

---

101 Reading here with manuscript H.

men and djinn."[102] That is to say, the advent of God's providence does the work of a hundred thousand efforts. Extra effort is well and good—even beneficial—but what is it next to providence?

The Prince asked, "Does providence bring effort?"

"Why should it not?" answered the Master. "When there is providence there is also effort." What effort did it cost Jesus to say from the cradle, *"Verily I am the servant of God: he hath given me the book of the gospel"* [19:30]? John the Baptist described him while still in his mother's womb. Speech came to Muhammad the Apostle of God without effort, for he said, *"He whose breast God hath enlarged."* [39:22]. When one first awakens from error there is grace; it is a pure gift of God's grace. If it were not so, why didn't others who were just like Muhammad have it? Grace and rebuke are like sparks that fly out of the fire. At first the spark is a "gift," but when you put cotton to it, nurse it along, and spread it, then the spark becomes "grace and rebuke." In the first instance man is small and weak: *man was created weak* [4:28]. But, just like fire, when you nurse that weak one he becomes huge and consumes a whole world; the little fire becomes large: *thou art of a noble disposition* [68:4].

*

I said, "Our master loves you very much."

The Master said, "Neither my coming here nor my speaking is commensurate with my love. I say what comes. If God wills, he will make these paltry words beneficial. He will lodge them in your breast and make great use of them. If he does not so will, you can take a hundred thousand words but they will not stick in your heart; they will pass away and be forgotten. They will be like a spark that falls on a singed rag: if God wills, that one spark will take and spread; if He does not will, a hundred sparks can fall on the rag, but they will all go out without a trace."

---

102 Identified as a dictum of Abu'l-Qasim Ibrahim ibn Muhammad Nasrabadi (d. 982).

*The hosts of heaven and earth are God's* [48:4]. These words are God's soldiers who break in and capture fortresses at his command. If He orders several thousand soldiers to go to a fortress but *not* to seize it, they will do as commanded. If He orders a single soldier to take a fortress, that one soldier will break in and seize it. He assigns a gnat to Nimrod, and it destroys him.[103]

It is said that for the one who knows, a *danaq* and a *dinar*, or a lion and a cat, are the same. If God gives his blessing, one *danaq* will do what a thousand *dinars* can do, and even more. If he withdraws his blessing from those thousand *dinars*, they will not be able to do what one *danaq* can. If he assigns a cat to a lion, it will destroy the lion as the gnat did Nimrod. If he assigns a lion, all lions will tremble before it, or else that same lion may become a donkey, just as some dervishes ride lions and just as the fire became *cold and a preservation* [21:69] for Abraham.[104] That fire turned into a rose garden because there was no command from God that it should burn him. In short, for those who realize that everything is from God, everything is the same.

We hope to God that you hear these words from within, for there lies the benefit. A thousand robbers may come from the outside, but they will not be able to open the door until another thief helps them by unlocking it from the inside. You can say a thousand words on the outside, but so long as there is no one on the inside to say that they are true, there is no benefit. It is like a tree: so long as there is no freshness in the root, it makes no difference how much you water it. There must first be freshness in the root for water to be of benefit.

---

103 According to Islamic legend, the tyrant Nimrod, the tormentor of Abraham, met a painful doom by means of a gnat God sent to gnaw at his brain. See Thackston, *Tales,* p. 149f.

104 Nimrod had Abraham cast into a fiery pit, but at God's command the fire became cool and peaceful *(bardan wa-salâman,* Kor. 21:69). Generally in Persian poetry the "coolness and peace" of the fire is interpreted as a rosegarden. See Thackston, *Tales,* p. 147f.

"Though one sees a hundred thousand lights, light rests only on the origin." Even though the whole world be enveloped in light, a man whose eye is not bright will not be able to see it. The principal thing is the receptivity in the soul. The soul is one thing, the spirit another. Don't you see how the soul roams abroad during sleep? While the spirit remains in the body, the soul travels and becomes something else. When Ali said, "Who knows his soul knows his Lord,"[105] he was speaking of this soul. If we say that he was speaking of this soul, then that is no small matter. If, on the other hand, we explain it as that soul, then the listener will understand it as this same soul because he does not know that soul.[106] For example, if you hold up a small mirror, it makes no difference whether what it shows looks big or small, for it is still that thing itself. It is impossible for this to be conveyed through the medium of words. In talking there is only enough to produce a hint of stimulation.

There exists outside of what we are saying a world for us to seek. This world and its pleasures are allotted to man's animal nature; they are fodder for his animality. The principal thing in man is in decline. Man is called a rational animal; therefore, he is two things. What feeds his animality in this world is passion and desire; but the food for his essential part is knowledge, wisdom and the vision of God. Man's animal nature avoids the Real, and his human nature flies from this world. *One of you is an unbeliever, and another of you is a believer* [64:2]. There are two personae in conflict in this being. "With whom shall luck be? Whom shall fortune favor?"

There is no doubt that this world is midwinter. Why are inanimate objects called "solid"? Because they are all

---

105 This famous expression of Sufi thought is most often quoted as a prophetic hadith *(man 'arafa)*. See note 11.

106 The problem arises with the Arabo-Persian use of *nafs* ("soul, self"). Like the Greek *psyche, nafs* is used both for the immortal soul of a human, which survives death, and also for the carnal, or lower, soul.

"frozen."[107] These rocks, mountains, and other coverings that garb this world are all "frozen." If the world is not midwinter, why is it frozen? The concept of the world is simple and cannot be seen, but through effect one can know that there are such things as wind and cold. This world is like the season of midwinter when everything is frozen and solidified. What sort of midwinter? A mental midwinter, not a tangible one. When that "divine" breeze comes, the mountains of this world will begin to melt and turn to water. Just as the heat of midsummer causes all frozen things to melt, so on the Day of Resurrection, when that breeze comes, all things will melt.

God surrounds you with word-soldiers both to repel your enemies and to be a means of overpowering the enemy. Internal enemies are the real enemy. After all, external enemies are nothing. What could they be? Don't you see how many thousands of unbelievers are prisoners of an unbeliever, who is their king? That one unbeliever is a prisoner of thought. We realize thus that thoughts are to be reckoned with, since by means of one feeble, mean thought so many thousands of people are held captive. Consider what might and splendor there is, how enemies are overpowered, and what worlds are subjugated where thoughts are limitless!

When I see distinctly that a hundred thousand forms without bound and hosts without end, multitude upon multitude, are held captive by a person who is held captive in turn by a miserable thought, then all these are prisoners of that one thought. How would they be if the thoughts were great, endless, grave, holy and sublime? We realize therefore that thoughts matter; forms are secondary, mere instruments. Without thoughts, forms are ineffectual "solids." Whoever sees only form is himself "frozen solid" and has no way to reach the intrinsic meaning. He is a child and immature, even though physically he may be a hundred years old. "We have returned

---

107 This line of reasoning is beased on an etymological similarity between *jamâd* ("solid, inanimate") and *munjamid* ("frozen").

from the minor struggle to the major struggle,"[108] that is, we were in combat with forms and were doing battle with a "formal" adversary. Now we are doing battle with thoughts so that the good thoughts may defeat the bad ones and expel them from the kingdom of the body.

In this struggle, this major battle, ideas matter and are operative without the means of the body. Inasmuch as the Active Intellect turns the celestial spheres without an instrument, so it can be said that ideas require no instrument. "You are substance; this world and the next are coincidentals. It is not fitting to seek substance in coincidentals. Weep for him who seeks knowledge from the heart; laugh at him who seeks reason from the soul." One should not dwell on coincidentals. The substance is like a musk sack, and this world and its pleasures are like the scent of musk, which does not last because it is coincidental. To seek the musk itself through its scent and not the scent itself—and not to be content with the mere scent—is good. However, to dwell on the musk scent is bad because one is holding onto something that does not last. Scent is an attribute of musk, but it lasts only as long as the musk is in this world. When it goes "behind the veil" into the other world, those who lived by the scent will die because the scent attached to the musk has now gone to that place where it can be manifested as Musk. Fortunate, therefore, is he who reaches the musk through its scent and "becomes" the musk itself. Thereafter, having become everlasting in the very essence of the musk and having taken on the properties of musk, he experiences no passing away. After that he can communicate the scent to the world, and the world will live through him. Of what he was before there is left to him nothing but a name. It is like a horse, or any other animal, that has turned to salt in a salt pit. There is nothing but a name left of its having once been a horse, for in deed and effect it *is* that

---

108 The prophetic hadith *(raja'nâ min)* is quoted several times in Rumi's father, Baha'uddin Valad's *Ma'arif*, I, 62, 84, 388. See also al-Munawi, *Kunuz*, p. 90.

ocean of salt. What harm does the name do it? It will not bring it out of its salty state. And even if you give the salt mine another name, it will not be less salty.

One, therefore, must pass beyond these pleasures and delights which are only shadows and reflections of the Real. One should not become content with this small amount, which, although is of God's grace and a shadow of His beauty, it is still not permanent. It is permanent in relation to God but not in relation to man. It is like a ray of sun shining into a house. Even though it is a ray of sunlight, it is still attached to the sun. And when the sun sets its light will cease. One must, therefore, *become* the sun in order for there to be no fear of separation.

There is "giving" and there is "knowing." Some people have gifts and talents but no "knowing." Others have the "knowing" but no "giving." One who has both is extremely fortunate and without equal. For the sake of example let us say there is a man going down a road. But he doesn't know whether it is the right road or the wrong road. He goes on blindly, hoping that he will hear a rooster crow or see some sign of a settlement. Now, what is this man in comparison with someone who knows the way and needs no sign or guide post? He knows what he is doing. Therefore, knowing is beyond everything else.

## THIRTEEN

The Prophet, with whom be peace, said, "The night is long: shorten it not with sleep. The day is bright: sully it not with sin." Night is long for speaking secrets and making requests without the interruption of people and the nuisance of friends and enemies. Peace and quiet can be attained, and God lowers the veil so that actions may be kept safe from hypocrisy and be devoted solely to Him. On a dark night a hypocrite can be distinguished from a sincere person: the hypocrite is put to shame by night.

Although all other things are hidden by night and revealed by day, the hypocrite is discovered by night, for he says, "Since no one will see, for whose benefit should I do this?"

He should be told, "Someone does see you, but you don't see Him. The person who sees you is the one who holds everyone in His mighty grasp and who is called upon in time of distress."

When people have toothaches, earaches, or sore eyes, or when they are in fear or insecurity, all people call upon Him in their hearts and trust that He will hear and fulfill their requests. Secretly they give alms to ward off calamity or for the recovery of a sick person, and they trust that He will find the alms acceptable. When He does give them health and recovery, their certitude dissipates and their vain fancies return. They say, "O Lord, what sort of condition was that? We called upon You in all sincerity from our prison corner. We never wearied of saying a thousand times, 'Say, He is God,' and You did grant our wishes. Now we are out of *that* prison, but we are still in need of You to take us out of *this* prison, the world of darkness, into the world of the prophets, which is light. Why does that same deliverance not come to us outside the prison and outside the state of pain?" A thousand different notions come down as to whether it is of benefit or not, and the influence of these notions causes a thousand indispositions and dullnesses. Where is that certainty that destroys vain notions? God then answers, "As I have said, your animal soul is an enemy to you and to me: *take not my enemy and your enemy for your friends*" [60:1].

Maintain your vigil over this enemy in prison, for while he is in prison, suffering calamity and pain, your deliverance is at hand and gains in strength. A thousand times you have been tried by being delivered of toothaches, headaches, and fear. Why then have you become chained to your body, preoccupied with caring for it? Do not forget the important thing. Always keep the carnal soul from getting what it wants so that you can attain eternal desire and be delivered from the prison of darkness, for *whoso shall have refrained his soul from lust, verily paradise shall be his abode* [79:40-41].

## FOURTEEN

Shaykh Ibrahim said that whenever Sayfuddin Farrukh had anyone beaten, he would distract himself by speaking to someone else while the beating was going on. In this manner no one could intercede on behalf of the one being punished.

Everything you see in this world is as it is in that world, but the things of this world are just samples of that world. Whatever is in this world has been brought from that world. *There is no one thing but the storehouses thereof are in Our hands, and We distribute not the same otherwise than in a determinate manner* [15:21].

Street vendors[109] carry trays around on their heads with many varieties of spices—a little pepper, a little mastic, and so forth. The supply is infinite, but there is room for only a little on these trays. Man is like one of these vendors or a druggist's shop, for small amounts of auditory capacity, rational capacity, intellectual capacity, virtue and knowledge from the storehouses of God's attributes have been placed in jars and on trays for him to peddle in this world as is fitting for him. Now then, men are engaged in a sort of peddling for God. Day and night the trays are filled, and you empty them—or squander them—so that you may make a profit thereby. By day you empty your tray; by night it is replenished. For instance, you see the brightness of an eye. In that world there are many, many eyes, a sampling of which has been sent to you and by means of which you look about the world. There is more to real sight than this, but man cannot bear more. All these

---

109 *Tâs-i ba'lînî* "Baalbek jar," which could also be read as *tâs-i na'laynî* "clog-shaped jar." In a note *(Fîhi mâ fîhi,* p. 282f.) Professor Furuzanfar quotes the lexicographer Ali-Akbar Dihkhuda that small containers of brass or tin in use in Iran in druggists shops and by nut vendors are still called *sar-tâs* and that they are hollowed out in shape like clogs. Professor Arberry translates it as "the bald man of Baalbek."

attributes are right here in front of us in infinite supply, in *a determinate manner We distribute the same*. Reflect then on how many thousands of creatures have come, century after century. This "sea" has teemed with them, and then it has been emptied again of them. Consider what a "storehouse" it is. Now, the more one is aware of the "sea," the more one is disappointed with just the trayful. Think of the world as a coin that came from a mint and returns again to the same mint: *we are God's, and unto Him shall we surely return* [2:156]. This "we" means that all our parts have come from there and are samples thereof, and everything, great and small—and animals too—will return thither. Things appear suddenly on this "tray"—and they cannot appear without the "tray"—because that world is subtle and cannot be seen.

Why should this seem strange? Don't you see how the breeze of spring appears and rustles through the trees, bushes, flowers, and herbs? You see the beauty of spring by means of these things, but when you examine the breeze itself you see none of them. It is not because such things as flowerbeds are not "in" the breeze; after all, are they not from its rays? No, within the breeze are waves of flowerbeds and herbs, but the waves are too subtle to be seen unless they are revealed out of their subtlety through some medium.

Likewise, these attributes are hidden in humans. They do not become apparent except through some internal or external medium such as speech, discord, war, or peace. You cannot see a human's attributes. When you look into yourself and, finding nothing, think yourself void of these attributes, it is not because you have changed from what you were, but because they are hidden within you. They are like water in the sea: water does not come out of the sea except through the medium of clouds, and it does not become apparent except through waves. A wave is a "fermentation" from within you that becomes visible without an internal medium. So long as the sea is still, you do not see anything. Your body stands on the shore while your soul is of the sea. Do you not see how many fish, snakes, fowl, and other creatures come forth from the sea, display themselves and then return once more to the sea? Your attributes— like ire, jealousy, passion—arise from this "sea." One might say then that they are "subtle lovers" of God. One cannot see them except by means of verbal "clothing." When they are "naked," they are too subtle to be visible.

## FIFTEEN

In a human being is such a love, a pain, an itch, a desire that, even if he were to possess a hundred thousand worlds, he would not rest or find peace. People work variously at all sorts of callings, crafts, and professions, and they learn astrology and medicine, and so forth, but they are not at peace because what they are seeking cannot be found. The beloved is called *dilârâm*[110] because the heart finds peace through the beloved. How then can it find peace through anything else? All these other joys and objects of search are like a ladder. The rungs on the ladder are not places to stay but to pass through. The sooner one wakes up and becomes aware, the shorter the long road becomes and the less one's life is wasted on these "ladder rungs."

*

"The Mongols seize property, but sometimes they give us property, which is strange. What is the sense in that?" someone asked.

"Whatever the Mongols seize," said the Master, "is as though it has come from God's hold and storehouse. It is as though you fill a jug or a vat from the sea and take it away. As long as the water is in your jug or vat it belongs to you . No one else has any jurisdiction over it. If anyone takes any of it without your permission, it is unlawful seizure. However, when it is poured back into the sea, it has left your possession

---

110 *Dil-ârâm*, literally, "that which gives the heart repose," a common term for the beloved.

and is free for all. Therefore, our property is unlawful for the Mongols, but their property is lawful for us."

*

"There is no monkery in Islam. Cohesion is a mercy."[111] The Prophet always strove for cohesion, for there are in the binding together of spirits great and weighty effects that do not obtain in individuality and isolation. Mosques are built so that the people of a quarter may gather in order for the "mercy" and benefit to be greater. Houses are separate one from another for "disbandment" and for hiding faults; that is their purpose. Congregational mosques were made for the people of a city to congregate in; visiting the Kaaba was made obligatory so that people from many cities and climes of the world might gather there.

"When the Mongols first came into this country, they were bare and naked; they rode on oxen, and their weapons were made of wood," someone said. "Now they have risen to power, they are well fed, and they have the finest Arabian horses and the best weapons."

"When they were downtrodden, feeble, and powerless, God found their need acceptable in His sight and befriended them. Now that they have grown so in stature and might, God will destroy them with the feeblest of creatures in order that they may realize that it was by God's favor and power that they conquered the world, not by their own force and strength. At first they were in a wilderness, remote from people, miserable, wretched, naked, and needy. The few of them who used to come as traders into the realm of the Khwarazmshah would buy muslin to clothe themselves. The Khwarazmshah hindered them and ordered their traders killed. He also levied taxes on them and barred the merchants from his lands. The Tatars went humbly before their own king and

---

111 The complete hadith *(lâ ruhbâniyyata)* is given in *FAM* 189: "There are no bridles or nose-rings or monkery in Islam; there is no celibacy or pererration in Islam." The second hadith *(al-jamâ'atu rahmatun)* is also abbreviated: "Cohesion is a mercy, and isolation torment" (see *FAM* 21 #76).

said, 'We have been destroyed.' The king sought ten days' respite from them and went into a deep cave, where he fasted the ten days, humbling and abasing himself. A cry came from God, saying, 'I have heard your plea. Come forth and be victorious wherever you go.' Thus it was that when they came out at God's command they were victorious and conquered the world."

"But the Tatars also believe in Doomsday," someone said, "for they say that there will be a *yarghu.*"

"They lie," said the Master. "They want to give themselves something in common with Muslims by saying, 'Oh yes, we too know and believe.' It is like the camel who was asked where he had been. 'I am coming from the bath,' he answered. 'Yes,' came the reply, 'I can tell by your heels!'

"Now, if they confess Doomsday, where are the signs of that belief? Their sin, oppression, and evil-doing are like ice and snow, frozen solid. When the sun of repentance and remorse—awareness of that world and fear of God—comes out, it melts the snow of sin away just as the sun melts ice and snow. If ice and snow were to say, 'I have seen the midsummer sun,' or, 'The midsummer sun has shone on me,' and yet remain ice and snow, no intelligent person would believe it. It is impossible for the midsummer sun to come out and not melt ice and snow. Although God has promised recompense for good and evil at Resurrection, still every instant examples of this can be seen. If a man is glad in his heart, it is recompense for having made someone else glad. If he is sad, it is for having made someone else sad. There are 'gifts' from that world and examples of the Day of Recompense in order that people may understand the much from the little, just as a handful of wheat is shown as a sample of a storehouse full.

"The Prophet, with all his greatness and glory, had a pain in his hand one night. An inspiration came to the effect that the pain was on account of the pain in Abbas' hand, the Abbas whom he had taken prisoner along with a group of captives

68

whose hands were bound.[112] Even though the binding of Abbas' hands had been at God's command, there was still recompense for it. Thus you should realize that the states of anxiety, quandary, and indisposition you suffer are on account of evil and sin you have done (even though you may not remember in detail what it is that you have done). You should know by the retribution that you have done much evil, although you may not know what you have done; you may have done it unaware or out of ignorance or because of an irreligious cohort who makes your sins seem so light that you don't consider them sin. But look at the recompense and see how elated you can be on the one hand and how remorseful on the other. Your remorse is absolute retribution for sin, and your elation is recompense for obedience.

"The Prophet was tormented for having twirled a ring around on his finger and was told, 'We did not create you for idleness and play. *Did ye think that We had created you in sport?* [23:115] You can judge from this whether your days are spent in disobedience or obedience.

"Moses was forced to involve himself with the people. Even though he was at God's command and was totally preoccupied with God, one side of him was made to be concerned with the people's welfare. Khidr, on the other hand, was made to be totally preoccupied with himself.[113] The Prophet was first allowed to be totally preoccupied with himself, but later he was commanded to summon the people, give good advice, and rectify their condition. The Prophet wept and wailed, 'O Lord, what sin have I committed? Why do You drive me from Your presence? I do not want to be involved with people.' Then God said, 'Muhammad, grieve not, for I will not let you become totally involved with people.

---

112 This episode is treated in section 1.

113 The story of Moses, the exoteric prophet, and the mysterious "servant of God," universally interpreted as the esoteric prophet/saint, the eternal Khidr (see Glossary of Persons), is given in Kor. 18:60–82; see also Thackston, *Tales*, pp. 247–50.

In that very involvement you will be with Me. Being with me as you are now will not be lessened one iota when you are concerned with the people. In every act you do you are in total union with Me.' "

\*

"Can any of the eternal judgments God has decreed be changed at all?" someone asked.

That which God has decreed from all eternity, ill for ill and good for good, can never change because God is the decreer. Who would say to do evil in order to have good? Does anyone ever plant wheat and reap barley, or plant barley and reap wheat? It is not possible. All the saints and prophets have said that the recompense for good is good and the retribution for evil, evil. *And whoever shall have wrought good of the weight of an ant, shall behold the same* [99:7-8]. By eternal decree you mean what we have said and explained, for it will never change. God forbid! If you want the recompense for good and evil to increase and thereby be changed, the more good you do, the more the recompense for good there will be; and the more injustice you do, the more retribution for evil there will be. This much can change, but the basis of the decree will not.

A babbler asked, "How is it that we sometimes see mean men happy and good men wretched?"

The mean person either did or contemplated doing good to be happy, and the good man who became wretched either did or contemplated doing evil to become so. It is like Iblis when he objected to Adam and said, *"Thou hast created me of fire, and hast created him of clay"* [7:12]. After having been chief among the angels, he was eternally accursed and exiled from God's presence. We too say that the reward for good is good and the reward for evil is evil.

\*

Someone asked if he would be punished if he vowed to fast for a day and then broke the fast.

The Shafiite school of thought is unequivocal in that atonement must be done because a vow is viewed as an oath, and anyone who breaks an oath must atone for it. However, according to Abu-Hanifa a vow is not the same as an oath, so atonement is not necessary. Now there are two types of vow, noncontingent and contingent. A noncontingent vow is like saying, "I am obliged to fast for a day," and a contingent vow is like saying, "I am obliged to fast for a day *if* such-and-such a thing happens."

A man lost his donkey and fasted for three days with the intention of finding it. After the three days he found his donkey dead. Upset, he turned his face to heaven and said, "In place of the three days I have fasted, I'll be damned if I don't eat six days during Ramadan! You just want to get more out of me!"

*

Someone asked the meaning of the *tahiyyât, salawât* and *tayyibât*.

These acts of devotion and worship do not come from us and do not pertain to us by ourselves. The actuality is that the *tayyibât* and *salawât* are God's, not ours. Everything is His and belongs to Him. Just as in spring people go out into the fields to do their planting, go on trips and build buildings—all this is "given" by spring. Otherwise they would stay as they were, cooped up in their houses and hovels. In reality, therefore, planting, sightseeing, and enjoyment of good things pertain to spring, but the real dispenser of these good things is God. People simply see the secondary causes and know things through them. For the saints, however, it is revealed that secondary causes are no more than "veils" that keep people from seeing and knowing the Causer. It is like someone speaking from behind a screen and people thinking that the screen itself is talking. They do not know that the screen has nothing to do with it and is merely a veil. Only when the speaker emerges from behind the screen does it become obvious that the screen was just a medium. God's saints see things being made and coming forth from outside of their secondary causes—just as the camel came out of the mountain,[114] as Moses' staff became a serpent,[115] as the twelve springs flowed from a solid rock,[116] as the Prophet split the moon without any implement just by pointing,[117] as Adam came into being without mother or father, and Jesus without father, as a rose garden grew from the fire for Abraham,[118] and so forth. Therefore, when the saints see such things, they realize that secondary causes are pretexts, that the motivator is something else, and that secondary causes are nothing but "wool over the eyes" to occupy the common folk. When God made a promise to give Zaccharias a child, he cried, "I am an old man, and my wife an old woman. My instrument of passion is weak, and my wife is beyond childbearing. O Lord, how can a child come of such a woman?" *He answered, Lord, how shall I have a son, when old age hath overtaken me, and my wife is barren?* [3:40] The reply came, "Beware, Zaccharias. You have lost your firm faith. I have shown you a thousand times things outside of their causes. That you have forgotten. Do you not realize that causes are pretexts? I am able at this instant to produce before your very eyes a hundred thousand children without woman and without pregnancy. Were I so to indicate, myriads of people would be produced, whole, mature and knowledgeable. Did I not give you birth in the world of spirits without father or mother? You have enjoyed past favors from me. Why do you forget that before coming into this existence?"

Prophets, saints, and other people—and their various good and evil states in accordance with their capacities and

---

114 The Arabian prophet Salih's miracle was to produce a giant camel from a mountain. See Thackston, *Tales,* pp. 117–28.

115 See note 9.

116 As in Exodus 17:6. See Thackston, *Tales,* p. 242.

117 One of the miracles ascribed to the Prophet Muhammad in popular piety is the *shaqq al-qamar,* the "splitting of the moon." The legend probably is derived from Kor. 54:1 ("the hour approacheth; and the moon hath been split in sunder").

118 See note 44.

essences—are like the slaves brought into Islamdom from heathen lands. Some are brought in at five years of age, some at ten, and some at fifteen. After those who were brought as small children have lived for many years among Muslims, they completely forget what their former state was like and remember nothing of it. Others, brought in a bit older, remember a little, while those who are brought in much older remember most of their former states. Likewise, spirits were in God's presence in "that world." As the Koran says, *Am I not your Lord? They answered, Yea: we do bear witness* [7:172]. Their food and sustenance were God's soundless, voiceless Word. Some who were brought out in infancy do not remember their former state and consider themselves strangers to the Word when they hear it. This group, having sunk totally into infidelity and error, is "veiled." Others remember a bit; their yearning for the "other side" can be stirred up. They are the "faithful." Still others see before their eyes their former condition exactly as it was in the past when they hear the Word. Their "veils" are completely removed, and they are joined in union. These are the saints and prophets.

Thus we advise our friends. When your "brides of intrinsic meaning" are manifested within you and the mysteries are revealed, beware! Again I say, beware lest you tell them to others. Expound them not, and do not relate the words you hear from us to just anybody. "Give not wisdom to the unworthy lest you wrong it; withhold it not from the worthy lest you wrong them." If you had a mistress or beloved concealed in your house and she had said to you, "Do not show me to anyone, for I am yours alone," would it ever be right to parade her around the marketplace and tell everybody, "Come and see this one"? Would your beloved like it? She would be furious with you and run off to another. God has forbidden these words to those "others."

It is like the people of hell who cry out to the inhabitants of heaven, saying, "Where is your generosity and virtue? What would happen if you were to cast down upon us as an act of charity some of the favor and grace God has bestowed upon you, as in the saying, 'and to the earth of the cup of the noble, a portion,' for we are burning in this fire. What harm would it do you if you were to throw down to us a little of the fruit or sparkling water of paradise?" *And the inhabitants of hell fire shall call unto the inhabitants of paradise, saying, Pour upon us some water, or of those refreshments which God hath bestowed on you. They shall answer, Verily God hath forbidden them unto the unbelievers* [7:50]. The inhabitants of paradise answer, God has forbidden us to do that. The seeds of this favor were in the world. Since you did not sow them or cultivate them there (and they were faith and devotion), what can you reap here? Even if we were to cast down some to you out of pity, since God has forbidden you these fruits, they would burn your throats and could not be swallowed. If you were to put them in a sack, it would split and they would fall out."

A group of hypocrites and aliens came to the Prophet, praising him and seeking an explanation of the mysteries. The Prophet signaled to his companions to "stop up their bottles," that is, to cover their jugs and vats, as if to say, "These people are unclean and poisonous animals. Beware lest they fall into your bottles and cause you harm by drinking unwittingly of your water." In this manner he told them to conceal wisdom from aliens and to hold their tongues in the presence of aliens, for they are rats, unworthy of this wisdom and favor.

*

The Master said, "Even if the prince who just left us did not understand our words precisely, still in general he knows that we pray to God for him. We take his nodding of the head and his love and affection in place of understanding. The peasant who comes to town may not understand the words of the call for prayer when he hears them, but he knows what they signify."

## SIXTEEN

Anyone who is loved is beautiful. The reverse, however, is not necessarily true. It does not follow that all beauties are loved. Beauty is part of being loved: being loved is primary, so when that quality is present, beauty follows necessarily. A part of a thing cannot be separated from the whole. The part must pertain to the whole. During Majnun's time there were girls much more beautiful than Layla, but they were not loved by him. When told, "There are girls more beautiful than Layla. Let us show them to you," he would always reply, "I do not love Layla for her external form. She is not external form; she is like a goblet which I hold and from which I drink wine. I am in love with the wine I drink therefrom. You see only the goblet and are not aware of the wine. Or what use would a golden goblet be to me if it were filled with vinegar or something other than wine? For me a broken old gourd filled with wine would be better than a hundred such goblets." One needs love and yearning to distinguish the wine from the cup.

Take, for instance, a hungry man who has not eaten for ten days and also a well-fed man who has eaten five times a day. Both of them look at a loaf of bread. The well-fed man sees the form of the bread while the hungry man sees the stuff of life. The loaf is like the goblet, and the enjoyment one derives from it is like the wine in the goblet. One can see the wine only with the eye of appetite and desire. Now, this appetite and desire are what you must acquire in order to be, not an observer of mere external form, but one who sees the real being of every beloved thing. The external forms of all created people and things are like goblets, while such things as knowledge, art, and learning are decoration on the goblet. Don't you see that when the goblet is shattered none of these "decorations" remains? The important thing therefore is the wine, which takes its shape from the goblet. Whoever sees and drinks the wine knows that *good works are permanent* [18:46].

There are two premises that an aspirant must conceive. First, when he says something is one thing, he is inevitably mistaken, for it is something else. Second, he must conceive of another word and another wisdom better and higher than his own, that is, he should say, "I don't know." We have come to the realization that this is what is meant by the dictum, "Asking is half of learning."

Everyone puts his expectations in someone, but that which is sought by all is God and in hopes of Him everyone spends his life. However, in this connection one must be discriminating in order to know just who in this fray does the striking and who is struck by the king's polo-stick in order to confess the oneness and unity of God. It is the drowned man over whom the water has complete control. The drowned man himself has no control over the water. Both a swimmer and a drowned man are in the water; the latter is borne by the water and controlled by it, while the swimmer is borne along by his own power and of his own volition. Every movement made by the drowned man—indeed, every act and word that issue from him—comes from the water, not from him. He is just a "vehicle." When you hear words from a wall, you know that it is not the wall; it is somebody who has made the wall seem to speak. The saints are like this. They have died before death[119] and become like that wall, without an iota of being left in them. They are like a shield in a powerful hand. The shield's movement is not of the shield (and this is what "I-am-Reality" means). The shield says, "I am not here at all; my movement is from the hand of the Real." When you can see the shield as God, do not struggle against Him, for those who strike blows against such a shield are in reality fighting with God and setting themselves against Him. From the time of Adam until now you have heard what happened to the likes of Pharaoh, Shaddad, Nimrod, the Tribe of Ad, Lot's people, Thamud, and so forth. That shield will exist until the Day of Resurrection, epoch after epoch, sometimes in the form of prophets and sometimes in the form of saints, in order that the pious may be distinguished from the impious and enemies from friends. Every saint is therefore a "proof" to the people. In accordance with their connection with him the people gain station and stature. If they are inimical to him, they are inimical to God. If

---

119 As in the hadith *(mûtû qabl);* see *FAM* 116 #352.

they love him, they love God. "Whosoever sees him sees Me, and whosoever seeks him seeks Me."[120] God's servants are privy to His sanctuary, and all traces of being and desire and all roots of treachery have been pruned and cleaned out from those who serve Him. They are to be served by the world; they are privy to the mysteries, for *none shall touch the same, except those who are clean* [56:70].

If one turns one's back on the tombs of the great saints, it is not out of rejection or heedlessness if one has turned one's face to their souls, for the words that issue forth from our mouth are their souls. If people turn their backs on the body and face the soul, there is no harm in that.

*

My disposition is such that I do not want anyone to suffer on my account. I am not pleased when my friends try to prevent some people from throwing themselves on me during the *sama'*. I have said a hundred times that no one should presume to speak for me. Only then am I content. I am loved by those who come to see me, and so I compose poetry to entertain them lest they grow weary. Otherwise, why on earth would I be spouting poetry? I am vexed by poetry. I don't think there is anything worse. It is like having to put one's hands into tripe to wash it for one's guests because they have an appetite for it. That is why I must do it. A man has to look at a town to see what goods the people need and for what goods there are buyers. People will buy those goods even if they are the most inferior merchandise around.

I have studied the various branches of learning and taken pains in order that the learned, the mystics, the clever and the profound thinkers, may come to me for an elaboration of something precious, strange, and precise. God too wanted this, for He gathered all this learning here and put me through all

---

120 There is a prophetic hadith *(man ra'ânî)*, "Who sees me sees God" (see *FAM* 63 #163); the version given here, however, is closer to a statement made by Bayazid Bistami, "Who sees you sees me, and who seeks you seeks me" (see Sahlaji, *Risalat al-nur*, p. 139).

that agony that I should occupy myself with this labor. What am I to do? In our country and among our people there is nothing more dishonorable than being a poet. Had we remained in our native land, we would have lived in harmony with their tastes and would have done what they wanted, such as teaching, writing books, preaching, practicing asceticism, and doing pious deeds.

\*

Prince Parvana said to me that the basis of everything is action. I asked him where the people of action were. Where are seekers of action so that I can show them some action? You are a seeker of talk. You have your ears set to hear something. If we don't say anything, you grow weary. Be a seeker of action so we can show you something. We are looking all over the world for a man to whom we can show action. Not finding a buyer for action but only for words, we occupy ourselves with talk. Since you are not a doer, how would you know what doing is? Action can be known through doing; learning is known through learning; form is known through form; content is known through content. Since there is no one else traveling this empty road, even if we are here and engaged in action, how should anyone ever see it? By this "action" I do not mean acts of prayer and fasting. These are just forms of acts. An "act" is inner content. From the time of Adam until the age of the Prophet prayer and fasting were never in their present form, but action has always been. The other is the form of action; action is meaning within man. When you say that a medicine has "acted," there is no visible form of action, only "meaning" within. When one says that a certain person is an agent in a city, one does not see anything of "form." One can tell that he is an agent by means of the works that pertain to him. So action is not what people have generally understood by the term, since they imagine "action" to be something visible. If a hypocrite goes through the form of action of religious duties, it profits him nothing because he has none of the "meaning" of sincerity and faith. The basis of things is all talk and speech. Now you know nothing of this "talk" and "speech." You despise it; yet talk is the fruit of the tree of action, for speech is born of action. God created the world through speech by saying *Be! And it was* [36:82]. Faith exists in the heart, but if you don't say it out loud, it is of no use. Prayer, which is a set of actions, is not correct without recitation of the Koran. Now by your saying that in this age words are not creditable, you deny this by means of words. Since words are not creditable, how is it that we hear you saying that words are not creditable? This too you have said by means of words.

Here someone asked whether or not there is harm in putting one's hopes in God and expecting a good recompense for having done good and good works.

Yes, one must have hope and faith, or, expressed another way, fear and hope. Someone asked me, since hope itself is a good thing, what fear is. "Show me fear without hope," I said, "or hope without fear, for these two are inseparable." Since you ask, I'll give you an example. When someone plants wheat, he of course hopes that it will grow. At the same time, however, he is fearful that some blight or disaster may befall it. It is obvious that there is no such thing as hope without fear. Neither fear without hope nor hope without fear can be imagined. Now, if one is hopeful and expectant of a good reward, one will certainly be more diligent in one's labor. Expectation is one's "wing"; and the stronger the wing, the higher the flight. When one is despondent, one becomes perfunctory and no longer serves well. A sick man takes a bitter medicine and gives up ten sweet things he enjoys. If it weren't for the hope he has of getting well, how could he tolerate such a thing?

"Man is a rational animal." Man is a mixture of animality and rationality, and his animality is as inseparable a part of him as his rationality. Even if he does not speak out loud, still he does speak inwardly: he is always speaking.[121] He is like a

---

121 That is, man is constantly engaged in rational intellection. See *nutq* in Glossary of Terms.

torrent in which mud is mixed. The clear water is his rational speech, and the mud his animality. The mud is only coincidental. Don't you see that when the mud and the shapes it takes go away or disintegrate, the power of rational utterance and the knowledge of good and evil remain?

The "man of heart" is the All. When you have seen him you have seen everything. The whole hunt is in the belly of the wild ass, as the saying goes. All the people in the world are parts of him, and he is the whole.

> All good and bad are part of the dervish.
> Whoever is not so is not a dervish.[122]

Now when you have seen a dervish you have certainly seen the whole world. Anyone you see after him is superfluous. Dervishes' words are the whole among words. When you have heard their words, whatever you may hear afterwards is repetitious.

> If you see him at any stage, it is as though
> You have seen every person and every place.

> O copy of the Divine Book which you are,
> O mirror of regal beauty which you are,
> Nothing that exists in the world is outside of you.
> Seek within yourself whatever you want,
> for that you are![123]

## SEVENTEEN

The Viceroy said, "In olden times the infidels used to bow down and worship idols. In this age of ours we do the same thing. What do we mean by considering ourselves Muslims

---

122 The line is from Rumi, *Divan*, I, *ghazal* 425, line 4476.

123 A quatrain by Najmuddin Razi, *Manarat al-sa'irin*, manuscript at Tehran, Malek Library.

when we bow and scrape to the Mongols and when we have so many other 'idols' within ourselves, idols of greed, passion, rancor, and envy? Inasmuch as we are obedient to all of these, we do both externally and internally the same as the infidels and yet consider ourselves Muslims!"

Still, there is something else here. Since you have thought of all this as bad and displeasing, your heart's eye must certainly have seen something incomparably great to make the other appear ugly and contemptible. Brackish water seems so to one who has tasted sweet water. "By their opposites are things made manifest." God, then, has placed the light of faith in your soul for you to see these things as ugly. Only in opposition to beauty do those things seem ugly. Other people, who do not have this "agony," are happy in what they are and say, "This is how it should be." God wishes to bestow upon you that which you seek, and in accordance with your aspiration you shall be given, as the saying has it, "Birds fly by means of their wings but the believer by means of his aspiration."

There are three kinds of creatures. The first are the angels, which are pure intelligence. To be obedient, worshipful, and constantly mindful of God is their nature and means of sustenance. That is what they feed on and live by, like a fish in water, whose life is of the water and whose bed and pillow are the water. Angels are not obliged to do what they do. Since they are abstract and free from lust, what favor do they incur for not being lustful or not having carnal desires? Being pure, they do not have to struggle against conceiving passions. If they perform acts of obedience, they are not counted as such because such is their nature and they cannot be otherwise.

The second kind are the beasts, which are pure lust and have no decisive intelligence. They are also under no moral obligation like poor man, who is a mixture of intelligence and lust. Half of him is angelic and half animal. Half serpent and half fish, his fish pulls him toward the water and his serpent toward the dust. They are in a constant tug-of-war. "He whose intellect overcomes his lust is higher than the angels; he whose lust overcomes his intellect is lower than the beasts."

> The angel is free because of his knowledge,
> the beast because of his ignorance.
> Between the two remains the son of man to struggle.[124]

Now some men have so followed their intellects that they have become totally angelic and pure light. These are prophets and saints who are free of fear and hope, *the persons on whom no fear shall come, and who shall not be grieved* [10:62]. There are others whose intellects have been so overcome by their lust that they have become totally bestial. Still others remain in the struggle. They are the group within whom a certain agony or anguish is manifested and who are not content with their lives. They are believers. The saints stand waiting to bring them to their own station and make them like themselves. The devils also lie in wait to pull them down to their level at the lowest depth.

> We want them, and others want them.
> Who will win? Whom shall they prefer?

*When the assistance of God shall come, and the victory . . .* [110:1]. The exoteric interpreters have interpreted this passage to mean that the Prophet's ambition was to make the world Muslim and to bring all men to God's way. When he perceived his own death approaching, he said, "Alas! I have not lived long enough to call the people." "Grieve not," said God, "for at the hour whereon you pass, I shall cause countries and cities, which you would conquer by armies and the sword, all of them I shall cause to become obedient and faithful. And the sign shall be that at the end of your allotted time you shall see people coming in flocks to become Muslim. When you see

---

124 The line occurs in Rumi, *Divan*, II, ghazal 918, line 9669.

that, know that your time for departure has come. Now extol and ask for forgiveness, for you will come to that pass."

The mystics, on the other hand, say that the meaning is as follows: man imagines that he can rid himself of his base characteristics by means of his own action and endeavor. When he strives and expends much energy only to be disappointed, God says to him, "You thought it would come about through your own energy and action and deeds. That is indeed a custom I have established, that is, that what you have you should expend on Our behalf. Only then does Our mercy come. We say to you, 'Travel this endless road on your own weak legs.' We know that with your weak legs you will never be able to finish the way—in a hundred thousand years you would not finish even one stage of the way. Only when you make the effort and come onto the road to fall down at last, unable to go another step, only then will you be uplifted by God's favor. A child is picked up and carried while it is nursing, but when it grows older it is left to go on its own; so now when you have no strength left you are carried by God's favor. When you had the strength and could expend your energy, from time to time in a state between sleep and wakefulness, We bestowed upon you grace for you to gain strength in your quest and to encourage you. Now that you no longer have the means to continue, look upon Our grace and favor and see how they swarm down upon you. For a hundred thousand endeavors you would not have seen so much as an iota of this. Now *celebrate the praise of the Lord, and ask pardon of Him* [110:3]. Seek forgiveness for your thoughts and realize that you were only imagining that all this could come from your own initiative. You did not see that it all comes from Us. Now that you have seen that it is from Us, seek forgiveness." *He is inclined to forgive* [110:3].

*

We do not love the Prince because of his administrative ability, his learning, or his deeds. Others love him for these things, but they do not see his "face"; they see only his "back." He is like a mirror, and these qualities are like precious pearls and gold affixed to the back of a mirror. Those who love gold and those who love pearls look at the back of the mirror. Those who love mirrors, however, do not look at the pearls and gold; they look always at the mirror itself. They love the mirror because it is a mirror, for its "mirrorness." Because they can see beauty in the mirror, they never grow tired of it.

On the other hand, anyone who has an ugly or defective face, because he sees ugliness in the mirror, will quickly turn it around and look at the jewels. Now, if they make thousands of designs on the back of the mirror and set them with jewels, how does that detract from the front of the mirror? God mixed animality and humanity in humans in such a way that both are apparent. "By their opposites are things manifested,"—that is, things can be identified only by means of their opposites. God, however, has no opposite. God said, "I was a hidden treasure and I wanted to be known,"[125] He said and therefore created this world, which is of darkness, in order for His light to be apparent. Likewise He made the prophets and saints, saying, "Emerge with My qualities to My people."[126] They are the focus of God's light in order that friend be distinguished from foe and stranger, for there is no opposite to substance in substance, only in form—as in opposition to Adam stands Iblis; in opposition to Moses, Pharaoh; in opposition to Abraham, Nimrod; in opposition to the Prophets, Abu-Jahl, and so forth. Therefore, through the saints, opposites to God become manifest, even though in substance He has no opposite. The more enmity and opposition grew, the more they succeeded and acquired renown. *They seek to extinguish God's light with their mouths: but God will perfect His light, though the infidels be averse thereto* [61:8].

---

125 The famous divine hadith *kuntu kanzan*, "I was a hidden treasure and wanted to be known, so I created creation that I might be known," given in *FAM* 29 #70.

126 The saying is attributed to Bayazid Bistami in Sahlaji, *Risalat al-nur*, p. 139.

The moon sheds its light and dogs bay.
Is it the moon's fault if dogs are so made?
The pillars of heaven are lit by the moon.
Who is that dog in the briar-patch of the earth?

*

There are many people who are tormented by God through favor, possessions, gold, and princely station, even though their souls would flee from such things.

A poor man saw a prince in the realm of the Arabs and, perceiving on the prince's brow the light of the prophets and saints, said, "Praise be to Him who torments His slaves with favors!"

## EIGHTEEN

Ibn Muqri reads the Koran correctly. That is, he reads the *form* of the Koran correctly, but he hasn't a clue as to the *meaning*. The proof of this lies in the fact that when he does come across a meaning he rejects it. He reads without insight, blindly. He is like a man who holds a sable in his hand. If offered a better sable he rejects it. We realize therefore that he does not know sable. Someone has told him that what he has is sable, and so he holds onto it in blind imitation. It is like children playing with walnuts; if offered walnut oil or walnut kernels, they will reject them because for them a walnut is something that rolls and makes a noise, and those other things do not roll or make noises.

God's treasure houses are many, and God's knowledge is vast. If a man reads *one* Koran knowledgeably, why should he reject any *other* Koran?

I once said to a Koran reader, "The Koran says: *Say, If the sea were ink to write the words of my Lord, verily the sea would fail, before the words of my Lord would fail* [18:109]. Now for fifty drams of ink one can write out the whole Koran. This is but a symbol of God's knowledge; it is not the whole of his

85

knowledge. If a druggist put a pinch of medicine in a piece of paper, would you be so foolish as to say that the whole of the drugstore is in this paper? In the time of Moses, Jesus, and others, the Koran existed; that is, God's Word existed; it simply wasn't in Arabic." This is what I tried to make that Koran reader understand, but when I saw that it was having no effect on him I left.

*

It is said that during the time of the Apostle, the Companions who memorized a chapter or half a chapter of the Koran were deemed extraordinary and were objects of admiration. They did this because they "devoured" the Koran. Now anyone who can devour a pound or two of bread can be called extraordinary, but a person who just puts bread in his mouth and spits it out without chewing and swallowing can "devour" thousands of tons. It is about such a one that is said, "Many a reader of the Koran is cursed by the Koran," that is, one who is not aware of the real meaning. Yet it is well that this is so. God shut some people's eyes in heedlessness in order for them to make the world flourish. If some people were not heedless of the next world, then no world would be built up here. Such heedlessness initiates worldliness. A child grows up in heedlessness; when his mind reaches maturity, he does not grow any more. The cause and originator of his growing is heedlessness, while the cause for the lack of growth is awareness.

What we say does not go beyond two cases. We speak either out of envy or out of compassion. God forbid it be out of envy because what is worthy of being envied is so destroyed by envy that it is no longer enviable. And then what is it? On the other hand, there are compassion and intercession, by means of which I wish to attract my dear friends to the concept.

The story is told of a man who wandered into the desert on his way to the pilgrimage and was overcome by great thirst. Finally, at a distance he saw a ragged little tent. Going there and seeing a woman, he cried out, "I can receive hospitality!

Just what I needed!" And there he descended. He asked for water, but the water they gave him was hotter than fire and more brackish than salt, and it burned his throat as it went down. Out of compassion he began to advise the woman, saying, "I am obliged to you insofar as I have been comforted by you, and my compassion for you has been stirred. Take heed therefore of what I say to you. The cities of Baghdad, Kufah, and Wasit are nearby. If you are in dire straits, you can get yourselves there in a few marches, where there is much sweet, cool water." And he also listed to her the great variety of foods, bathhouses, luxuries, and pleasures of those cities.

A moment later her Bedouin husband arrived. He had caught a few desert rats, which he told the woman to cook. They gave some to the guest, who, destitute as he was, could not refuse.

Later that night, while the guest was asleep outside the tent, the woman said to her husband, "You've never heard the likes of the tales this man had been telling." And she told her husband everything he had related to her.

"Don't listen to such things," the Bedouin said. "There are many envious people in the world, and when they see others enjoying ease and comfort they grow envious and want to deprive them of their enjoyment." People are just like that. When someone advises them out of compassion, they attribute it to envy.

If, on the other hand, one has a "basis," in the end one will turn to substance. Since on the Day of Alast a drop was sprinkled on such a man, in the end that drop will deliver him from confusion and tribulation.

Come now, how long will you remain estranged from us in your confusion and melancholy? What, on the other hand, is one to say to a people who have never heard the likes of it, neither from him nor from their own teachers?

> There being no greatness among his forebears,
> He cannot abide to hear the great mentioned.

To turn to the substance of a thing, although not pleasant at first, becomes sweeter the further you go. In contrast, form appears beautiful at first, but the more you stay with it the more disenchanted with it you become. What is the form of the Koran in comparison with its substance? Look into a man to see what his form is and what his substance is. If the substance of a man's form were to go away, he would not be let loose in the house for even a moment.

Mawlana Shamsuddin used to tell of a large caravan, en route to a certain place, that could find neither settlement nor water. Suddenly they came across a well that had no means for drawing water. They brought a bucket and some rope and let the bucket down into the well. When they started to draw it up, the rope broke. They let down another bucket, but it too broke loose. Then they tied some of the members of the caravan to the rope and lowered them into the well, but they did not come back up either. An intelligent man among them said, "I'll go." So they lowered him down. When he was almost to the bottom, a horrible black thing appeared. "I'll never escape from this," said the man. "Yet, let me gather my wits and not go to pieces so I can see what is going to happen to me."

"There is no use making a ruckus," the black thing said. "You are my prisoner and will never go free unless you give me a correct answer."

"What is your question?"

"What is the best place?" it asked.

Here the intelligent man thought, "I am helpless as his prisoner. If I say Baghdad or any other place, it will be as though I have insulted his place." Therefore he said, "The best place is where one is at home. If it is in the depths of the earth, that's the best. If it's in a mousehole, that's the best."

"Well said!" said the thing, "You are free. You are a real man. I free not only you but also the others for your sake. Henceforth I will shed no more blood. Because of my love for you I bestow upon you the lives of all the men in the world."

And he gave the people of the caravan all the water they wanted.

Now, the purport of all this is the intrinsic meaning. One can express this very same intrinsic meaning in another form, but those who adhere to convention can have it only their way. It is difficult to talk to them. If you say the same thing another way, they won't listen.

## NINETEEN

It is related that some people once said to Tajuddin Quba'i, "These learned men come among us and cause the people to lose their belief in religion."

"No," he answered, "they can't *come* among us and make us unbelievers. They can do that only if—God forbid!—they *be* from among us." For example, if you put a gold collar on a dog, it's not going to be called a hunting dog because of the collar. The ability to hunt is inherent in a dog, whether it has a collar of gold or of wool. A man is not a scholar by virtue of his cloak and turban. Scholarship is a virtue in one's essence, and it makes no difference whether that virtue be under a cloak or under a tunic. At the time of the Prophet there were some who had designs on religion. In order to undermine the faith of mere ritual imitators, they garbed themselves in the prayer robe because they would have been unable to succeed in their plot without making themselves out to be Muslims. If a European or a Jew were to impugn the faith, who would listen to him? *Woe be unto those who pray, and who are negligent at their prayer; who play the hypocrite, and deny necessaries to the needy* [107:4-7]. These words sum it all up. You have the light, but you have no humanity. Seek humanity, for that is the goal. The rest is a lot of talk. When talk goes on too long, the purpose is easily forgotten.

A greengrocer who once loved a lady sent a message with the lady's maid, saying, "I am thus, and I am so. I am in love; I burn; I have no peace; I am tormented. Yesterday I was so; last night such befell me." And thus he went on at great length. When the maid came to her mistress she said, "The greengrocer sends his regards and says that he wants to do thus and so with you."

"So bluntly?" asked the lady.

"Well," replied the maid, "he made a long story, but that was the gist of it."

It's the gist that counts; the rest just gives you a headache.

## TWENTY

Night and day you struggle to refine the character of woman and to purify her impurity. It would be better to purify and refine yourself through her than to purify her through you. Go to her and submit to whatever she says, absurd though it may seem. Even if zeal is a manly virtue, abandon it because this one good attribute allows bad ones to enter you. For this very reason the Prophet said, "No monkery in Islam!" The way of monks was to dwell in solitude off in the mountains, to eschew women and to abandon the world. God showed the Prophet a narrow and obscure way to refine himself, and that was to marry women, endure their tyranny, listen to their absurdities and let them ride roughshod over him.127 *Thou art of a noble disposition* [68:4]. To suffer and endure the tyranny of others is to cleanse away one's own impurity through them. Your character becomes good through forbearance, and theirs becomes bad through domineering and aggressiveness. When you realize this, purify yourself. Consider them as garments by means of which you can cleanse yourself and be purified. If you cannot vanquish your carnal soul, then deliberate rationally with yourself and say, "Let me think that we have not been married. She is a woman of pleasure, a courtesan, to whom I go when my passion gets the

---

127 Publisher's note: On the one hand, similar words might have been spoken to a woman with a difficult husband. On the other, Rumi here reflects some of the prevailing notions of his time; and yet he had many mature female disciples and a fundamental respect for womanhood. As he says in his *Mathnawi*: "Woman is a ray of God. She is not just the earthly beloved. She is creative, not created."

better of me." In this manner you will ward off from yourself pride, envy, and jealousy. In the end you will have no further need for this rational deliberation, and not only will you take pleasure in struggle and endurance, but you will also experience spiritual states through their absurdities. Afterwards, when you will perceive the inherent advantage for yourself, you will become a disciple of forbearance, even without the rational deliberation.

The story is told of the Prophet's return with his Companions from an expedition. "Let the drums be beat," he said. "Tonight we will stay by the city gate and enter tomorrow."

"O Apostle of God," they asked, "what is the good of that?"

"Because if you found your wives with other men, you would be pained. And sedition might arise thereby," he answered. One of the Companions, however, did not heed the Prophet's words and, entering the town, found his wife with another man.

Now, it is the way of the Prophet that one should endure pain by warding off jealousy and indignation and by enduring the pain of one's expenditures on women—along with a hundred thousand other untold agonies—in order for the Muhammadan world to appear. The way of Jesus is to struggle in solitude and not to indulge one's passions; the way of Muhammad is to endure the tyranny and grief caused by men and women. If you cannot go the way of Muhammad, then take the way of Jesus lest you be deprived altogether. With sufficient inner peace you can endure a hundred indignities because you either see or secretly believe in the fruits others have reported. "Since such a thing exists," you say to yourself, "let me be patient until the fruits of which they have spoken come to me." If you have set your heart on them you will see them. "Because of the pains I endure," you will say, "I will find a treasure, even if I don't have it right now." And you *will* find a treasure. You will find even more than what you had expected or hoped for. If these words have no effect immediately, after a time, when you have matured more, they will have great effect.

What is woman? No matter what you say, she is what she is, and she is not going to change her ways. Words not only have no effect but actually cause her to grow worse. Take, for example, a loaf of bread and put it under your arm. Don't let anybody have any. Say, "Under no circumstances will I give any of this to anybody! Not only will I not *give* any, I won't even *show* it to anybody!" Even if it were something that had been thrown away, something the dogs would not eat because bread was so abundant and cheap, as soon as you begin to withhold it, everybody is bound and determined to get some of it. They will come begging and demanding to see the loaf of bread you have withheld and stashed away. Especially if you keep that same loaf of bread for a year and persist in not giving it away or showing it, their desire will exceed all bounds, for "man is greedy for what he is denied."[128] The more you tell a woman to keep herself covered, the more she itches to show herself and the more other people desire to see her. There you sit, whipping up desire on both sides and thinking you are being righteous. What you are doing is actually the essence of corruption. If she has a natural disposition averse to evil deeds, whether or not you forbid her to do evil, she will proceed in accordance with her own pure natural disposition. Of this you may rest assured and not trouble yourself. If she is the opposite, she will still go her own way, and forbidding her will actually do nothing but increase her desire.

*

These people say, "We saw Shamsuddin of Tabriz. Master, we did see him." You pack of fools, did you *see* him? Someone who can't see a camel up on the roof tells you he's found the eye of a needle and threaded it! It's a good story they tell of the man who said, "Two things make me laugh: a black man painting his fingernails black and a blind man sticking his head out of a window." These people are just like that. Their blind

---

128 For the prophetic hadith *(ibnu âdama la-harîs)* see *FAM* 92 #260.

insides stick their heads out of the windows of their bodies. What do they think they're going to see? What does their approval or disapproval mean? For the rational they are the same inasmuch as these others have seen nothing to approve or disapprove; no matter what they say, they speak nonsense. One must first acquire sight and then look. Even when one has acquired sight, how can one see things that are not meant to be seen?

There are in the world many saints with sight who have achieved union, but there are yet other saints beyond them who are called the Veiled Ones of God. The former saints cry out humbly, "O God, show us one of your Veiled Ones," but until they truly desire them, until they are to be seen, no matter how "sighted" their eyes may be, they will not be able to see them. Tavern girls who are whores are not frequented or seen by anybody until they are needed. How then can anyone see or recognize the Veiled Ones of God without their will? It is not an easy task.

The angels said, *"We celebrate thy praise, and sanctify thee* [2:30]. We are pure love, we are spiritual, we are pure light. Those humans are a bunch of murderous gluttons who shed blood." This was said in order that man might tremble for himself before the spiritual angels, who have no wealth, position or veils, who are pure light and whose food is God's beauty. Pure love, far-sighted and keen of vision, they dwell in a state between the negative and positive. Before them man should tremble and say, "Woe is me! What am I? What do I know?" And if light shines upon him and a yearning develops within him, he should offer a thousand thanks to God and ask, "How am I worthy of this?"

This time you will enjoy more fully Shamsuddin's words that belief is the sail on the ship of man's being. When the sail is set it carries him to great places. When there is no sail, words are nothing but wind.

*

It is very good that between lover and beloved there should be absolute informality. Formalities are for outsiders. Informality is forbidden to any condition other than love.

I would expound at length on these words, but the time is not right, and one must strive mightily and "dig many wells" to reach the "pool of the heart." Either the people are weary or else the speaker is weary and making excuses—and a speaker who cannot extricate people from their boredom is not worth two cents.

Neither is a lover able to give proof of his beloved's beauty nor is anyone else able to convince the lover of anything that would provoke hatred for his beloved. It is obvious therefore that logical proofs are of no use here. In this case one must simply *be* a seeker of the love relationship. Now, if I exaggerate in a line of poetry concerning the lover ("You whose form is fairer than a thousand substances . . ."), it is not true hyperbole, for I see that the disciple has expended his own substance in favor of his master's form. Every disciple is in need of a master when he first rises above concepts.

Baha'uddin asked, "Doesn't he quit his own concept, not for the master's form but for his concept?"

It is not fitting that it should be so because, if it were, then both would be masters. Now it is necessary for you to strive to acquire inner illumination in order to escape and be safe from the fires of confusion. Worldly states such as princely and ministerial ranks flash briefly like lightning within a person who has acquired such an inner illumination—just as the states of the unseen world, such as fear of God and longing for the world of the saints, flash briefly like lightning and pass quickly away within the worldly. The "people of God" have turned completely to God and belong to Him. They are occupied with and drowned in God. This-worldly desires, like an impotent man's lust, appear but, finding no foothold, pass quickly away. The worldly are just the opposite with regard to the states of the next world.

## TWENTY-ONE

Sharif Paysokhta says:

> That holy author of grace
> who can dispense with the world,
> the soul is totally he;
> yet he is independent of the soul.
> He encompasses the range of your thought,
> of that he is the focus, yet independent.

These words are highly shameful. They are neither flattery of a king nor self-praise. Little man, what joy does it give you that he is able to dispense with you? This is not how friends talk, but how enemies talk, for it is an enemy who says, "I have nothing to do with you. I can do without you." Consider a man who is an ardent lover and who, in a state of ecstatic joy, would say of his beloved that she is indifferent to him. He would be like a boiler room stoker who says: "The sultan is indifferent to me, a mere stoker. He can do without all stokers." What joy does this wretched stoker derive from the sultan's indifference to him? What the stoker should say is this: "I was on the roof of the furnace when the sultan passed. I greeted him, and he looked long at me. As he passed by he was still looking at me!" Such words as these would give the stoker joy. What kind of praise of the king would it be to say that he is indifferent to stokers? What joy does it give the stoker?

"He encompasses the range of your thought . . ." Little man, to what will your thought range, except that men can do without your thoughts and fancies? And if you make up tales about them out of your imagination, they will grow weary and run away. What fancy is there of which God is not independent? The Verse of Self-Sufficiency[129] was revealed for the infidels. God forbid it be for the faithful! Little man, His self-sufficiency is a proven fact. If you have a spiritual state that

---

129 The Verse of Self-sufficiency *(istighnâ)* is Koran 92:8, "But whoso shall be covetous, and shall be wholly taken up with this world."

is of any worth, then His not being independent of you is in proportion to your spiritual might.

*

Shaykh-i-Mahalla said: "First there is seeing and only afterwards come speaking and hearing. Anyone can see the sultan, but only the elite can talk to him." This is crooked, shameful, and upside-down, for Moses first spoke and heard and only later asked to see. The station of conversing belongs to Moses, the station of vision to Muhammad.[130] How then can those words be right?

In the presence of Shamsuddin of Tabriz someone said, "I have proven the existence of God, indisputably." The next morning Mawlana Shamsuddin said, "Last night the angels came down and blessed that man, saying: 'Praise to God, he has proven our God. May God grant him long life. He has done no injury to mortals.' " O little man, God is a given fact. His existence needs no logical proof. If you must do something, then prove that you yourself have some dignity and rank in His presence. Otherwise He exists without proof. *Neither is there anything which doth not celebrate His praise* [17:44]. Of this there is not doubt.

*

The jurisprudents are clever and hit the mark ten times out of ten in their own profession, but between them and the other world a wall has been raised to maintain their realm of *licet* and *non licet*. If they were not closed in by that wall, they would not want to do what they do and their job would be left in abeyance. This is similar to our great master's saying that the other world is like a sea and this world is like foam. God wanted the foam to flourish, so He put people on the back of

---

130 Moses is known as Kalîmullâh, "the one who converses with God," an epithet drawn from the "conversations" he had with God on Mount Sinai (Koran 7:143, 19:52, as in Exodus 3 and 19:20). In the Koranic version when Moses asked God to reveal himself, he replied, "Thou wilt not see Me" (7:143). God's first revelation to Muhammad, on the other hand, was in the form of a vision of Mt. Hira (see Koran 53:6–11).

the sea to make it prosper. If they did not occupy themselves with this job, people would destroy each other and as a matter of course the foam would fall into ruins. Therefore, a tent was pitched for the king, and certain people were set to occupy themselves with its maintenance. One says, "If I didn't make rope, how could the tent stand?" Another says, "If I didn't make stakes, what would they tie the ropes to?" And each one knows that they are all slaves to the king who will enter the tent and gaze upon his beloved. If the weaver gives up weaving and tries to become a vizier, the whole world will go naked. He was therefore given a certain pleasure in his craft and is happy. That nation, then, was created to keep the world of foam in good order, and that world was created to maintain that saint. Blessed is he for whose maintenance the world was created: he was not created to maintain the world. Each person was therefore given such pleasure and happiness in God's labor that if he were to live a hundred years he would go right on doing his job. Every day his love for his labor increases. His expertise is born of practicing his craft, and he derives joy and pleasure therefrom. *Neither is there anything which doth not celebrate His praise* [17:44]. The rope maker has one kind of praise and the carpenter who makes the tent poles has another. The stake maker praises God one way and the canvas weaver another, and the saints who inhabit the tent and contemplate in perfect delight praise Him yet another way.

*

If I am silent, the people who come to me will get bored. But since what we say has to be suited to them, *we* grow weary. They go and speak unkindly of us and say that we got bored with them and ran away. How can the kindling run away from the pot? The pot may run away when it cannot endure the fire, but when the fire appears to run away, it is not running away at all but is withdrawing because it sees that the pot is weak. Therefore, however it may seem, the truth is that it is the pot that runs away. Our running away then is really their running away. We are a mirror, and if there is a desire to run away in them, it appears in us. We do the running away for them. A mirror is that in which one sees oneself. If they think we are bored, the boredom is really theirs. Boredom is a quality of weakness, and this is no place for boredom or weariness.

*

It happened to me that once in the bath I was acting excessively humble toward Shaykh Salahuddin, and he was being excessively humble toward me. As I complained of his humility, the thought occurred to me that I was overdoing my own meekness and that it would be better to do it gradually. First you should rub someone's hands and then his feet until little by little he becomes so accustomed to it that he no longer notices. You must not, of course, inconvenience him, and you must match courtesy with courtesy. Then you will accustom him by degrees to your humility. As one acts in this manner with friends, so also one must act in this same manner with enemies, that is, little by little, gradually. For example, first of all you give an enemy advice a little bit at a time. If he doesn't listen, you slap him. If he still doesn't listen, you drive him away. In the Koran it is said, *Rebuke them and remove them into separate apartments, and chastise them* [4:34]. Thus go the affairs of this world. Don't you see how spring's serenity and affability in the beginning spread their warmth little by little and then increase. See how the trees sprout little by little at first, then put out buds and then garb themselves in leaves and fruit and then, like dervishes and Sufis, offer to give away everything they have.

If man rushes into the works of this world and the next and exaggerates at the beginning, his labor is not easy. Here is the disciplined way: a man who normally eats a maund of bread should eat a dram less every day. Gradually, after a year or two, he will cut his consumption in half, and the body will not notice the reduction. Acts of devotion, retreat, obedience to divine law and ritual prayer are just like this. A man who wants to pray wholeheartedly and enter on God's Way should first observe the five prescribed daily prayers. Later he can increase the number infinitely.

## TWENTY-TWO

As a matter of principle Ibn Chavush should guard against backbiting with regard to Shaykh Salahuddin—both for his own good and also so that this dark covering might be lifted from him. Why does Ibn Chavush think that so many people have abandoned their homes, fathers and mothers, families, relatives, and tribes and worn out the iron in their boots traveling from "Hind to Sind" in hopes of meeting a man who has the aroma of the other world? How many people have died of regret because they were unsuccessful in meeting the likes of this man? In your own house you have encountered such a man in the flesh and turned your back on him! This is not only a great misfortune but an act of heedlessness.

Ibn Chavush used to say to me: "The Shaykh of Shaykhs Salahuddin is a great man. His greatness is apparent in his countenance, the very least being that from the day I entered your service I never ever heard him mention your name without calling you 'our lord and master,' and not once did he ever alter this mode of expression." Is it not the case that Ibn Chavush's corrupt self-interest has so blinded him that now he says that Shaykh Salahuddin is nothing? What evil has Shaykh Salahuddin done him other than to see him falling into a pit and tell him not to fall? And this he says because he feels compassion for him out of all people. But he hates that compassion.

If you do something displeasing to Salahuddin you will find yourself subject to his wrath. And how will you clear yourself of his wrath? Every time you are about to be covered and blackened by the smoke of hell he will counsel you and say: "Do not dwell in my wrath, but move from the abode of my wrath into the abode of my grace and mercy. When you do something that pleases me you will enter the abode of my affection and grace, and thereby your heart will be cleansed and become luminous." He counsels you for your own good, but you consider his compassion and advice as selfish self-interest. Why should a man like that have an ulterior motive or harbor enmity toward you? Isn't it so that every time you long for forbidden wine or hashish or the *sama'* or anything else, you are pleased with your every enemy, forgive them, and are inclined to kiss their hands and feet? At that point infidel and believer are alike as far as you are concerned.

Shaykh Salahuddin is the root of spiritual joy. The oceans of joy are with him. How could he harbor hatred or selfish interests with regard to anyone? God forbid! He speaks out of compassion and commiseration about all God's servants. What other interest could he possibly have in these "locusts" and "frogs"? What are these beggars worth to one who possesses such greatness?

Is it not said that the Water of Life is in the land of darkness? The darkness is the body of the saints, where the Water of Life is. The Water of Life can be found only in the darkness. If you hate the darkness and find it distasteful, how will you find the Water of Life? Isn't it true that you will not be able to learn sodomy from sodomites and harlotry from harlots except by enduring a thousand hateful things? In order to succeed in learning what you want, wouldn't you have to endure beatings and acts contrary to your will? How then would it be if you were to want to acquire eternal, everlasting life, which is the station of the saints? Do you think that in that case you would not suffer anything hateful or have to abandon anything you possess? What the shaykh will prescribe for you is what the shaykhs of old used to prescribe—namely, that you abandon your wife and children, property, and position. Even when they said, "Leave your wife so that we may take her," it was endured. But you won't tolerate the simplest thing you are advised to do. You may hate something even if it is good for you.

What do these people think? They have been stricken by blindness and ignorance. They do not consider how a person in love with a boy or a woman may grovel and fawn and sacrifice all his wealth, or how he may beguile his beloved by spending his all in order to placate him or her. He may weary of other things, but of this pursuit he never wearies. Is the shaykh's love—or God's love—less than this? Yet at the least command or advice he turns away and abandons the shaykh. By such action it is understood that he was no lover or aspirant, for, had he been either, he would have endured what we have said many times over. For his heart dung would have been honey and sugar.

## TWENTY-THREE

I have to go to Toqat because it's warm there. It's warm in Antalya too, but the people there are mostly Greeks. They don't understand our language, although there are a few who do. We were speaking one day to a group that included some infidels, and during our talk they were weeping and going into ecstatic states. "What do they understand? What do they know?" someone asked. "Not one out of a thousand Muslims can understand this kind of talk. What have these people understood that they weep so?" It is not necessary for them to understand the words. What they understand is the basis of the words. After all, everyone acknowledges the oneness of God and that He is the Creator and Sustainer, that He controls everything, that everything will return to Him, and that either eternal punishment or forgiveness emanate from Him. When they hear words that are descriptive of God they are struck with a commotion, yearning, and desire because their objects of desire and search are made manifest in these words. Although the way may differ, the goal is one. Don't you see that there are many roads to the Kaaba?

Some come from Anatolia, some from Syria, some from Persia, some from China, some across the sea from India via the Yemen. If you consider the ways people take, you will see a great variety. If, however, you consider the goal, you will see that all are in accord and inner agreement on the Kaaba. Inwardly there is a connection, a love and affection, with the Kaaba, where there is no room for dispute. That attachment is neither infidelity nor faith—that is, it is not confounded by the different ways of which we have spoken. All the dispute and quarrelling that were done along the way (such as one saying to another, "You're an infidel; you're wrong,") while the one appears so to the other—when they reach the Kaaba, it becomes obvious that the dispute was over the way, while their goal was the same all along.

For example, if a cup were alive, it would love the cup maker devotedly. Now, once this cup has been made, some will say that it should be placed on the table just as it is; some will say the inside should be washed; some will say the outside should be washed; some will say the whole thing should be washed, while still others will say that it does not need washing at all. The difference of opinion is confined to such things; all are in agreement that the cup had a creator and a maker and that it did not make itself. Over that there is no disagreement.

Now let us consider humans: inwardly, in the depths of their hearts, they all love God, search for Him, and pray to Him. All their hopes are in Him, and they acknowledge no one as omnipotent or in absolute dominion except Him. Such an idea is neither infidelity nor faith. Inwardly it has no name, but when the "water" of that idea flows toward the "drain spout" of the tongue, it congeals and acquires form and expression. At this point it becomes "infidelity" or "faith," "good" or "evil." It is like plants growing in the ground. At first they have no specific form of their own. When they poke their heads out into the world, initially they are fragile, delicate, and colorless. The farther they proceed into this world, the thicker and coarser they become. They take on different colors. When believers and infidels sit together, as long as they say nothing expressly, they are in accord and their thoughts are not hampered. There is an inner world of freedom where thoughts are too subtle to be judges—as the saying goes, "We judge by externals, and God will take care of innermost thoughts." God creates those thoughts within you, and you cannot drive them away with any amount of effort.

As for the saying that God has need of no instrument, don't you see how He makes those thoughts and ideas within you without any instrument, without any pen or ink? Those ideas are like birds of the air and gazelles of the wild, which cannot be lawfully sold before they are caught and caged. It is not within your power to sell a bird on the wing because delivery is a condition of sale. How can you deliver what you do not control? Therefore, so long as thoughts remain within, they are nameless and formless and cannot be judged as indicating either infidelity or Islam. Would any judge say, "You have inwardly acknowledged thus and so," or "You have inwardly sold thus and such a thing," or "Come and swear that you have not inwardly had thus and such a thought"? He would not because no one can judge what goes on inside you. Thoughts are birds on the wing. However, when they are expressed, they can be judged as pertaining to infidelity or Islam, as good or evil.

There is a world of bodies, another of imaginings, another of fantasies, and another of suppositions, but God is beyond all worlds, neither within nor without them. Now, consider how God controls these imaginings by giving them form without qualification, without pen or instrument. If you split open your breast in search of a thought or idea and take it apart bit by bit, you won't find any thoughts there. You won't find any in your blood or in your veins. You won't find them above or below. You won't find them in any limb or organ, for they are without physical quality and are non-spacial. You won't find them on your outside either. Since His control of your thoughts is so subtle as to be without trace, then consider how subtle and traceless He must be who is the Creator of all this. Inasmuch as our bodies are gross objects in relation to ideas, so also subtle and unqualifiable ideas are gross bodies and forms in relation to the subtlety of the Creator.

If the holy spirit were to unveil itself,
human intellect and soul would seem as substantial as flesh.[131]

God cannot be contained in this world of phantasmagoria—nor yet in any world. If you could be contained in the world of phantasmagoria, then it would

---

131 From Rumi, *Divan*, VI, p. 265, ghazal 3053, line 32,498.

follow of necessity that He could be comprehended by a maker of notions and He would no longer be the creator of phantasmagoria. It is obvious therefore that He is beyond all worlds.

*Now hath God in truth verified unto His apostle the vision wherein He said, Ye shall surely enter the holy temple of Mecca, if God pleases, in full security* [48:27]. Everyone says, "Let us enter the Kaaba," Some, however, say, "Let us enter the Kaaba if God please." These latter, who are exceptional, are lovers inasmuch as a lover does not see himself as in control or as an agent with free will; a lover considers himself as subject to the beloved's control. Therefore, he says, "If the beloved wishes, let us enter." Now the holy temple, in the view of the externalists, is that Kaaba to which people go; but for lovers and the elite it is union with God. Therefore, they say, "If God please, let us reach Him and be honored by seeing Him." On the other hand, it is rare for the beloved to say, "If God please." It is like a stranger's tale, which requires a stranger to listen or to be able to listen. God has servants who are beloved and loved and who are sought by God, who performs all the duties of a lover with respect to them. Just as a lover would say, "If God please, we will arrive," God says, "If God please" on behalf of that stranger. If we were to occupy ourselves in explaining this, even the saints who have attained union would lose the train of thought. How then is one to tell such mysteries and states to ordinary people? "The pen reached this point and broke its nib."[132] How is a person who cannot see a camel on a minaret going to see a hairline crack on the camel's tooth? Let us return to our original topic.

Those lovers who say, "If God please"—that is, "the Beloved is in control; if the Beloved wishes, we will enter the Kaaba"—are absorbed in God. There no "other" can be contained, and to mention any "other" is forbidden. How can there be room for an "other" when, until one effaces one's

---

132 From Khaqani, *Divan*, p. 429, line 1.

own self, there is no room for God? "No one other than the householder is in the house."

As for the saying, "*Now hath God in truth verified unto His apostle the vision*" [48:27], this "vision" is the dream of lovers and those devoted to God. Its interpretation is revealed in the other world. As a matter of fact, all the conditions of this world are dreams, the interpretation of which is revealed in the other world. When you dream that you are riding a horse and attain your goal, what does the horse have to do with your goal? If you dream that you are given sound dirhems, the interpretation is that you will hear good and true words from a learned man. What resemblance is there between dirhems and words? If you dream that you are hanged on the gallows, it means that you will become chief of a people. And what does a gallows have to do with chieftainship? Likewise, as we have said, the affairs of this world are dreams. "This world is like a sleeper's dream."[133] The interpretations of these dreams are different in the other world from the way they appear here. A divine interpreter interprets them because everything is revealed to him.

When a gardener comes into a garden and looks at the trees, he does not have to examine the fruit on each one to tell which is a date tree, which is fig, pomegranate, pear, or apple. Since the divine interpreter knows, there is no need to wait for Resurrection for him to see the interpretations of what has happened and what the result of a dream will be, for he has seen beforehand what the result would be—just as the gardener knows beforehand what fruit will be given by each branch as a matter of course.

Everything in this world—like wealth, women, and clothes—is sought because of something else, not in and for itself. Don't you see that if you had a hundred thousand dirhems and were hungry or unable to find food, you couldn't eat those dirhems? Sexuality is for producing children and satisfying passion. Clothing is to ward off the cold. Thus do all

---

133 For the hadith *(al-dunyâ ka-hulm)* see *FAM* 141.

things form links in a chain to God. It is He who is sought for His own sake and who is desired for Himself, not for any other reason. Since He is beyond everything and is nobler and more subtle than anything, why would He be sought for the sake of what is less than Him? Therefore it can be said that He is the ultimate. When one reaches Him, one has reached the final goal; there is no surpassing there.

The human soul is a locus of doubt and ambiguity, and by no means can one ever extricate the doubt and ambiguity from it without becoming a lover. Only then does no doubt or ambiguity remain. "Your love for a thing makes you blind and deaf."[134]

When Iblis refused to bow down to Adam, in disobedience to God's command, he said, *"Thou has created me of fire, and hast created him of clay"* [7:12]—that is, my essence is of fire and his of clay. How is it right for a superior to bow down to an inferior? When Iblis was cursed and banished for his sin and opposition and contention with God, he said: "Alas, Lord, you made everything. This was your temptation of me. Now you curse me and banish me."

When Adam sinned, God expelled him from paradise and said: "O Adam, when I took you to task and tormented you for your sin, why did you not contend with me? You had a line of defense, after all. You could have said, 'Everything is from You. You made everything. Whatever You will comes to be in the world; whatever You will not can never come to be.' You had such a clear, right defense. Why did you not state it?"

"O Lord," said Adam: "I knew that, but I could not be impolite in Your presence. My love for You would not allow me to take You to task."

The Divine Law is a fountainhead, a watering place. It is like a king's court, where the king's commands and prohibitions are many, where his dispensation of justice for the elite and common alike is limitless and beyond reckoning. It is extremely good and beneficial. The stability of the world rests

---

134 The hadith *(hubbuka li'l-shay')* is given in *FAM* 25.

on his orders. On the other hand, the state of dervishes and mendicants is one of close conversation with the king and knowledge of the ruler's own knowledge. What is it to know the science of legislation in comparison with knowing the legislator's own knowledge and having converse with the king? There is a great difference. His companions and their states are like a school in which there are many scholars. The director pays each scholar according to his ability, giving to one ten, to another twenty, to another thirty. We also speak to each person according to his ability to comprehend. "Speak to the people in accord with their understanding."[135]

## TWENTY-FOUR

Every edifice is built for a certain purpose. Some build in order to display their generosity, some in order to gain renown, and some for heavenly reward. But the true goal in exalting the rank of saints and glorifying their tombs and graves should be God. The saints themselves have no need of glorification. They are glorified in and of themselves. If a lamp wants to be placed on high, it wants it for the sake of others, not for its own sake. Whether above or below, wherever it is, a lamp sheds light. It only wants its light to reach others. If the sun above in the sky were below, it would be the same sun but the world would remain in darkness. It is therefore above, not for its own sake, but for the sake of others. In short, the saints transcend "above" and "below" and the glorification of people.

When a bit of ecstasy or a flash of grace from the other world manifests itself to you, at that moment you are totally indifferent to "above" and "below," to "lordly rank, "leadership," even to your own self, which is the closest thing of all to you. How then could the saints, who are mines and sources of that light and ecstasy, be bound by "above" or "below"? Their glory is in God, and He is independent of

---

135 The prophetic hadith *(kallim al-nâs)* is given in Ayn al-Qudat, *Tamhidat,* 6.

"above" and "below." "Above" and "below" are for us who have physical existence.

The Prophet said, "Do not give me preference over Jonah, son of Matthew, simply because his 'ascension' was in a whale's belly and mine was at the Throne of God in heaven."[136] By this he meant that if you do prefer him, do not give him preference over Jonah just because Jonah's apotheosis was in a whale's belly and his was in heaven—because God is neither above nor below. God's manifestation is the same above as it is below; it is the same even in the whale's belly. He transcends "above" and "below." They are all the same to Him.

Many people do things for purposes contrary to God's purpose. God wanted Muhammad's religion to be exalted and evident and to remain for ever and ever, but look at how many different interpretations have been made of the Koran—volumes ten by ten, eight by eight, and four by four. The purpose of the authors is to display their own learnedness. Zamakhshari in his *Kashshaf* explained so many minutiae of grammar, lexicography, and rhetorical exposition in order to show how learned he was; nevertheless, the real purpose was accomplished, and that was the glorification of Muhammad's religion.

All people then do God's work, ignorant though they may be of God's purpose and even if they have in mind another purpose entirely. God wishes the world to continue; people occupy themselves with their desires and gratify their lusts with women for their own delectation, but from it come children. In this manner they are doing something for their own pleasure while it is actually for the maintenance of the world. They are therefore serving God, although they have no such intention. Similarly, people who build mosques spend so much on doors, walls, and roofs. The credit, however, goes to

---

136 Cf. the divine hadith *(lâ yanbaghî li-'abd)*, "No servant of mine should say, 'I am better than Jonah son of Matthew,'" is given in al-Suyuti, *al-Jami' al-saghir*, II, 81.

the kiblah, the object of glorification which is the more honored, even though the donors may have no such intention.

The greatness of the saints is not in external form. The elevation and greatness they possess are unqualifiable. A *dirhem* is, after all, "above" a *pul*, but what does it mean to be "above" a *pul*? It is not in external form, for if you put a *dirhem* on the roof and a gold piece downstairs, the gold piece is still most assuredly "above" the *dirhem*, no matter what—just as rubies and pearls are "above" gold, no matter whether they are physically "above" or "below." Similarly the husk stays on top of the gristmill, while the flour falls below. If the flour stayed on top, how could it be flour? The superiority of flour is not then because of its physical form. In the world of intrinsic meaning, since it has that "substance," it is "above" in any case.

## TWENTY-FIVE

That person who just came in is beloved and humble. It is in his nature to be so. He is like a limb that has so much fruit that it pulls the limb down, while the limb that has no fruit, like the poplar, holds its head up high. When there is too much fruit, the limb has to be propped up lest it be weighed down altogether.

The Prophet was exceedingly humble because all the "fruits" of the world, from first to last, were gathered on him. He was then necessarily the most humble of all. "No one was able to precede the Messenger of God in greeting"—that is, no one could offer greetings before the Prophet did because he, being so extremely humble, always greeted others first. If he chanced not to offer greetings first, he was still the humble one and was the first to speak because the manner of greeting had been heard and learned from him. Everything possessed by the ancients and moderns is a reflection of him: they are shadows of him.

If a man's shadow enters the house ahead of the man himself, in actuality the man is ahead even though his shadow may seem to precede physically. After all, however much a shadow may precede, it is derived from a man. These characteristics do not belong to the present but to that former time. They have been in man's atoms and parts, some bright, some half-lit, some dark. They may manifest themselves in the present, but the brightness and illumination belong to a former time. Man's atoms were clearer and brighter in Adam, and he was more humble.

Some people have regard to beginnings and some to ends. Those who look at the ends are powerful and great because their sights are on finalities and results. Those who look at the beginnings are even more select. They say: "What use is there of looking at the ends? When wheat is sown in the beginning, barley will not grow in the end. When barley is sown, wheat is not going to grow." Their view is then on the beginning.

There is another group more select still who look neither to the beginnings nor to the end. They do not think of beginnings or ends; they are absorbed in God. Another group is absorbed in the world and look not to beginnings or ends out of extreme heedlessness; they are fodder for hell.

It is obvious that Muhammad was the origin, for God said to him: "Were it not for you, I would not have created the heavens."[137] Whatever exists—such as nobility, humility, authority, and high station—all are gifts from him, shadows of him, inasmuch as they were manifested through him. Whatever this hand does it does as a "shadow" of the mind because the mind's "shadow" lies above it. No matter that the mind has no shadow; it does have a "shadowless shadow," just as the concept of "being" exists without physical being. If there were no shadow of the mind over man, none of his limbs would work—the hand would not grasp correctly; the foot would not be able to walk correctly; the eye would not see; the ear would not hear. These limbs and organs then perform correctly and as they should because of the shadow of the mind. In reality, all these functions come from the mind. Limbs and organs are mere instruments. Similarly, there is a

---

137 The famous divine hadith *(lawlâka lamâ)* is given in *FAM* 172.

great man, the vice regent of his age, who is like the Universal Intellect. The minds of men are like his limbs. Everything they do is from his shadow. If they do something incorrectly, it is because the Universal Intellect has withdrawn its shadow. Similarly, when a man begins to go mad and do untoward acts, everyone realizes that his mind has left and no longer casts its shadow over him, that he has fallen away from the shadow and refuge of the mind.

The mind is of the same species as the angels, although angels have a winged form and the mind does not. Nonetheless, in actuality they are the same thing and have the same nature. One must not take form into consideration since they perform the same function in actuality. For example, if you dissolve the angels' form, they become pure intellect, with nothing of their wings remaining externally. We realize then that they were totally intellect that had been embodied. In fact, they are called "embodied intelligences." Similarly, if you make a bird with feathers and wings out of wax, it is nonetheless wax. Don't you see that when you melt it down, the bird's feathers, wings, head, and feet revert to wax? Nothing at all remains that can be discarded: it all becomes wax. We realize then that it was wax all along and the bird that was made from it was only wax. It was molded into a body and decorated, but it was wax. Similarly, ice is nothing more than water. When you melt it, it is nothing but water. Before it turned to ice it was water and could not be held in the hand. When it froze it could be held in the hand or put in the lap. The difference between the two is no more than that. Ice is just water. The two are the same thing.

Here is the situation of man: they brought angels' feathers and tied them onto a donkey's tail in hopes that the donkey, by means of those angel feathers and by conversing with angels, might take on angelic characteristics.

Jesus grew wings of intellect
and flew above the celestial spheres.
If his donkey had half a feather

111

it would not have remained a donkey.[138]

And what wonder would it have been had it become
human? God is capable of anything.

After all, when a child is newly born it is worse than a
donkey. It puts its hand into filth and then puts it to its mouth
to lick it. Its mother slaps it to keep it from doing that. A
donkey is a clean thing by comparison. When it urinates it
spreads its legs so that its urine won't drip on it. If God can
turn a baby, which is worse than a donkey, into a human
being, what wonder would there be if He turned a donkey into
a human? Nothing is surprising for God.

At Resurrection all of man's limbs, hands, and feet, and so
forth, will speak one by one. The philosophers explain this
away by saying that a hand cannot speak except by means of
some sign or other, which will be in place of speech—
something like a wound or scab will appear on a hand so that
one might say that the hand "speaks" or "tells" that it was
burned. If scarred, the hand might "speak" and "tell" that it
had been cut by a knife. If black, the hand "says" that it was
rubbed against a black pot. The "speaking" of the hand and
other limbs will be of this sort.

The Sunnis say: "God forbid! Absolutely not! This very
hand will speak palpably just as the tongue does. On the Day
of Resurrection a man may deny that he has ever stolen, but
his hand will say plainly, 'Oh, yes, you did steal, for it was I
who took.' The man will face his hands and feet and say, 'You
did not speak before. How is it you can speak now?' They will
answer, *'God hath caused us to speak, who giveth speech unto all
things* [41:21]. He causes me to speak who causes everything to
speak, who causes doors and walls and stones and mud clumps
to speak. The creator who can endow all those things with
speech gives me speech also—just as He gives your tongue the
power of speech.'" Your tongue is a piece of flesh; your hand is
a piece of flesh, and so is speech. Is the tongue intelligent?

---

138 The verse is from Sanai, *Divan*, p. 339, line 6506.

From the many things you have seen it should not appear impossible that it might be. Otherwise, the tongue is just a pretext for God. When He commands it to speak it will, and it will say whatever He tells it to.

Speech comes in proportion to man's capacity. Our words are like the water the superintendent of waterworks turns on. Does the water know to which field the superintendent is sending it? It may be going to a cucumber field, a cabbage patch, an onion plot, or a rose garden. I know that when a lot of water comes there must be a lot of parched land somewhere. When only a little water comes, then I know that the plot is small, only a kitchen garden or a little walled garden. "He inculcates wisdom through the tongues of preachers in proportion to the aspirations of the listeners."[139] Say I am a shoemaker: there is plenty of leather, but I cut and sew in proportion to the size of the foot.

> I am a man's shadow, I am his measure.
> How much is his stature? That much am I.[140]

In the fields beneath the earth there is a little animal that lives in total darkness. It has neither eyes nor ears because where it makes its home it needs neither. Since it has no need, why should it be given eyes? It is not because God has a lack of eyes and ears, or because He is stingy, but because He gives in proportion to need. What is not needed is burdensome. God's wisdom and grace remove burdens. Why should they impose a burden on anyone? For example, if you give a tailor carpentry tools such as an adze, a saw, and a file and tell him to take them, they would become burdens on him since he cannot use them. God therefore gives things by need. Just like the worm that lives beneath the earth in darkness, there are people who are happy and content in the darkness of this world and have no need for the other world or any desire to see it. What

---

139 The prophetic hadith *(allâhu yulaqqinu)* is given in *FAM* 198 #634.

140 Rumi, *Divan*, IV, p. 33, ghazal 1680, line 17, #614.

would they do with the "eye of insight" or the "ear of understanding"? They get along in this world with the sensible eye they have. And since they have no intention of going to the other side, why should they be given the power of insight, which they cannot use?

> Think not that there are no travelers on the road,
> or that those of perfect attribute leave no trace.
> Just because you are not privy to the secrets
> you think that no one else is either.[141]

At this time the world subsists through heedlessness. If there were no heedlessness, this world would cease to be. Desire for God, memory of the other world, "inebriation," and ecstasy are the architects of the other world. If everyone were attuned to that world, we would all abandon this world and go there. God, however, wants us to be here so that there may be two worlds. To that end He has stationed two headmen, heedlessness and heedfulness, so that both worlds will flourish.

## TWENTY-SIX

If outwardly I neglect to thank you or to express my gratitude for the kindnesses, favors, and support you give both directly and indirectly, it is not out of pride or arrogance, nor is it because I do not know how one ought to repay a benefactor in word or deed, but because I realize that you do these things out of pure belief, sincerely for God's sake. And so I leave it to God to express gratitude for what you have done for his sake. If I say that I am grateful, and acknowledge my admiration for you in praise, it would be as though you had already received some of the recompense God will give you. Humbling oneself, expressing gratitude, and admiring another are worldly pleasures. Since you have taken pains in this world to bear the burden of monetary expense and social position, it

---

141 Not traced.

would be better for the recompense to be wholly from God. For this reason I do not express my gratitude, as to do so would be this-worldly.

Money cannot be eaten. It is sought after for other than itself. People buy horses, serving girls, and slave boys and seek high office with their money so that they will be praised and approved. It is the world itself which is great and respected and which people praise and esteem.

*

Shaykh Nassaj of Bukhara was a great, spiritual man. The great and learned used to come to him and sit respectfully in his presence. The shaykh was illiterate. When they desired to hear interpretation of the Koran and *hadith* from him, he would say: "I don't know Arabic. You translate the verse or *hadith* for me and I'll tell you what it means." So they would translate a verse of the Koran, and he would begin to interpret and actualize its meaning, saying, for instance, that the Prophet was in such-and-such a situation when he spoke this verse and the conditions of the situation were thus-and-so. And he would expound in detail on the level of that situation, the ways to it, and the climax. One day a descendant of Ali was praising a certain judge in his presence and saying: "There is not such a judge in all the world. He doesn't take bribes. He dispenses justice impartially among the people with sincerity and devotion to God."

"What you are saying about his not taking bribes," said Shaykh Nassaj, "is certainly untrue. You, an Alid of the descent of the Prophet, praise and extol this man by saying that he doesn't take bribes. Is this not bribery? What better bribe could there be than for you to talk about him so to his face?"

*

The Shaykhu'l-Islam of Termez was once saying that the reason Sayyid Burhanuddin could expound so well on mystical truths was that he read the books of the masters and studied their esoteric treatises.

Someone asked him why it was, seeing that he too read and studied the same books, that he didn't speak like Sayyid Burhanuddin.

"He has the suffering and striving and action," he answered.

"Why don't you speak of those things?" he was asked. "You just tell of what you have read."[142]

There is the root of the matter. That is what we are talking about. You too should speak of that. They did not have the agony of the other world. Their hearts were totally set on this world. Some have come to eat bread and others just to look at it. They want to learn these words to peddle them. These words are like a beautiful bride. What love or affection will a beautiful girl have for someone who buys her in order to sell her again? Since the only pleasure such a trader has is in selling the girl, he might as well be impotent. Inasmuch as he buys a girl only to sell her, he does not have the manliness to be buying her for himself. If a fine Indian sword falls into an effeminate man's hand, he will only take it in order to sell it. If he chances upon a champion's bow, he will only sell it since he does not have the arm to pull it. He wants the bow for the sake of the string, and he has not even the aptitude for the string. He is in love with the string, and when he sells it, he will buy powder and rouge. What else can he do?

These words might as well be Syriac for all you understand of them! Beware lest you say you understand. The more you think you have understood, the farther you are from understanding. To understand this means not to understand. All your troubles and problems arise from that understanding. That understanding is a fetter; you must escape it to become something.

It would be absurd for you to say, "I filled my skin from the sea, and the sea was contained in my skin." What you should say is, "My skin was lost in the sea." Reason is a good

---

142 This passage occurs almost verbatim in Faridun ibn Ahmad Sipahsalar, *Risala*, p. 121.

and desirable thing to bring you to the king's gate, but when you get there, you must divorce yourself from reason. From then on reason is to your detriment and will hamper your progress. When you reach the king, submit yourself to him. You will have nothing more to do with whys and wherefores. For example, you have an uncut piece of cloth you want made into a cloak or tunic, so your reason takes you to the tailor. Up to that point reason has done well to bring the cloth to the tailor, but from that point on you must divorce yourself from reason and turn yourself over to the tailor. Similarly, reason does well to take a sick man to a doctor, but once in the doctor's presence reason has nothing further to do; one must submit oneself to the doctor.

Those who know what it is to cry out have ears to hear your inner cries. It is obvious when someone has inner substance and empathy. Among a whole train of camels, one intoxicated camel is obvious because of its eyes, its way of walking, its foam, and so forth. *Their signs are in their faces, being marks of frequent prostration* [48:29]. Everything a tree root "eats" appears as branches, leaves, and fruit on top of the tree. If it does not eat and withers, how is that to remain hidden? The secret of this loud hue and cry they raise is that they understand many words from one word and they comprehend many allusions from one word. When a man who has read the *Wasit*[143] and other lengthy tomes hears one word from the *Tanbih*,[144] which commentary he has read, he understands from one topic many principles and problems. He could write many *Tanbih*s from that one word—that is, he could say, "I understand what underlies these things. I see

---

143 The *Kitab al-wasit al-muhit bi-athar al-basit* (*GAL* I, 424) is a detailed jurisprudential commentary by Abu-Hamid al-Ghazali (d. 1111) on his own *Kitab al-basit fi'l-furu'*, itself a commentary on the *Nihayat al-matlab* of his teacher Imam al-Haramayn al-Juwayni (d. 1085).

144 Apparently the book meant here is the *Tanbih fi'l-furu'* by Abu-Ishaq Ibrahim ibn Ali al-Firuzabadhi al-Shirazi (d. 1083), one of the best known handbooks on Shafiite jurisprudence (*GAL* I, 387).

because I have taken pains and stayed awake at night and found the treasures." *Have we not opened thy breast?* [94:1]. The "opening" *(sharh)* of the heart is infinite. When one has read that commentary *(sharh),*[145] one understands many symbols. One who is still a neophyte will understand of a given word only the meaning of that one word. What can he know? What hue and cry will beset him? Speech comes in accordance with the listener's capacity. Wisdom does not come out by itself if one does not draw it out. Wisdom comes in proportion to the amount one draws it out and feeds on it. If one does not do this and asks why speech does not come, the answer is, "Why don't you draw it out?" One who does not use the faculty of listening does not induce a speaker to speak.

In the time of the Prophet there was an unbeliever who had a slave, and this slave was a Muslim and a man of integrity. One morning the master told his slave to carry some bowls for him to the bath. Along the way they passed a mosque where the Prophet and his companions were praying. "Master," the slave said, "please hold this bowl for a moment so that I can perform the noon prayer. I'll return to you immediately afterward." So saying, he entered the mosque. The Prophet came out; the Prophet's companions also came out, but the slave remained alone in the mosque. The master waited until lunch time and then cried out, "Slave, come out of there!"

"He won't let me go," he replied.

When this state had gone on too long, the master stuck his head into the mosque to see who it was that would not let his

---

145 Rumi puns on the two meanings of *sharh,* ("splitting open" and "commentary, explanation"). The "opening" of the heart, or breast, refers obliquely to the legend of the Prophet's childhood, when it is said the angels descended and split open his breast and inserted light into his inner being. The legend is derived from Koran 94:1 *(a-lam nashrah laka sadraka),* "Have we not opened thy breast?" The "split breast" and "explanation" pun is also used by Rumi at the beginning of his *Masnavi* (1:3) "I want a breast torn to shreds *(sharha-sharha)* so that I may tell an explanation *(sharh)* of the pain of yearning."

slave go. Seeing a pair of shoes and someone's shadow but no movement, he asked, "Who won't let you come out?"

"The same one who won't let you come in," he replied. "The one you can't see."

One always loves what he has not seen or heard or understood. Night and day he searches for it. I am devoted to what I do not see. One grows tired and abandons what one has seen and understood. It is for this reason that the philosophers reject the notion of visions. They say that when you see, it is possible for you to grow tired. But this is not so. The Sunnis say the vision is a time when He appears in one way, but He appears a hundred different ways every instant: *every day is He employed in some new work* [55:29]. Although He may manifest himself in a hundred ways, no two are ever the same. This very instant you are seeing God in various traces and deeds. Every moment you see in various ways that no two of His acts resemble each other. In time of joy there is one manifestation, in time of sorrow another, in time of fear another, in time of hope another. As varied as are God's acts and the manifestations of his acts, so is the manifestation of His essence. You too, who are a part of God's power, appear a thousand different ways every moment and never remain fixed in any one fashion.

There are some of God's servants who approach God via the Koran. There are others, the more elite, who come from God only to find the Koran here and realize that it is God who has sent it. *We have surely sent it down; and We will certainly preserve the same* [15:9]. The commentators say this is about the Koran. This is all well and good, but there is another meaning here, namely: "We have placed in you a substance, a desire to seek, a yearning, of which We are the keeper. We will not suffer it to be wasted and will bring it to fruition."

Say "God" once and stand firm, for all calamities will rain down upon you.

Someone once came to the Prophet and said, "I love you."

"Be careful of what you are saying," said the Prophet.

Again the man repeated, "I love you."

119

"Be careful of what you are saying," the Prophet warned again.

But a third time he said, "I love you."

"Now stand firm," said the Prophet, "for I shall kill you by your own hand. Woe unto you!"

In the time of the Prophet someone said, "I don't want this religion. By God I don't want it! Take this religion back. Ever since I entered into this religion of yours I have not had one day of peace. I have lost my wealth; I have lost my wife; I have no children left; I have no honor, strength, or passion left."

The reply was, "Wherever our religion goes, it does not come back until it has plucked one out by the roots and swept his house clean." *None shall touch the same, except those who are clean* [56:79].

So long as you have an iota of self-love left within you, no beloved would pay any attention to you. Neither would you be worthy of union nor would any beloved grant you admittance. One must become totally indifferent to the self and inimical to the world in order for the beloved to show his face. Now, our religion will not turn loose of a heart that has found stability until it brings it to God and divorces it from everything that is unsuitable. The Prophet said the reason you find no peace and constantly grieve is because grieving is like vomiting. So long as any of those original joys remain in your stomach you will not be given anything to eat. While a person is vomiting he cannot eat anything. When he has finished vomiting, then he can eat. You too must wait and suffer grief, for grieving is vomiting. After the vomiting is over, a joy will come that has no grief, a rose that has no thorns, a wine that causes no hangover. Night and day in this world you are searching for rest and peace, but it is not possible to acquire them in this world. Nonetheless, you are not without this quest for even an instant. Any peace you find in this world is as unstable as a passing lightning flash. What kind of lightning? A lightning full of hail, rain, snow, full of tribulation. For example, say someone wants to go to Antalya but takes the road to Caesarea. Although he may never abandon hope of reaching Antalya, it is impossible to get there by the road he has taken. On the other hand, if he does take the Antalya road, though he be lame and weak, eventually he will arrive since that is where the road ends. Since neither the affairs of this world nor the affairs of the next world are accomplished without suffering, then suffer for the next world lest your suffering go for nought.

You say, "O Muhammad, take my religion away, for I find no peace."

"How can our religion turn a person loose before it brings him to the goal?" he will answer.

The story is told of a teacher who was so destitute that during the winter he had nothing but a length of linen. By chance a flood had caught up a bear in the mountains and swept it down with its head under the water. Some children saw the bear's back and cried out: "Teacher, here is a fur coat fallen in the ditch. Since you are cold, take it out." The teacher was in such need and so cold that he jumped into the ditch to get the fur coat. The bear dug its claw into him and held him in the water. The children cried, "Teacher, either bring the fur out or, if you can't, let it go and come out!"

"I've let the fur go," he said, "but it won't let me go! What am I to do?"

How then is yearning for God to let you go? It is a cause for thanks that we are not in our own hands but in God's. An infant knows only milk and its mother. God does not leave it in that state but causes it to advance to the stage of eating bread and playing. From there He advances it to the stage of rationality. In relation to the other world we are in the stage of infancy: this world is just another mother's breast. He will not leave you until He brings you to the point that you realize that this state is infancy and nothing more. "I am amazed by a people who have to be dragged to paradise in chains and fetters."[146] *Take him, and bind him* [69:30], then burn him in

---

146 Essentially the same as the hadith *('ajiba rabbunâ)* given in *FAM* 103 #305.

121

paradise; then burn him in union; then burn him in beauty; then burn him in perfection: burn him!

Fishermen do not pull in a fish all at once. When the hook has caught in the fish's mouth, they pull it a bit so that it will bleed and lose its strength. Then they keep letting it out and pulling it in until its strength is completely sapped. When the hook of love catches in a man's mouth, God pulls it gradually so that all the excess strength and "blood" in him go away little by little. *God contracteth and extendeth* [2:245].

That there is no god but God is the belief of the common folk. The belief of the elite is that there is no "he" but He. It is like someone who dreams that he is a king seated on a throne and around him stand his slaves, chamberlains, and generals. He says, "I must be a king. There is no king but I." This is what he says in his dream, but when he wakes up and sees that there is no one in the house but himself, then he will say, "I'm here and there is no one here but me." Now, one needs an open eye; an eye asleep cannot see this. It is not its duty to see this. Every sect rejects every other sect and says: "We are right. Revelation belongs to us. These others are wrong." And the others say exactly the same about them. Thus do the "two-and-seventy creeds" reject each other.[147] Of one accord, they say that nobody else possesses revelation. Thus they are all in agreement that none of the others has revelation and that of the whole only one has it. Now, one must be a discerning and wise believer to know which one that one is. "The believer is sagacious, discriminating, understanding, intelligent."[148] Faith is that very power of discrimination and comprehension.

Someone said: "Those who do not know are many, and those who do know are few. If we occupy ourselves with distinguishing between those who don't know and have no

---

147 The "two-and-seventy creeds" as a metaphor for all heterodox and heretical sects comes from a saying of the Prophet: "The Jews split into seventy-one sects; the Christians split into seventy-two. My community will split into seventy-three, all but one of which will go to hell."

148 This hadith *(al-mu'minu kayyis)* is given in *FAM* 67 #178.

substance and those who do have substance, it will take a long time."

Even though those who do not know are many, when you know the few you know all. Similarly, when you know a handful of wheat, you know all the grainhouses in the world. If you have tasted a bit of sugar, no matter how many hundreds of different kinds of sweets may be made from it, you know from the sugar you have tasted that they have sugar in them. A person who has eaten sugar and does not recognize it later must be stupid.

If these words seem repetitious to you, it is because, since you have not yet learned the first lesson, we have to say the same thing over every day.

There was once a teacher who had had a child for three months, but the child had not progressed beyond "A has nothing." The child's father came and said, "We have not been remiss in our remuneration, but if we have tell us so that we can pay you more."

"Oh, no," said the teacher, "you are not at fault. It's just that the child has not progressed." He summoned the child and said, "Say, 'A has nothing.' "

"Has nothing," said the child, who could not say "A."

"You see," said the teacher, "since he has not gone beyond this and hasn't learned even this much, how can I give him a new lesson?"

We say "praise to God Lord of the Universe,"[149] not because there is any lack of bread or victuals, for that is unlimited, but because the guests are full and cannot eat any more. Now, these "bread and victuals" do not resemble the victuals of this world because the victuals of this world can be fed by force, however much you want, without having the appetite for it. Since the victuals of this world are inanimate they will go wherever you take them. They have no spirit to keep themselves from the unworthy—unlike divine food,

---

149 The phrase is said at the end of a meal or by a guest to signal that he has eaten his fill.

wisdom, and which is a living favor that comes to you
shes you as long as you have the appetite and show
tion. When you no longer have the appetite and
......, since it cannot be fed by force, it withdraws under
cover and hides from you.

Speaking of saintly miracles, one can go from here to the
Kaaba in a day, or in a moment. There is nothing strange or
miraculous about that. The desert wind can perform the same
"miracle," for in a day or an instant it can go wherever it
wants. A miracle is what brings you from a low state to an
exalted one; it is what transports you from there to here, from
ignorance to intelligence, from inanimacy to life. At first you
were dust; you were inanimate and were brought into the
world of plant life, whence you traveled into the world of
animality, and thence into the world of humanity. These are
miracles. God gave you the ability to travel over these various
stages and routes by which you came. You had no inkling that
you would come or by what route or how you had come or
that you were being led; yet you see clearly that you have
come. Likewise you will be transported to a hundred various
other worlds. Do not deny it. Even though you know nothing
of it, accept it.

A bowl filled with poison was presented to Umar. "What
is this good for?" he asked.

"If it be considered inexpedient to kill someone openly,"
they said, "he can be given a little of this and he will die
quietly. If you have an enemy who cannot be killed by the
sword, he can be killed surreptitiously with a little of this."

"This is a wonderful thing you have brought," he said.
"Give it to me to drink, for within me is a powerful enemy no
sword can reach. In all the world there is no one more inimical
to me."

"There is no need for you to drink all of it," they said.
"Just a bit is enough. All of it would kill a hundred thousand
men."

"This enemy is no ordinary person," Umar said. "He is an
enemy equivalent to a thousand men and has vanquished a

hundred thousand people." Taking the cup, he gulped it all down at once.

Those who were present all became Muslims on the spot and said, "Your religion is true."

"You have all become Muslims," said Umar, "but this infidel has still not become a Muslim.

Now, what Umar meant by faith was not the faith of the masses. That kind of faith he had and more, for he had the faith of the truly devoted. What he meant was the faith of the prophets and the elect, the "eye of certainty." That is what he expected.

The fame of a certain lion had spread throughout the world. A certain man so wondered at this lion that he set out from afar for the jungle where the lion was in order to see it. When he reached the jungle, having endured hardship for a year and having traversed many leagues, he saw the lion at a distance and stopped, unable to go any farther. "You have come so far for love of this lion," he was told, "and this lion has the peculiar characteristic of not harming anyone who approaches him bravely and pets him lovingly. The lion only grows angry at those who are afraid of him. He attacts those whom he suspects of harboring an evil opinion of him. Now that you have traveled for a year and come so close to the lion, why have you stopped? Step forward!"

But the man did not have the courage to take even one step forward. "All those steps I took," he said, "were easy. But now this one step I cannot take."

What Umar meant by faith was that one step toward the lion in the lion's presence. That one step is very rare—it pertains to only the elect and the chosen few. Indeed, this is what a step is; anything else is a mere footprint. Such faith comes only to the prophets, who have washed their hands of their lives.

*

A beloved is a good thing because a lover derives strength and life from the image of his beloved. Why should this be strange? Layla's image gave Majnun strength and sustenance.

Where a "metaphoric" beloved has such power and influence as to strengthen the lover, why should you think it strange for an actual beloved's image to give strength both visibly and invisibly? Why speak of image? It is the soul of reality. It should not be called an image. The world subsists through an image. You call this world a reality because it is visible and tangible, and those intrinsic ideas of which the world is a branch you call images. The reality is just the opposite; this world is the image. The intrinsic idea can produce a hundred worlds like this one, which can rot, be destroyed, and pass into nothingness. It can then produce new, better worlds without growing old itself. It transcends newness and oldness. Only its branches can be qualified with oldness and newness; and as originator of these, it transcends both.

An architect formulates a house in his mind, making an image of a certain width, a certain length, with a portico and courtyard of certain dimensions. This is not called an image because the reality is born of the image, as a branch of the image. If a non-architect were to imagine such a form it would be called a fancy. A man who is not a builder and doesn't know how to build is commonly said to have fancies.

## TWENTY-SEVEN

It is better for people not to ask questions of a fakir because questions provoke him to invent lies. Why? Because when a materialistic person asks him a question, he has to answer. Since his answer is truth, he cannot speak it. The asker is not capable or worthy of such an answer: his lips and mouth are not worthy of such a morsel. Therefore, the fakir is obliged to invent a lie as an answer to be in harmony with the asker's capacity and ability and in order to be rid of him. Although everything a fakir says is truth and not a lie, still, in relation to what the true answer is for the fakir himself, the answer is a lie, however right—and even more than right—it may be for the one who hears it.

A dervish once had an apprentice who begged for him. One day he brought some food from his begging and the dervish ate it. That night the dervish experienced nocturnal emission.

"Who did you get this food from?" he asked the apprentice.

"A beautiful girl gave it to me," he replied.

"By God," said the dervish, "I have not had a nocturnal emission for twenty years. This is a result of her morsel."

Thus a dervish must be on his guard and not eat the food of just anybody, for dervishes are subtle and easily effected by things. Things show up on them just as a bit of soot shows up on a pure white garment. On a dirty garment, on the other hand, one that has turned dark and lost its whiteness through years of grime and filth, nothing will show up no matter how much grease and grime dribble onto it. Being thus, a dervish should not eat any morsel from the unjust, those who are tainted or gross materialists, for such morsels will effect them. Through the influence of such strangers' morsels corrupt thoughts will show up on him, just as that dervish experienced nocturnal emission because of the girl's morsel. And God knows best.

## TWENTY-EIGHT

The litanies of aspirants consist of striving and serving God and of dividing their time for every labor so that their time is apportioned, as though they have force of habit as an overseer to put them to their tasks. For example, one should rise at dawn, the appropriate hour for devotions, when the soul is calmer and purer. Every person performs what service is appropriate and suitable to his noble soul. *We range ourselves in order; and we celebrate the divine praise* [37: 165-66]. There are a hundred thousand degrees. The purer a man is, the farther forward he is advanced; the less he is, the farther back he is demoted. "Send them back even as God has sent them back."[150] This is a long story, and there is no escaping its

---

150 The prophetic hadith *(akhkhirûhunna)* is found in *FAM* 60 #154.

length. Whoever abbreviates this story abbreviates his own life and soul—except one preserved by God.

As for the litanies of those who have attained union—and I speak in accordance with understanding—at dawn the holy spirits and pure angels, along with those *whom none knows but God* [14:9] and whose names are kept concealed from people out of extreme jealousy, come to visit them. *And thou shalt see the people enter into the religion of God by troops* [110:2]. *And the angels shall go in unto them by every gate.* [13:23]. You may be seated next to them and neither see them nor hear those words, greetings, and laughter. Why should this be strange? An ill person near death may have visions, and another person sitting by his side has no knowledge of them and does not hear what is being said. And before death no one sees realities, which are a thousand times subtler than a vision one can't see or hear, unless he is ill.

A visitor, knowing the delicacy and might of the saints and realizing how many angels and pure spirits have come at first dawn into the shaykh's presence, waits incalculably because he must not interrupt the shaykh during such litanies.

The king's servants stand at his door every morning ready to serve. It is their "litany" for each one to have a fixed station and a fixed duty. Some serve from afar, and the king never sees them or pays them attention; but the king's servants see who has performed him service. When the king goes out, his "litany" is to have servants attend to him from every side because servitude is not something that lasts.

The saying, "Adopt the qualities of God" has been realized; the saying, "I will be His hearing and sight."[151] has become a reality. This is a very powerful station; to speak of it is a shame. It cannot be understood by spelling out the words. If a

---

151 The last part of the famous *hadith al-nawâfil (lâ yazâlu 'abdî)*, "My servant continues to draw nigh to Me through supererogatory acts until I love him; and when I love him I am his hearing, sight, and tongue; through me he hears, through me he sees, and through me he speaks." See Ayn al-Qudat, *Tamhidat*, 271.

little of its power were actualized, then the word itself would become unpronounceable and nothing would remain, neither physical nor psychic force. The "city of existence" is destroyed by the armies of light. *Verily kings, when they enter a city by force, waste the same* [27:34]. If a camel comes into a small house, the house will be ruined; but within the ruins will be a thousand treasures.

> Treasure abounds in ruins;
> A dog in a flourishing city is still a dog.[152]

Now that I have spoken at length about the stage of aspirants, what can I say of the stage of those who have achieved union, except that it has no end? The former does have an end, and that is union. What then is the end for those who have already attained that union that knows no separation? No red grape ever returns to a green state; no ripe fruit ever becomes unripe again. ·

> I hold it unlawful to speak of these things to men,
> But when You are mentioned I go on at length.[153]

By God, I won't go on at length. I'll cut it short.

> I drink my heart's blood
> and you think it's wine I'm drinking.
> You rob me of my soul
> and think you are giving me a gift.

Anyone who abbreviates this, it is as though he leaves the right road and takes the road to a deadly desert, thinking that some trees are near at hand.

---

152 From Sanai, *Hadiqat*, p. 347, line 3.

153 From a quatrain given in Muhammad ibn al-Munawwar, *Asrar al-tawhid*, p. 26.

# TWENTY-NINE

The Christian surgeon said: "A group of Shaykh Sadruddin's companions were drinking wine with me and said, 'Jesus is God as you Christians claim. We know this to be the truth, but we conceal our belief and deny it publicly on purpose in order to preserve the community.' "

"The enemy of God has lied," said the Master. "This is the talk of a man intoxicated with the wine of the misled, vilified and vilifying Satan, who was driven from God's presence. How is it possible for a weak person, who fled the wiles of the Jews from one place to another and whose physical form was less than two cubits, to be the preserver of the seven heavens? The breadth of each heaven would take five hundred years to cross, and to get from one to the next would take another five hundred years. Then there are the earths, each of which would take five hundred years to cross, and again five hundred years to reach the next one. Below God's Throne is a sea the depth of which would not reach His ankles. This much, and many times more, belongs to God. How can your reason accept that the disposer and controller of all that could be the weakest of all forms? Then too, who was the creator of heaven and earth before Jesus? (Glory be to God, whose might is far beyond what the unjust uphold!)"

The Christian said, "The dust went to dust and the pure to the pure."

"If Jesus' spirit were God," said the Master, "then where did his spirit go? The spirit returns to its origin and maker, and if he were the origin and maker, where would it go?"

"This is how we found things, and so, as a community, we adopted it,"[154] said the Christian.

---

154 A reference to the Koranic passage (5:104), "And when it was said unto them, 'Come unto that which God hath revealed, and to the apostle'; they answered, 'That religion which we found our fathers to follow is sufficient for us.' What, though their fathers knew nothing and were not rightly directed?"

"If you 'found,' or inherited from your father, tarnished, worthless, counterfeit coins, wouldn't you exchange them for gold of sound assay, free from alloy and adulteration? Or would you keep the counterfeit and say, 'We found it so'? If you were left with a crippled hand from your father but then found a physician and medicine that could cure your hand, wouldn't you take the medicine? Or would you say, 'I found my hand thus, crippled, and I do not desire to change it'? If you found brackish water in the village where your father had died and where you were brought up, but were then led to another village where the water was good, the vegetation good and the people healthy, wouldn't you want to move there and drink the sweet water so that your ailments and diseases would leave you? Or would you say, 'We found this village and its brackish water which bequeaths disease; therefore, we will cling to what we have found'?"

No one would do this. No one possessed of reason and sound senses would say such things. God gave you a mind, sight, and discrimination separate from that of your fathers. Why then do you count your own mind and sight as nothing and follow a mind that will destroy you and not lead you aright?

Yutash's father was a shoemaker, but when he reached the sultan's court he learned the manners of kings. He was given the highest rank of all, the Keeper of the Sword. He did not say: "We found our father a shoemaker. We do not want this rank. Sultan, give me a shop in the market-place so I can practice shoemaking."

Even a dog, with all its baseness, when it learns to hunt for the sultan, forgets what it inherited from its parents, such as living in garbage heaps and desolate places and desire for carrion. It follows the king's horses and chases after game. So also the hawk, once it is trained by the king, does not say: "We inherited mountain crags and eating dead things from our fathers. We will pay no heed to the king's drum or to his hunt."

If an animal is intelligent enough to cling to what it finds better than what it inherited from its parents, then it is horrible and corrupt for a human being, who is superior to all beings of the earth by virtue of reason and discrimination, to be less than the animals. God forbid! Yes, it would be proper to say that Jesus' Lord ennobled him and placed him among the elect and that whoever serves and obeys him serves and obeys the Lord. And if God sent a prophet better than Jesus and manifested through Jesus, then it would be obligatory to follow that prophet for God's sake, not for the sake of the prophet. Nothing is worshipped for its own sake except God; nothing is loved for its own sake except God. All things other than God are loved for the sake of God. The end is God, that is, the end is that you should love and seek a thing for other than itself until you reach God—and then you will love Him for himself.

To clothe the Kaaba is folly.
The "My" in "My House"
is enough to caparison the Kaaba.[155]

"To make up the eyes with kohl is not the same as to have black eyes."[156] Just as shabby, tattered clothes may conceal wealth and grandeur, so do fine clothes and raiment conceal the countenance and perfect beauty of the poor. When the fakir's robe is tattered, his heart is opened in expansion.

## THIRTY

Some heads are graced by golden crowns. Golden crowns and jewelled diadems detract from the beautiful tresses of other heads because the tresses of beauties are traps of love, which is the heart's throne. A golden crown is a lifeless thing; the wearer is the heart's beloved.

---

155 The line is from Sanai, *Sayr al-'ibad*, p. 101, line 705.

156 Quoted from Mutanabbi, *Diwan*, p. 331.

We sought Solomon's ring in all things. We found it in spiritual poverty, and there we found repose. Nothing was so pleasing as this.

After all I am a whoremonger (*ruspi-bara*).[157] I have done this since I was small. I know that this removes obstacles; this burns the veils. This is the origin of all forms of obedience; the rest is secondary. Until you cut a sheep's throat, what is the use of its trotter or tail? Fasting leads to non-existence, for, after all, all joy's are there. *God is with those who patiently persevere* [2:249].

The root of everything in the market place—shops, beverages, merchandise or trade—is a need within man's soul; but the "root" is hidden and does not move or become apparent until a thing becomes a "must." Similarly, every nation, every religion, every saintly and prophetic miracle, every prophetic state has a "root" in the human spirit, but until it becomes a "must" it does not budge or show itself. *Everything do We set down in a plain register* [36:12].

Are good and evil one thing or two? Insofar as they are contradictory, then the answer is that they must absolutely be two since nothing can contradict itself. However, from the point of view of their being inextricable, evil must come from good because good is the abandonment of evil, and it is absurd to think of abandoning evil unless it exists. If there were no motivation for evil, then good would never be abandoned. In that case there would not be two different things, which proves that good is the abandonment of evil.

The Mazdeans say that Yazdan is the creator of good and Ahriman the creator of evil. To this we say that good is not separate from evil: there can be no good unless there is evil also because being good means a cessation of evil. It is impossible for evil to cease without there having been evil to begin with. Joy is the cessation of grief, and it is impossible for grief to cease unless it exists. The two are therefore one and indivisible.

---

157 Rumi's intent here is unclear.

I said that a thing's benefit does not become apparent until it passes away. It is like speech: until the separate letters pass away in utterance, the benefit does not reach the listener. If anyone speaks ill of a mystic, he is in reality speaking well of him because the mystic avoids characterization for which he can be blamed. He is inimical to such qualification. Therefore, when one speaks ill of a bad quality, he speaks ill of the mystic's enemy and thereby praises the mystic, who avoids blameworthy things. And one who avoids the blameworthy is praiseworthy. "By their opposites are things apparent." In reality then the mystic knows that the critic is not his enemy or censurer.

I am like a pleasant garden, and around me is a wall covered with filth and thorns. A passerby who sees only the wall and its filth speaks ill of the garden. Why should this anger the garden? To speak ill of the garden harms none but the passerby himself. One must accept the wall in order to gain access to the garden, but when one criticizes the wall one remains outside the garden and "destroys" oneself. Thus the Prophet said, "I am the laughing slayer,"[158] that is, I have no enemy with whom I can be wrathful. The Prophet slays an unbeliever in one way lest the unbeliever slay himself in many different ways. Of course he laughs as he slays.

## THIRTY-ONE

Policemen are always chasing thieves, and thieves are always running from the police. Wouldn't it be novel if a thief were to chase a policeman?

God asked Bayazid what he wanted. "I want not to want,"[159] replied Bayazid. Now a human being is limited to two states: either he wants something or he doesn't. Not ever to want is not a human characteristic, for it would mean that

158 The phrase *(anâ 'l-dahûku 'l-qatûl)* is quoted as a prophetic hadith, but the source has not been traced.

159 As the phrase occurs in Sahlaji, "Risalat al-nur," p. 96, Bayazid says to God, "I want not to want other than what you want."

one has become void of self and ceased to be. If anything is left of the self, then the human characteristic of either wanting or not wanting something must still be present. When God wishes to perfect a man and turn him into a complete shaykh, He causes him to enter the state of perfect union and unity, where neither duality nor separation exists. All your agonies arise from wanting something that cannot be had. When you stop wanting, there is no more agony.

Men are of various types, and there are various degrees along the way. Some are brought through strife and effort to the stage where they are able not to put into action what they desire mentally. This is within human capability; however, that there should be no inner "itch," desire, or thought is not within man's capability. It can be removed only by God's attraction. *Say, Truth is come, and falsehood is vanished* [17:81].

"Enter, O believer," hell will say, "for your light extinguishes my fire."[160] When a believer has real and perfect faith, he does just what God wants, whether you call it his own attraction or God's.

It is said that after the Prophet and the elder prophets, no one else will receive prophetic inspiration. Why should this be? Indeed inspiration does come down to humans, but it is not called prophetic inspiration. That is what the Prophet meant when he said, "The believer sees by means of God's Light."[161] When one sees by God's Light, one sees everything, the beginning and the end, the present and the absent. How could anything shut out God's Light? If it can be shut out, then it is not God's Light. The intrinsic meaning of inspiration is present even though it may not be called by that name.

When Uthman became caliph he mounted the pulpit. The people waited to see what he would say, but he remained silent and said nothing. As he looked at the people, they were overcome by such a state of ecstasy that neither could they leave nor did they know where they were. Not a hundred

---

160 The hadith *(juz yâ mu'min)* is given in *FAM* 52 #134.

161 The prophetic hadith *(al-mu'minu yanzuru)* is found in *FAM* 14.

homilies or sermons could have put them into such a state. They learned more valuable lessons, and more mysteries were revealed to them than could ever have been acquired through any amount of deeds or preaching. Until the end of the session Uthman kept looking at them in silence. As he was about to come down, he said, "It is better for you to have an active leader than a talkative one." And he spoke truly, for if the end of rhetoric is to impart something of benefit and to transform character, it can be imparted much better without speech than with. Therefore, what he said was perfectly correct.

Let us examine where he called himself "active," although while he was in the pulpit he made no overt "act" that could be seen. He made no pilgrimage, gave no alms, preached no sermon. We realize therefore that "acts" and "deeds" do not consist of external forms alone. External forms are the "form of action," while the action itself is of the soul. Here the Prophet says, "My companions are like the stars: whichever of them you follow, you will be led aright."[162] One looks at a star and is guided; yet no star "speaks." No indeed. Simply by looking at the stars one knows the right way from the wrong way and reaches one's destination. Thus, it is possible for you to look at God's saints and for them to take control of you without saying a word. Your destination will be attained, and you will be transported to your goal, union. "Let any who desire look upon me. My mien is a harbinger to those who imagine that love is easy."[163]

In God's world there is nothing more difficult than to tolerate the absurd. For example, say you have read a book and decided upon the correct reading and phrasing. Then someone sitting next to you reads the same book wrongly. Can you abide it? Of course not. It is impossible. When you haven't read the book—and hence not discerned the wrong from the right—it does not make any difference to you whether he reads

---

162 The prophetic hadith *(ashâbî ka'l-nujûm)* is given in *FAM* 19 #44.

163 The line is quoted from Mutanabbi, *Diwan,* p. 39.

it correctly or wrongly. To tolerate the absurd, therefore, takes great effort.

The prophets and saints do not shy from exerting effort. The first effort they have in their quest is to kill the carnal self and to abandon concupiscence and desire. That is the "major struggle." When they have attained union and taken their places in the station of security, then wrong and right are revealed. Although they know right from wrong, they are still in great struggle because all the deeds of the people are wrong. This they see, but they are tolerant. If they were not and were to speak out to expose the people's wrongness, not one person would stay with them. No one would be so much as civil to them. God, on the other hand, gives them such great patience and latitude that they can be tolerant. They speak out on only one of a hundred mistakes so as not to make things too difficult. The rest of the mistakes they ignore or even praise and say that they are right. Then, gradually, one by one, they can rectify all the mistakes.

In this same manner a teacher instructs a child in handwriting. When he first comes to write, the child scribbles a line and shows it to the teacher. In the teacher's view it is all wrong and horrible; but, by virtue of his skill and consideration, he says: "It is all very nice. You have written very well. Very good, very good. Just this one letter here you have written badly. It ought to be like this. Oh, yes, and that one too you have written incorrectly." Only a few letters out of the whole line does he call bad, and he shows the child how they ought to be written. The rest he praises lest the child be frustrated. The child's inability is corrected through such praise, and he is taught and helped gradually.

\*

If God wills, we hope that God will facilitate the Prince's goals. It is hoped that whatever he has in his heart (and so also that good fortune that he does not have in his heart, not knowing what he wants) be made easy for him so that when he sees it and when those favors reach him, he will be ashamed of these first wants and desires and say: "Such a thing was in store for me! With such favor and beneficence as this, I marvel how I could have desired those other things!"

What does not come into man's imagination is called a "gift" because whatever passes through his imagination is in proportion to his aspiration and his worth. However, God's gift is in proportion to God's worth. Therefore, the gift is that which is suitable to God, not what is suitable to the imagination or ambition of God's servant. "What no eye has seen nor ear heard nor has occurred to the mind of man"[164]— that is, no matter how much eyes have seen, ears heard, or minds conceived the gift you expect of Me, My gift is above and beyond all that."

## THIRTY-TWO

The attribute of Certainty is the perfect shaykh; Good and True Thoughts are his disciples, according to their varying degrees, such as Thought, Prevailing Thought, Most Prevailing Thought, and so forth. As every thought expands, it comes clearer to Certainty and farther from Doubt. "If Abu Bakr's faith were to be weighed. . . ."[165]

All right thoughts suckle and increase at the breast of certainty. That nursing and increasing is a sign that increase of thought is being acquired through knowledge and practice. This continues until each thought passes completely away from itself into certainty; and when all thoughts have become certainty, no doubt remains.

This shaykh and his disciples, as they are manifested in the world of bodies, are forms of Shaykh Certainty, and his disciples are proof that these forms are changeable age after age and era after era, while Shaykh Certainty and his sons, Right

---

164 The famous divine hadith *(a'dadtu li-'ibâdî)*, "What no eye . . . have I prepared for my righteous servants," occurs in *FAM* 93 #264.

165 The prophetic hadith *(law wuzina îmân)*, "If Abu-Bakr's faith were weighed against the faith of the universe it would outweigh it," is given in al-Ghazali, *Ihya'*, I, 87 *(juz'* i, *bâb* v).

Thoughts, abide immutable in the world throughout the passage of the ages. Again, erroneous, stray, and wrong thoughts are banished by Shaykh Certainty. Every day they grow farther from him, every day they become baser because every day they acquire more of what increases bad thoughts. *There is an infirmity in their hearts, and God hath increased that infirmity* [2:10].

Now the masters eat dates while the prisoners eat thorns. *Do they not consider the camels?* [88:17] . . . *except him who repenteth, and believeth, and doth that which is right* [19:60].

*Unto them will God change their former evils into good* [25:70]. Every acquisition one has made in corrupt doubt now becomes a powerful rectifier of thought, like an expert thief who reforms and becomes a policeman. All the tricks of thievery that he used to practice now become powers on behalf of good and justice. Indeed, he is superior to policemen who were not formerly thieves because a policeman who has committed theft knows the ways of thieves—that is, the habits of thieves are not unknown to him. Such a person, if he becomes a shaykh, is perfect, the guide of the world and the rightly-guided of the age.

## THIRTY-THREE

"Keep away from us!" they said.

"Do not come near us!"
How can I keep away when you are my need?[166]

It must be realized that everyone, everywhere, is inseparable from his need. Every living thing is inseparable from its need. One is constantly accompanied by one's need. It is closer to one than one's mother and father. It constantly cleaves to one. Bound by that need, one is tugged this way and that, as by a bridle. One cannot have bridled oneself because a

---

166 Not traced.

human being seeks freedom, and it is absurd for one who seeks freedom to seek bondage. Of necessity, therefore, there must have been someone else to do the bridling. For example, if one seeks good health, one does not injure oneself because it is impossible to seek both ill health and good health.

Being inseparable from one's need, one is also inseparable from the giver of that need. When a man has been bridled, he is of necessity attendant upon the bridler, but the reason for his being weak and powerless is that his gaze is on the bridle and not the bridler. If his gaze were upon the bridler, he could escape from the bridle: the bridle would be the bridler. He was bridled in the first place because he would not follow the bridler without a bridle. Of course *we will stigmatize him on the nose* [68:16]. We will put a ring in his nose and pull him against his will, since without the ring he will not come to us.

> They say, "Is there play after eighty?"
> I say, "Is there play before eighty?"[167]

God, of His grace, bestows on the aged a youthfulness the young cannot know. Such youthfulness refreshes, causes one to leap and laugh, and gives a desire to play. An elder who sees the world as new and is not weary of the world desires to play, leaps and bounds, and grows robust.

"Great is the appellation of old age if, when grey hairs appear, one's steed of playfulness leaps."[168] The glory of old age is more powerful than the glory of God, for the spring of God's glory appears and then the autumn of old age prevails over it, never to relinquish its autumnal nature. The frailty of spring is the grace of God, for with every tooth shed the smile and blossom of God's spring diminishes, with every grey hair the freshness of God's grace is lost, and with every weeping of

---

167 This line is quoted anonymously in Ibn Qutayba, *'Uyun al-akhbar,* IV, 53, line 6.

168 Ibidem, line 7.

autumnal rain the garden of realities is spoiled. May God be exalted over that which the unjust say!

## THIRTY-FOUR

I saw him in the form of a wild animal, and over him was the skin of a fox. I determined to catch him, but he was at a small window looking down the stairway. Then he waved his hands and jumped this way and that.

Then I saw Jalal of Tabriz with him in the form of a beast. He shied off, but I caught him as he was trying to bite me. I put my foot on his head and squeezed down hard until everything that was in it spilled out. Seeing how beautiful his skin was, I said, "This is worthy to be filled with gold and gems, pearls and rubies, and even more!" Then I said, "I have taken what I wanted. Run away, shy one, to wherever you will. Leap in whatever direction you see fit!" But he leapt rather out of fear of being dominated, although in being dominated lay his happiness. There is no doubt that he was formed from meteor dust and what-not, and that his heart was drenched, and that he desired to comprehend everything. He set off down that road to which he struggled to keep on and in which he took such pleasure, but he was unable to do it because the mystic has states that cannot be caught in those nets. Such prey cannot be trapped in such nets. If he is sound and hale, the mystic is free to determine whether or not he will be captured. No one can apprehend him except by his own determination.

You sit in your covert waiting for the prey. The prey sees you, your place, and your stratagem. He is free to determine. The ways he traverses cannot be limited. He does not pass by your hiding place, for he passes by ways he himself has laid down. *God's earth is spacious* [39:10]. *And they shall not comprehend any thing of His knowledge, but so far as He pleaseth* [2:255].

When these subtleties fall upon your tongue and your comprehension, they are no longer subtleties but rather have degenerated because of their connection with you. Similarly, nothing sound or corrupt remains as it was when it has fallen into the mystic's mouth and comprehension but turns into something else, wrapped up and swathed in favors and miracles. Don't you see how the staff no longer remained in the quiddity of "staff" when Moses' hand was around it? Likewise, the Moaning Pillar and the Stick in the hand of the Prophet, prayer in Moses' mouth, iron in David's hand, and the hills with him[169]—none of these remained as it was but became something else, other than what it had been. So also, when subtleties and invocations fall into the hands of creatures of dark and gross materiality, they cease to remain as they were.

> The Kaaba is a tavern while you are obedient.
> As long as it is yours, it is with you in essence.[170]

"The unbeliever eats with seven stomachs."[171] That ass chosen by our ignorant servant eats with seventy stomachs.[172] Even if he were to eat with one stomach, he would still be eating with seventy stomachs because everything from the despicable is despised, just as everything from the lovable is loved. If the servant were here, I would go to him and advise

---

169 The story of the Moaning Pillar *(al-ustuwana al-hannana)* is told by Rumi in the *Masnavi* (1:2113f). The Prophet Muhammad first preached to his followers while leaning against a pillar, but when the number of Muslims increased and many complained of not being able to see the Prophet, a pulpit was built for him to stand on. The pillar moaned and complained of being abandoned by the Prophet, so he planted it in the ground so that it would bear fruit for the believers in paradise. David is known as the first to make chain mail from iron (Kor. 21:80); the hills and birds were also compelled to praise God along with David as he recited his psalms (Kor. 21:79). For the story of Moses' staff, see note 9.

170 The line occurs in Sanai, *Hadiqat*, p. 112, line 8.

171 The prophetic hadith *(al-mu'minu ya'kulu)*, "The believer eats with one stomach but the unbeliever with seven," is given in *FAM* 145 #449.

172 The "ass" spoken of here appears to be a fraudulent shaykh who has duped the simple servant.

him. I would not leave him until he drove the ass far away because his religion, heart, soul, and intellect are being corrupted. I wish he had driven him to other corruptions like wine-drinking and singing-girls. That could be rectified if he were in contact with a master of grace. But he filled his house with prayer carpets. Would that he were rolled up in them and burned so that the servant would be delivered from him and his evil! He corrupts his belief in the master of grace and slanders him in his presence, while he is silent and destroys himself. He has caught him with prayer beads, litanies, and prayer carpets. Perhaps one day God will open the servant's eyes and he will see what he has lost and how far he has roamed from the compassion of the master of grace. Then he will strike him on the neck and say, "You have destroyed me so that my heavy loads and the forms of my deeds have gathered upon me, just as the master of grace saw in his revelations that the foulnesses of my deeds and corrupt and sinful beliefs were piled in a corner of the house. Although I was trying to hide them behind my back from the master of grace, he knew what I was concealing from him and said, 'What are you hiding?'" By Him in whose hand is my soul, if I were to call those foul forms to come forth to me one by one, the eye would see and they would expose themselves and tell what is concealed within them. May God deliver those who suffer injustice from the likes of these bandits who prey upon God's way through false devotion.

Kings play with polo sticks on the playing field in order to show the people of the city, who cannot be present at battle, a representation of how champions fight, how enemies' heads are lobbed off and roll like balls on the playing field, and how they charge, attack, and retreat. This play in the field is a miniature representation of serious battle. The prayer and *sama'* of the people of God are to show spectators how they are in secret concert with God's commands and prohibitions pertaining to them. The singer at a *sama'* session is like an imam at prayer, for the people follow him. When he sings ponderously, they dance ponderously; when he sings lightly, they dance lightly as a representation of the inner following of the herald of command and prohibition.

## THIRTY-FIVE

It strikes me as odd how those who have memorized the Koran are unable to penetrate the state of the mystics. As the Koran states, *Obey not any who is a common swearer* [68:10]. A slanderer is precisely one of whom is said, "Do not listen to anything So-and-So says," for with you he is *a despicable fellow, a defamer, going about with slander, who forbiddeth that which is good* [68:11-12].

The Koran is an amazingly jealous piece of magic. It contrives to say frankly in an opponent's ear what he understands but cannot comprehend or take any delight in. If it were otherwise, it would snatch him away, for *God hath sealed up* [*their hearts and their hearing*] [2:7]. What a wondrous grace He has to set a seal on those who hear without understanding and who deliberate without understanding. God is gracious, His wrath is gracious, and His "locking up" is gracious; yet unlike His locking up is His "unlocking," the graciousness of which is beyond description.

If I am broken into pieces, it will be on account of the infinite grace and will of His unlocking and the unqualifiableness of His opening. Do not accuse me of being sick and dying! Such an attribution is a blind. What will kill me is His grace and incomparability. The blade that is approaching is for warding off the eyes of "others" so that strange, ill-omened, impure eyes not comprehend the slaughter.

## THIRTY-SIX

Form is secondary to love, for without love form has no value. That which cannot exist without the principal is secondary. Since God cannot be said to have form, and since form is secondary, He cannot be called secondary.

If anyone says that love cannot be imagined or concretized without form and that therefore its secondary aspect is form, we ask why love cannot be imagined without form. Indeed, it is the motivator of form. Thousands of forms, both representational and actualized, are stirred up by love. Although there is no painting without a painter and no painter without a painting, the painting is still secondary and the painter primary—"like the movement of the finger with the movement of the ring."

So long as there is no "love" for a house, an architect cannot conceive or design a house. Similarly, wheat sells one year at the rate of gold and the next at the rate of dirt, but the form of the wheat is always the same. The value and price of the wheat's form depend upon the "love" for it. Likewise, the craft you seek and love may have great worth for you, but in an age when there is no demand for it, no one learns or exercises it.

People say that in the end love is being in want and need for a certain thing; therefore, the state of needfulness is primary and the thing needed secondary. I say that these words you speak are spoken out of need. After all, these words arise out of your need—that is, when you had a desire for these words, they were "born." Therefore, the state of need preceded, and these words were born from that. The need existed prior to the words. If anyone were to ask how an object can be secondary if, after all, the object of the need was these words, I say that the secondary is always the object, just as the object of a tree's roots is the branch of the tree.

## THIRTY-SEVEN

The allegation they have made against this girl, being a lie, will proceed no further. In this group's imagination something has settled.

The human imagination and inner workings are like an entryway through which one comes first before entering a house. This whole world is like a house, and everything that comes inside the entryway must of necessity appear in the house. Take, for example, this house in which we are seated. Its form first appeared in the architect's mind; then it became a house. Therefore, we say that this whole world is a single house. Imagination, thought, and ideas are the entryway to the house. Know for certain that whatever you see having appeared in the entryway will appear in the house. And everything, good and evil, that appears in this world appears first in the entryway; only then does it appear here.

When God desires various things to appear in this world—such as miracles and wonders, or gardens, orchards, and meadows, or sciences and crafts—He places a desire, a demand, for them in the inner workings of human beings so that they may appear from there. Whatever you see in this world exists in the other world. For example, everything you see in a dewdrop exists in the ocean, for the dew drop is of the ocean. Similarly, the creation of the heavens and earth, the Canopy and Throne of God, and all other marvels—God placed a desire for them in the souls of the saints, wherefore the world became apparent.

How can you listen to people who say that the world is uncreated? The saints and prophets, who are more ancient than the world, say that it is temporally created. God placed a desire for the creation of the world into their spirits, and only then did it appear. They, therefore, actually know that it is temporally created; they report from their own vantage point.

For example, we are sitting in this house, and we are sixty or seventy years old. Since this house was built only several years ago, we have seen that there was a time when it did not exist. Animals such as scorpions, mice, snakes, and other vermin that were born and have lived their whole lives within the walls of this house saw it already built when they were born. If they say that this house has existed from eternity, that is no proof for us, who ourselves have seen that this house came to be in time.

Exactly like the animals that have sprung from the walls of this house, there are people who have sprung from the house called the world and who have no substance. From this place they arise and into this same place they sink. If they call the world eternal, it is no proof for the prophets and saints, who existed before the world for thousands and thousands and thousands of years. Why speak of years? Why speak of numbers? It is beyond reckoning, beyond all count. They saw the world come into temporal existence just as you saw the creation of this house in time.

After all that, the little philosopher asks the Sunni how he knows that the world was temporally created. You ass, how do you know that the world has existed eternally? After all, when you say that the world is eternal, what you mean is that it is not temporally created. This is a statement based on a negative. Statements based on affirmatives are easier to make than statements based on negatives. When you make a negative proof, it is like saying that So-and-So has *not* done something. It is difficult, however, to know any such thing. It necessitates having been with that person from the beginning of his life to the end, day and night, during his sleep and waking hours, in order to say that he has absolutely never done such a thing. And even that is not incontrovertible. The person bearing witness may have fallen asleep or the subject may have gone to the bathroom where it was not possible to accompany him. For this reason testimony based on a negative statement is not admissible because it is not within the realm of possibility. On the other hand, testimony based on an affirmative is within the realm of possibility and quite simple. One need only say, "I was with him for a moment, and during that one moment he said thus and so and did thus and so." Such testimony is acceptable because it is within the realm of human capability.

Now, you dog, it is easier to give testimony for the temporal creation of the world than for the world's having existed eternally because the gist of the latter is that it is not temporally created, which is a statement based on a negative. However, since neither has any proof, and you have not seen whether the world is temporally created or ever-existent, you say to someone, "How do you know it is temporally created?" He rejoins, "You lout, how do you know it has always existed?" In the end it is your claim that is the more difficult to prove and the more logically absurd.

## THIRTY-EIGHT

The Prophet was sitting with his companions when some infidels began to interfere. He said, "You are all agreed that in the world there is someone who receives inspiration and that not everyone is so inspired. That person is marked by certain signs in his deeds, words, and countenance. Indeed, in his every part there are signs of that inspiration. When you see those signs in someone, turn toward him and know that he is powerful enough to be your protector."

The infidels were confounded by these words and had nothing more to say. Later they took their swords and returned to vex and insult the Companions.

"Have patience," the Prophet said, "lest they say that they have prevailed over us. They want to force a public display of religion, but God will make this religion manifest when He wills." And for a time the Companions made their prayers in secret and concealed the name of the Prophet until, after a while, an inspiration came, saying, "You too take up the sword and fight!"

The Prophet is not called "unlettered" because he was unable to write. He was called that because his "letters," his knowledge and wisdom, were innate, not acquired. Is a person who made inscriptions on the moon unable to write?[173] What is there in the world that such a person does not know, when all learn from him? What can the partial intellect have that the Universal Intellect has not? The partial intellect is not capable of inventing anything it has not seen before.

The compositions, skills, and new foundations laid by men are not new artifices: their likes have been seen before and merely added to. Only the Universal Intellect can invent things anew. The partial intellect is merely instructable. It is in need

---

173 See note 117.

of instruction, and the instructor is the Universal Intellect. Similarly, when you investigate all trades, you will find that they all originated with inspiration and that they were learned from the prophets, who are the Universal Intellect. Remember the story of the raven: when Cain killed Abel and stood not knowing what to do with the body, one raven killed another, dug out the earth, buried the dead raven and scratched the dirt over the body. From this Cain learned how to make a grave and bury a body. All trades are like this.

Whoever possesses partial intellect is in need of instruction. The Universal Intellect is the giver of all things. Those who have united the partial with the Universal Intellect and become one are prophets and saints. For example, the human hand, foot, eye, and ear, and all other human sensory organs, are capable of being instructed by the mind. The foot learns how to walk, the hand how to grasp, the eye and ear how to see and hear from the mind. If there were no mind, would any of these sensory organs be able to perform its function?

Now, relative to the mind, this body is coarse and gross, while the heart and intellect are subtle. The gross subsists through the subtle, from which it derives whatever it has. Without the subtle the gross would be useless, foul, coarse, and unworthy. Similarly, relative to the Universal Intellect, partial intellects are tools that are instructed by and benefit from the Universal Intellect; but they are gross in comparison to the Universal Intellect.

\*

Someone said, "Mention us in your intention. The intention is the main thing. If there are no words, never mind. Words are secondary."

Does this man think that after all, the intention existed in the world of spirits before the world of bodies and that therefore we were brought into the world of bodies to no good purpose? This is absurd, for words are useful and beneficial. If you plant only the kernel of an apricot pit, it will not grow; but if you plant it together with its shell, it will grow. Therefore, we realize that external form is important too.

Prayer is internal: "There is no prayer without the presence of the heart."[174] However, you must necessarily perform it in external form, with physical bendings and prostrations. Only then do you gain full benefit and reach the goal. *Those . . . who persevere in their prayers* [70:23]. This is the prayer of the spirit. Prayer of the external form is temporary; it is not everlasting because the spirit of this world is an endless ocean. The body is the shore and dry land, which is limited and finite. Therefore, everlasting prayer belongs only to the spirit. The spirit does indeed have a type of bow and prostration; however, bowing and prostrating must be manifested in external form because there is a connection between substance and form. So long as the two do not coincide there is no benefit. As for your claim that form is secondary to substance, that form is subject and the heart king, these are relative terms. You say that Y is secondary to X. As long as there is no secondary thing, how can X be called primary? It is by means of the secondary that the other becomes primary. If there were no secondary, the other would have no name. When you say "female," you imply "male"; when you say "lord," you imply "subject"; when you say "ruler," you imply "ruled."

# THIRTY-NINE

Before Husamuddin Arzanjani entered the service of the poor and took up the company of the dervishes, he was a great debater. Wherever he went, he debated and deliberated in earnest. He did it well and was a good speaker, but when he joined the dervishes his pleasure in debate paled. "Love is severed only by another love."[175] "Whosoever wishes to sit with God Almighty, let him sit with the Sufis."[176] These

---

174 The hadith *(lâ salât)* is given in *FAM* 5 #10.

175 The hemistich of poetry is said to be from Fakhruddin Gurgani's *Vis u Ramin;* exact location not traced.

176 The dictum *(man arâda)* is given in *FAM* 198 #635.

intellectual pursuits, relative to the states of fakirs, are mere games and a waste of one's life.

*Verily this present life is only a play and a vain amusement* [47:36]. When a man reaches maturity and attains full reason, he does not play anymore. If he does, he does it in secret and shame lest anyone see him. Intellectual knowledge, idle talk, and worldly whims are all "wind," while man is "dust." When wind and dust are mixed, they hurt the eyes wherever they go. Nothing comes of them but confusion and complaint. Now, although man is only dust, he weeps at every word he hears, and his tears are like flowing water. *Thou shalt see their eyes overflow with tears* [5:83]. When water, instead of wind, flows over the dust, the opposite will occur, for doubtless when dust is watered fruits, greenery, herbs, and flowers grow.

This way of poverty is a way for you to attain all your hopes. Whatever you may have desired you will doubtlessly attain in this way, whether it be the conquest of armies and victory over enemies, or seizing property and subjugation of people, or superiority over one's peers, or eloquence in speaking and writing, or anything else. When you have chosen the way of poverty, you will attain all these things. Unlike other ways, no one who took this way ever had a complaint. Of a hundred thousand who took contrary ways and struggled, perhaps one reached his goal. And even that was not to complete satisfaction because every way has its own turns and detours to the attainment of the goal. The goal can be attained only by means of those turns and detours. That way is long, full of affliction and obstacles thrown up by those detours against final attainment. But when you enter the world of poverty and practice it, God bestows kingdoms and worlds upon you that you never imagined. You are embarrassed by what you had hoped for before. "Oh," you say, "how could I have sought such a mean thing when such a marvellous thing existed?" Here, however, God says, "Although now you are detached, undesirous, and disdainful of that 'mean' thing, yet it did once cross your mind. But you abandoned it for Our sake.

Our generosity knows no limit. Of course, I will make it easily available for you."

Before attaining fame, the Prophet saw the eloquence of the Arabs and desired to be as eloquent and elegant of speech as they were. When the world of the unseen was revealed to him, he became intoxicated in God and lost all interest in that desire. God said to him, "I give to you that very eloquence and elegance of speech you desired."

"O Lord," he replied, "of what use is it to me? I am free of the desire for it. I don't want it."

"Grieve not," said God, "for both the eloquence and your indifference to it shall stand, and you shall suffer no loss thereby." And God indeed gave him such speech that the whole world, from his own time until this present day, have made many volumes of commentary to explain it. Still they continue to do so, but even until now they have fallen short of comprehending it. Then God said, "Your companions, out of weakness and fear for their heads and fear of the envious, whisper your name. I will publish your greatness abroad, and it shall be cried out five times a day in loud voices and graceful tones from lofty minarets throughout the climes of the world from the east to the west."

Anyone who gives himself over totally to this way will find all his goals, worldly and religious, made easy. Of this way no one ever complains.

Our words are true coin; the words of others are artificial. The artificial is secondary to the true. True coin is like a man's leg, whereas the artificial is like a wooden form in the shape of a human leg. Now, the wooden leg has been "stolen" from the original leg: its measure has been taken from the real one. If there were no such thing as a leg in the world, how would anyone know what the artificial one was? Therefore, some words are true coin and some are artificial; but, since they resemble each other, one must be discerning in order to tell the true from the false. Discernment is faith, and lack thereof is infidelity.

Don't you see that in Pharaoh's time, when Moses' staff became a serpent and the sorcerers' sticks and ropes also became serpents, those who had no discernment saw them all as the same thing and made no distinction, whereas those who did have discernment understood the difference between sorcery and the real and became believers by means of that discernment.

We realize therefore that faith is discernment. After all, the basis of the science of jurisprudence is inspiration; however, when it got mixed up with the ideas, emotions, and the application of people, that grace disappeared. Now what resemblance does it bear to the subtlety of revelation? It is like the water that flows from a spring in Turut into the city here. See how clear and pure it is. As it enters the city and passes through the gardens, quarters, and houses of the citizenry, so many people bathe their hands and feet and faces and limbs, clothes and carpets in it, and the urine and filth of the quarters and of horses and camels are poured in and mixed with it. See what it is like when it comes out on the other side of town. Even though it is the same water, it will turn dirt into mud; it will slake the thirst of the thirsty; and it will turn the desert green. Still it takes a discerning person to comprehend that the purity that water once had has gone and that unpleasant things have been mixed in with it. "The believer is discriminating, sagacious, understanding, and rational."[177] An old man is not rational when he is occupied with play; although he may be a hundred years old, he is still immature and childish. And a child, when not preoccupied with play, is an old man. Here age is of no consideration.

*Incorruptible water* [47:15], that is what is necessary. "Incorruptible water" is that which cleans all the impurities of the world but which is not infected thereby but remains as pure and clear as it was, neither breaking down in the stomach nor becoming adulterated or polluted. And that is the Water of Life.

---

177 The prophetic hadith *(al-mu'minu kayyis)* is given in *FAM* 67 #178.

A man shouted out and wept during prayer. Is his prayer void or not? The answer is contingent. If he cried out because another world, beyond the tangible, was shown to him—now that, after all, is called "water of the eyes"—and it depends on what he saw. If he saw something that is of the species of prayer and perfecting of prayer, then that is the object of prayer. His prayer is correct and more than complete. If, on the contrary, his eye wept because of this world or out of agony because an enemy had triumphed over him, or if he was envious of someone who possessed something he did not, then his prayer is incomplete and void. We realize therefore that faith is discernment to distinguish between the real and the false and also between the true and the imitation. Whoever has no discernment is deprived. Anyone who does have discernment will benefit from these words we speak, while our words are wasted on any who have no discernment. It is like two rational and qualified townsmen who go out of compassion to give testimony on behalf of a rustic. The rustic, in his ignorance, says something that contradicts the two so that their testimony has no effect and their good offices are wasted. For this reason they say that the rustic has his testimony with himself.

When the state of inebriation comes over one, one is too drunk to consider whether or not there is a discerning person here who is worthy of these words, and so one pours them out at random. It is like a woman whose breasts are so full and painful that she gathers the puppies of the quarter and pours out her milk over them. For these words to fall into the hands of the undiscerning is like giving a priceless pearl to a child who does not appreciate its worth. Because it has no discernment, when the child goes a little further, an apple can be placed in its hand and the pearl taken from it. Discernment, therefore, is a great thing in substance.

When Bayazid was a child, his father took him to school to learn jurisprudence. When brought before the teacher, he asked, "Is this the jurisprudence of God?"

"This is the jurisprudence of Abu-Hanifa," they said.

"I want the jurisprudence of God!" he said.

When taken before the grammar teacher, he asked, "Is this God's grammar?"

"This is Sibawayh's grammar," the teacher said.

"I don't want it," he replied. Everywhere he was taken he said the same thing. Unable to do anything with him, his father left him alone. Still following his quest, he came later to Baghdad. As soon as he saw Junayd, he cried out, "This is God's jurisprudence!" And how should a lamb not recognize its mother, having been nourished on her milk? Bayazid was born of intellect and discernment. So let the external form go.

There was once a shaykh who kept his disciples standing with their hands folded in service. "O Shaykh," they said, "why don't you let the group sit down? This is not the practice of dervishes but the custom of princes and kings."

"No," he said, "be silent! I want them to show respect like this so that they may benefit therefrom."

Although respect is in the heart, the outside is the title page of what is within. Now what does this "title page" mean? It means that a letter can be known by its cover. It can be known for whom it is meant and with whom it is. From the title page of a book one can find out what chapters and divisions are inside. By an external show of respect, such as bowing the head or standing up, one can know what kind of inner respect men have for God. If they do not make external shows of respect, then it is obvious that they are inwardly indifferent and have no respect for men of God.

## FORTY

Jawhar, the sultan's servant, said: "During a man's lifetime he is coached five times on the articles of faith. These words he does not understand and cannot remember correctly. What is he going to be asked after he dies, seeing as how he will have forgotten the answers to the questions he has learned?"

I say that when a man forgets what he has learned, he becomes, as it were, a clean slate, fit for questions not learned beforehand. You, who have been listening to my words for some time now, accept some of my words. You have heard their likes before and accepted them previously. Some of my words you half accept, and some you hesitate over. Can anyone *hear* this rejection, acceptance, or internal indecision of yours? No, for there is no organ for hearing it. No matter how hard you listen, no sound from within reaches the ear. If you search your interior you will find no "speaker." Your coming to visit me like this is itself a type of asking formed without the vocal organs or tongue, as if to say, "Show us a way and make clearer what you have already shown." And our sitting like this with you, whether silent or speaking, is a response to those inner questions of yours. When you leave here and return to the king's service, that is a question addressed to the king and an answer. Every day the king silently asks his servants, "How do you stand?" and "How do you eat?" and "How are you looking?" If anyone looks askance at him, the response will most certainly be askance, and he will not be able to bring himself to respond straight. It is like someone who is tongue-tied: he is not able to form his words correctly no matter how hard he may try.

When the goldsmith beats a nugget, he asks the gold something, and it responds to him as to whether it is pure or alloyed.

> The crucible itself tells you, when you are strained,
> Whether you are gold or gold-plated copper.[178]

Hunger is "asking" something of nature. It is as if it is saying: "There is a crack in the wall of the body's house. Hand me a brick. Hand me some mortar." Eating is a "response," as though nature says: "Here, take it." Not eating is also a "response," as though nature is saying: "There is no need yet. The brick has not dried out yet. You shouldn't tap the brick quite yet."

---

178 The line is from Sanai, *Hadiqat*, p. 382, line 1.

A physician comes and takes your pulse. That is the "asking." The beat of your vein is the response. His examining your urine is an unostentatious "asking" and "responding." Casting seeds into the ground is "asking" for a particular kind of fruit; the growth of the tree is a response without the ostentation of the tongue, since the response comes without words. The "asking" must be equally wordless. When the seed is rotten, the tree will not sprout. And this too is a question and answer. "Have you not learned that no answer is an answer?"

A king read three petitions from a subject but wrote no answer. The subject wrote a complaint, saying, "I have petitioned thrice. If my petition is acceptable, please say so. If not, please say so." On the back of the petition the king wrote, "Have you not realized that no answer is an answer?"

"The answer to a fool is silence."[179] The not-growing of a tree is a "non-answer" and therefore an answer. Every move man makes is a "question," and everything that happens to him, grief and joy, is an "answer." When one hears a pleasant answer one must be thankful, and the thanks must be in accord with the question the answer to which one received. If the answer is unpleasant, one must quickly ask forgiveness and not ask such a question again. *Yet when the affliction which We sent came upon them, they did not humble themselves, but their hearts became hardened* [6:43]—that is, they did not understand that the answer was in accord with their question. *And Satan prepared for them that which they committed* [6:43]—that is, they saw the answer to their own question and said, "This ugly answer is not appropriate to that question." They did not know that smoke comes from the kindling, not from the fire. The drier the kindling, the less smoke there is. When you entrust a garden to a gardener and an unpleasant odor comes, blame the gardener, not the garden.

---

179 The attribution as a hadith *(jawâbu 'l-ahmaq)* is found in *FAM* 118 #357.

A man was asked why he had killed his mother. "I saw an unseemly thing," he said.

"You should have killed the stranger," he was told.

"Then I would have to kill one every day," he replied.

Now, whatever happens to you, discipline your soul lest you have to do battle with someone every day. If others say *all is from God* [4:78], we say that necessarily chastising one's soul and abandoning the world are also from God.

This is like a man who was shaking apricots down from a tree and eating them. When the owner of the orchard found out he said, "Don't you fear God?"

"Why should I?" the man replied. "The tree belongs to God and I, a servant of God, am eating of what belongs to Him."

"I must make a reply to you," the owner said. "Bring some rope, tie him to this tree, and beat him until the reply is clear."

"Don't *you* fear God?" the man cried out.

"Why should I?" asked the orchard owner. "You are God's servant, and this is God's stick I am beating His servant with."

The gist of all this is that the world is like a mountain. Everything you say, good or evil, is echoed off that mountain. If you imagine that you made a nice sound but the mountain gave an ugly reply, it is absurd to think that a nightingale could sing to the mountain and that it could reply with the voice of a crow, a human, or a donkey. Know then for certain that it is you who have made the donkey noise.

When you come to a mountain, make a pleasant sound.
Why bray like a donkey at the mountain.[180]

The azure dome makes you sound beautiful.[181]

---

180 Quoted from Sanai, *Hadiqat*, p. 145, line 8.
181 The line is from Sanai, *Divan*, p. 29, line 441.

## FORTY-ONE

We are like bowls floating on the surface of water. How the bowls go is not determined by the bowls but by the water.

Here someone said, "This is generally applicable; yet some realize that they are on the water while others do not."

If it were generally applicable, then the particularization of the saying, "The heart of the believer is held between two of the Merciful's fingers,"[182] would not be correct, nor would the saying, *The Merciful hath taught the Koran* [55:1-2]. These cannot be called generally applicable. God taught all things that are known. Why then single out the Koran? In the saying, *He created the heavens and the earth* [6:1], why single out the heavens and the earth since He created all things generally?

There is no doubt that all bowls are floating on the water of divine might and will, but it would be impolite to ascribe anything vulgar to God, such as calling Him the creator of dung or of farting. He is rather called the Creator of the Heavens or the Creator of the Intellects. Therefore, there is a reason for this particularization even though it may be generally applicable. For something to be particularized is an indication of its selectness. At any rate, the bowls are floating on water. The water carries one in such a fashion that all the other bowls look at it. Another bowl is carried by the water in such a fashion that all the others instinctively run away from it, ashamed. They are inspired by the water to run away and enabled by it to do so, saying, "O God, increase the distance between us!" Of the former they say, "O God, bring us nearer to it!"

Now, the person who sees this as generally applicable will say that with respect to being subjugated, the subjugation of both to the water is equal. In reply to this one may say, "If you saw the grace and beauty of the former bowl's turning upon the water, you would not be concerned with the generally applicable characteristic."

---

182 The hadith *(qalbu 'l-mu'min)* is given in *FAM* 6 #13.

Similarly, one's beloved has existence in common with all manner of filth, but does it ever occur to any lover that his beloved has something in common with filth from the general standpoint that both are corporeal—both are spatial entities, created temporally and subject to decay—or other such generally applicable characteristics? Such a thought would never occur to him. He indeed would not take kindly to anyone who would remind him of these "generally applicable" attributes; he would consider such a person as his own personal devil. Therefore, since you have it within you to regard things from the general point of view—meaning that you are not capable of seeing our particular beauty—then it is not seemly to dispute with you because our disputations are mixed with beauty, and to reveal beauty to those unworthy of it is wrong. "Impart not wisdom to the unworthy lest you wrong it; deny it not to the worthy lest you wrong them."

This knowledge is speculation, not disputation. Roses and fruit trees do not bloom in autumn, for that would be disputation—that is, it would be a confrontation with the "opponent" autumn—and it is not in the rose's nature to come into confrontation with autumn. If the regard of the sun has done its job, then the rose comes out in temperate, moderate weather. Otherwise, it turns its head in and returns to the root. Autumn may say to it, "If you are not a dried-up twig, if you're a real man, come out and face me!" But the rose replies, "Before you I *am* a dried-up twig and a coward. Say what you will."

> O king of the truthful,
> have you ever seen a worse hypocrite than me?
> With those alive to you I am alive;
> with those dead to you I am dead.[183]

You, Baha'uddin, if an old hag with no teeth and a face as wrinkled as a lizard's back were to come to you and say: "If

---

183 The line is from Rumi, *Divan*, III, p. 166, ghazal 1371, line 14,477.

you're a real man, here I am! Here's the steed. Here's your fair
damsel. Here's the field. Show your manliness if you're a
man."—you would say: "God forbid! By God, I am no man.
What they say is a lie. If you are a mate, it is better to be a
coward." If a scorpion were to come with its stinger poised at
one of your limbs and say—"I have heard that you are a jovial
man. Laugh so that I can see how you laugh."—you would say:
"Since you have come I have no laughter or joviality within
me. What they say is a lie. All my incentive to laughter is just
now preoccupied with the hope that you will go away."

Someone said, "You sighed and my ecstasy ended. Do not
sigh lest my ecstasy go away." There are times when ecstasy
will leave you without sighing, depending on the situation. If it
were not so, God would not have said, *Abraham was pitiful*[184]
*and compassionate* [9:114]. One should not make a show of any
act of obedience, for all ostentation is ecstasy. You say what
you do in order for ecstasy to come. If there is someone who
induces ecstasy, you go to that person in order to have ecstasy.

This is like shouting to a sleeping man, "Get up! Hurry!
The caravan is leaving."

"Don't shout at him," they say, "for he is in ecstasy, and
his ecstatic state may be broken."

"That ecstasy is destruction," you say, "while this one is
salvation from destruction."

"Don't disturb him," they say, "for this shouting prevents
him from thinking."

"This shouting will make the sleeping man think.
Otherwise, what can he be thinking of in his sleep? After he
wakes up he will think."

There are then two types of shouting. If the shouter is
ahead of the other in knowledge, then it will result in an
increase in thought because the warner possesses knowledge
and divine wakefulness. Having waked the other from his sleep
of negligence, he informs him of his own world and drags him
there. As a result the sleeper's level of thought is raised,

---

184 "Pitiful," (*awwâh*), literally "sighing," to fit the context.

inasmuch as he has been called to from a sublime condition. On the other hand, if the awakener is below the sleeper in intelligence, when he wakes the sleeper up, his gaze is brought down. The wakener being lower than the sleeper, the sleeper's gaze is consequently lowered, and his thought goes to the lower world.

## FORTY-TWO

These persons who have been or are presently engaged in study think that if they come in attendance here they will either forget what they have learned or become "drop-outs." On the contrary, when they come here their knowledge comes alive.

Learning is like an empty outline. When it acquires a soul it is like a lifeless form coming to life. All this knowledge originates there in the "non-phonic, non-sonic" world and is translated into the phonic, sonic world here. In the other world speech is without sound and words. *God spake unto Moses, discoursing with him* [4:164]. Yes, God "spoke" to Moses but not through sound or words, not by means of a throat or tongue. One needs a throat and lips in order to produce words, but God transcends such things as lips, mouth, and throat. So the prophets converse with God in the non-phonic, non-sonic world in a way that cannot be comprehended by the imagination of these partial intellects. However, the prophets come out of the non-phonic world into the world of words and become as children for the sake of these children here, as the Prophet said, "I was sent to call."[185]

Now, although this congregation, stuck in words and sound as they are, cannot touch this state, they do derive strength from the prophet or saint and grow. They are comforted by him, like a child who finds comfort and strength in his mother, even though he may not recognize her every detail—as fruit finds comfort in the branch and grows sweet

---

185 The prophetic hadith *(bu'ithtu dâ'iyan)* is given in *FAM* 64 #169.

and ripens, unaware of the tree. In such a manner people are strengthened and nourished by the words of the great one, even though they do not know him and cannot comprehend him.

Within all souls there is a conviction that there is something, that there is a great world beyond reason, beyond words and sounds. Don't you see how all these people are inclined to visit madmen? They say, "It may be that this is 'it.'" It is true that "it" exists, but they have mistaken its locus. "It" does not exist in the intellect, but not everything that does not exist in the intellect is "it." Every walnut is round, but not every round thing is a walnut. There is a clue to it in what we have said. Although it may exist in a state that cannot be put into words and codified, still the intellect and soul are strengthened and nourished by it. It does not exist in these madmen about whom people gather, for neither are they transported out of themselves nor do they find comfort in these madmen—though they think they do. What they find we do not call comfort. A child separated from its mother may find comfort momentarily with another, but we do not call that comfort: it is simply a case of mistaken identity.

Physicians say that whatever is agreeable and appetizing to the constitution will give a person strength and purify the blood, but only as long as the person is without illness. For instance, a mud-eater finds mud agreeable, but we cannot say that it is beneficial to the temperament. Similarly, a cholerous person may like sour things and not like sugar, but that does not signify agreeability because it is based on a distemperament. The truly agreeable is what a man likes in the first place before he falls ill.

For example, if a man's arm has been wrenched or broken and hangs crooked, the surgeon will set it straight and fix it back as it was in the first place. The man will not find this operation agreeable and will be pained by it. In fact he would rather leave his arm crooked, but the surgeon will say, "You liked your arm straight as it was in the first place, and you were content that it should be so. When it was made crooked, you suffered pain. Now, you may prefer to leave it crooked, but this 'pleasure' is false and has no significance."

In a like manner, the spirits found it agreeable to adore God in the world of sanctity and to be totally absorbed in Him, like the angels. If they experience pain and distemperament by the connection with bodies and then are pleased to "eat mud," as it were, prophets and saints, acting as "physicians," tell them: "You are not really pleased. Your pleasure is false. You are really pleased by something else, but you have forgotten it. What is really agreeable to your original sound temperament is what you liked in the first place. You now find this distemperament agreeable. You think it is agreeable and do not believe the truth."

A mystic was seated before a grammarian. The grammarian said, "Words can be only one of three things: verbs, nouns, or particles."[186]

The mystic rent his garment and wailed, "Twenty years of my life, twenty years of striving and searching have been in vain. I labored all these years in hopes of there being a word outside of these, but you have destroyed my hope."

Although the mystic *had* found that word and attained his goal, he said what he did to make the grammarian take heed.

The story is told that as children Hasan and Husayn saw a man making his ablutions wrongly, in a manner not in accord with the law. They wanted to teach him how to make ablutions properly, so they went to him and one of them said, "This one tells me that I am making my ablutions wrong. We will both make ablutions here in front of you. You see which of us is doing it in accordance with the law."

When they made their ablutions the man said, "My sons, your ablutions are perfectly correct and in accordance with the law. Poor me! It was my ablutions that were wrong."

The more guests there are, the more the house is enlarged, the more it is decorated, and the more food is prepared. Don't you see that when a child is small in stature, his ideas, which

---

186 The traditional division of all parts of speech in Arabic grammar.

are like guests, are in proportion to the "house" of his body? He knows nothing beyond milk and his nurse, but as he grows up his "guests," or ideas, become more numerous. His house is enlarged with reason, comprehension, and discernment. When the guests called love come they will not fit into the house, and so it is pulled down and built anew. The king's trappings, his retinue, troops, and camp followers will not fit into the house. This gate is not worthy of those trappings. Such an infinitely numerous retinue can fit only in an infinite space. When these trappings are hung, they give off all illuminations; they dissolve all obscurity and reveal hidden things—in contrast with the trappings of this world, which increase obscurity. The former trappings or veils are opposite to the latter.

I complain of wrongs I will not specify
in order that people may be ignorant of my excuse
and my reproach.
Who knows whether the candle's wax tears are shed
on account of its converse with the fire
or its separation from the honey of the hive?

Someone said that this was written by Qadi Abu-Mansur of Herat. Qadi Mansur usually speaks in an obscure style, characterized by contrivance and rhetorical embellishment, whereas Mansur could not contain himself and spoke out bluntly.[187] The whole world is a prisoner of destiny, while destiny is a prisoner of the Beautiful One. The Beautiful One reveals all and conceals nothing.

Someone said, "Recite a page of the Qadi's words." Having recited, the Master said: "God has some servants who tell a veiled woman, 'Lift your veil so that we may see your face and know who and what you are. So long as you pass by veiled, we cannot see you, and there is confusion in my mind as to who and what this person is. I am not such as to become infatuated

---

187 See Glossary of Persons under Hallaj, who is often called by his father's name, Mansur.

by you if I see your face. For a long time now God has made me pure and innocent of you. I am secure enough not to be aroused or tempted by the sight of you. On the other hand, if I do not see you, I am confused as to what person this is. I am unlike other, carnal people who, seeing the faces of beauties openly, fall into temptation and are confused. With regard to them, is it better not to unveil the face lest they be tempted. Before the "people of the heart" it is better to unveil the face in order to escape temptation.'"

Someone said: "In Khwarazm no one falls in love: there are so many beauties that as soon as you see one and become infatuated, you see another even more beautiful. So one grows weary of the whole thing." If one does not fall in love with the beauties of Khwarazm, one must fall in love with Khwarazm itself because of its innumerable beauties. That "Khwarazm" is spiritual poverty, where there are so many beauties of substance and spiritual forms that no matter which one you approach and find contentment with, another appears and drives the first one from your mind. And so on ad infinitum. Let us then become lovers of the soul of poverty, in which there are such beauties.

## FORTY-THREE

Sayf of Bukhara went to Egypt.

Everyone loves mirrors. Everyone loves a mirror of his own attributes and good qualities. Ignorant of the actuality of one's own face, one reckons the veil to be one's face and the mirror to be a mirror of one's face. Uncover your face so that you may discover that I am a mirror of your face, and you will know that I am a mirror.

In reply to one who says he has realized that the prophets and saints are operating on a mistaken contention and that there is nothing in them but contention, it may be said: "Are you talking through your hat, or are you speaking from a vision? If you have visions and speak from them, then the vision has been actualized into being and that is the most precious and most noble thing in existence. It is also a touchstone of the prophets' veracity, for they claimed nothing but vision, which you have acknowledged. Then too, vision can be manifested only through an object of vision because 'to see,' being a transitive verb, requires a thing seen and a seer. The thing seen is what is sought, and the seer is the seeker, or the other way around. By your very act of denial, the seeker, the sought, and the act of seeing have been confirmed as existent. And the God-man relationship is a case where the negation is affirmation of its existence necessarily."

It is said that certain people are disciples of a dimwit and venerate him. To this I say that the "dimwit shaykh" is not inferior to a stone or an idol, whose devotees venerate and extol it, place their hopes in it, long for it, ask it for things, and cry to it. The stone does not know or feel any of these things, but God has made it a means for devotion in them, although it itself knows nothing.

A *faqih* was beating a boy. "Why are you beating him?" he was asked. "What is his crime?"

"You don't know what this bastard does! He spoils it all!"

"What does he do? What sin has he committed?"

"He runs away at the time of climax."

What he meant was that when he was beaten his image ran away and spoiled the climax. There is no doubt that the *faqih*'s love was for his mental image of the boy, but the boy knew nothing of that.

These people love their own mental image of this useless shaykh, who is ignorant of their states of separation, union, and ecstasy. However, even though mistaken and misplaced love for an image may cause ecstasy, it is not like making love to an actual beloved, who is aware and sensitive to the lover's condition. The pleasure of a man who embraces a stone column in the dark, thinking it to be his beloved and crying and lamenting, is not like the pleasure of one who embraces his living, aware beloved.

## FORTY-FOUR

When a person makes up his mind to travel to a place, he has rational thoughts, such as: "If I go there, it will be advantageous to me. I will be able to accomplish many things. My affairs will be ordered; my friends will be glad; and I will overcome my enemies." This is his proposition; however, God's intention may be something else entirely. Of so many strategies man has made and so many proposals he has thought up, not one has been achieved satisfactorily; nonetheless, he continues to rely on his own strategy and freedom of choice.

Man proposes, unaware of the disposal:
In the face of the Lord's disposal, proposal vanishes.[188]

This is like someone who dreams that he is a stranger in a city. He knows no one there, and no one knows him. So he wanders about, perplexed. This person, filled with regret and sadness, asks, "Why have I come to this city, where I have no friends or acquaintances?" He slaps his hand and bites his lip. When he wakes up he sees neither city nor people, so he realizes that all his sorrow and regret were pointless. He regrets having worked himself into such a state and considers it a waste. When he goes back to sleep and sees himself by chance in another such city, he begins all over again to feel regret and sorrow at having come to that place. It doesn't occur to him that when he was awake he had regretted his former sorrow—realizing that it had been a waste, only a pointless dream. Now that is how it is. Thousands and thousands of times people have seen that their proposals and plans have come to nought and that they have made no advancement toward their desires; however, God casts forgetfulness over them and, forgetting all that, they follow their own ideas and choice. *God goeth between a man and his heart* [8:24].

---

188 Rumi quotes a line of his own poetry; see Rumi, *Divan*, II, p. 67, ghazal 652, line 6800.

While he was still a king, Ibrahim Adham went on a hunt. Charging after a gazelle, he became utterly separated from his army. Although his horse was drenched in sweat, he galloped on. After passing the end of the plain, the gazelle turned around and said: "You were not created for this! You were not brought out of non-existence into being in order to hunt me down. Suppose you catch me. Then what?" Hearing this, Ibrahim cried out and threw himself down from his horse. There was no one in that wilderness but a shepherd whom he begged to take his regal, jewel-studded garments, his arms, and his horse. "Take these," he said, "and give me your felt cloak. But tell no one, and give no one any sign of me." Putting on the felt cloak, he set off on his way.

Now, consider his intention. What was it? What was God's intention? Ibrahim wanted to make the gazelle his prey, but God made him the prey of the gazelle in order that you might realize that things happen in the world as He wills, in harmony with His kingdom and true to His intention.

Once, before he became a muslim, Umar went to his sister's house. She was reciting aloud from Chapter *TaHa* of the Koran, but when she saw her brother, she fell silent and hid the book. Umar drew his sword and said, "Tell me what you were reciting and why you have hidden it away, or I will cut your head off this very instant with my sword and give no quarter!"

Knowing the intensity of his wrath and ferocity and fearing for her life, his sister confessed, "I was reciting from the words that God has sent down in these latter times to Muhammad."

"Recite them, then, that I may hear," said Umar. So she recited Chapter *TaHa*. Umar grew a hundred times more wrathful and said: "If I were to kill you now, it would be an undignified slaying. First I shall go and cut his head off and then I shall see to you!" And so, full of wrath and brandishing his naked sword, he set out for the Prophet's mosque.

When the chieftains of Quraysh saw him headed in that direction, they said: "Umar is intent on Muhammad. If anyone is going to do anything, it will be he." Umar, who was very powerful and manly, vanquished and returned with the severed heads of any army he faced. (Even the Prophet always said of him, "O God, sustain my religion through Umar or Abu-Jahl," for those two were renowned in their time for their prowess and manliness. When Umar finally became a Muslim, he wept and said, "Apostle of God, if you had mentioned Abu-Jahl first and said, 'O God, sustain my religion through Abu-Jahl or Umar,' what would have become of me? I would have remained on the wrong path.")

Anyway, while he was on his way to the Prophet's mosque, sword in hand, Gabriel brought the Prophet an inspiration to the effect that Umar was coming to accept Islam and that the Prophet should embrace him. The moment Umar entered the mosque he saw plainly a shaft of light fly from the Prophet and pierce his heart. He let out a cry and fell unconscious. Affection and love were born in his soul and, in this great love, he wanted to be obliterated and consumed in the Prophet.

"Now, Prophet of God," he said, "offer me the faith and speak that blessed word that I may hear." When he became a Muslim, he said, "In thanksgiving and in expiation for having come to you with sword drawn, I shall henceforth give quarter to no one I hear belittling you. With this very sword I will straightaway separate his head from his body!"

As Umar was coming out of the mosque, his father approached and said, "You have changed your religion!" Umar immediately struck off his head and walked on, blood-stained sword in hand. When the chieftains of Quraysh saw the sword, they said, "You swore to bring back a head. Where is it?"

"Here it is," he answered.

"You brought this head from that place?" one of them asked.

"No," replied Umar, "this is not that head, but another."

Now, if you consider what Umar's intention was and what God's will was, you will realize that all things turn out as He wills.

Umar stalks the Apostle, sword in hand:
He falls prey to God and is smiled upon by fortur

If you too are asked what you have brought, say, "I have
brought a head." If they say, "We have seen this head before,"
tell them that this is not that head but another. A head *(sar)* is
that in which there is a secret *(sirr);* otherwise a thousand
would not be worth a cent.

You have read the verse that says: *And when we appointed
the holy house of Mecca to be a place of resort for mankind, and a
place of security; and said, "Take the station of Abraham for a
place of prayer"* [2:125], Abraham said, "O Lord, since you have
ennobled me with your robe of contentment and chosen me,
provide my progeny also with this favor."

God replied, *"My covenant doth not comprehend the
ungodly"* [2:124]—that is, those who are unjust are not worthy
of My favor.

Then Abraham, realizing that God's favor was not for the
unjust and rebellious, made a condition and said, "O Lord, give
those who have faith and are not unjust a share in your
sustenance and withhold not from them."

"Daily bread is available at large," said God. "All have a
share in it. All creatures may take advantage of this
'guesthouse,' but My garb of contentment, acceptance, and
favor are the lot of the chosen elect."

The literalists say that what is meant by this is the Kaaba,
since anyone who takes refuge there is safe from calamity and
becomes "forbidden game" that must not be harmed, chosen of
God. This is true and good, but it is only the exterior of the
Koran. The mystics say that the "house" is man's interior.
They pray, "O Lord, empty the interior of carnal temptations
and preoccupations. Purify corrupt and vain thoughts and
melancholy so that no fear remain there, so that security
become manifest, and so that it become totally the locus of

---

189 See Rumi, *Divan,* II, p. 40, ghazal 598, line 6303.

your inspiration. Let there be no entrance for demons and satanic temptations, just as God has placed shooting stars in the heavens to prevent the devils from listening to the angels' secrets and to keep them from calamity. O Lord, station the guard of your favor over our interiors to keep us safe from the temptations of devils and the tricks of the carnal soul." This is what the esotericists and mystics say.

Everybody has his own way of doing things. The Koran is a two-sided brocade. Although some benefit from one side of it and some from the other, they are both right because God wants both groups to derive benefit. It is like a woman who has a husband and also a nursing infant: each derives a different pleasure from her, the infant from the milk in her breasts and the husband from being mated to her. People who take external pleasure from the Koran and "drink its milk" are "infants of the way," but those who have attained perfection have a different enjoyment and understanding of the meaning of the Koran.

Abraham's Station and Oratory near the Kaaba is a spot where the literalists say one should perform two *rak'a*s of prayer. This is certainly well and good. However, for the mystics Abraham's Station is where one should be like Abraham and hurl oneself into the fire for God's sake,[190] thereby transporting oneself through effort and endeavor to his station, or near to it. Then one will have sacrificed oneself for the sake of God—that is, one will no longer have any concern or fear for one's lower soul. Two *rak'a*s of prayer at Abraham's Station are good, but the prayer should be such that the standing part is in this world and the prostrating part in the other world.

The meaning of the Kaaba is the heart of the prophets and saints, the locus of God's inspiration, of which the Kaaba is but a branch. If there is no heart, what purpose is served by the Kaaba? The prophets and saints, having totally abandoned

---

190 For the story of Abraham's being cast into a fire by Nimrod, see Thackston, *Tales*, p. 147f.

their own desires, follow God's desire and do whatever He commands. They are vexed by and view as inimical anyone who is not in His favor and grace, be it father or mother.

> We have given over into your hands
> the reins of our heart:
> What you called cooked I call burned.

*

What I say is an analogy, not a parallel. An analogy is one thing, a parallel another. By way of analogy God likened His light to a lamp, and He likened the existence of the saints to the lamp-glass, also by way of analogy.[191] If His light would not fit into the spacial world, how could it fit into a lamp or glass? How could the rays of God's light fit into the heart? Yet when you search you will find it there, not from the point of view of containment such that it could be said that the light is *in* that place. You will find it *through* that place, just as when you look in a mirror you see yourself, although your likeness is not really *in* the mirror. Things that seem unintelligible become intelligible when put as analogies. It is like, say, when you close your eyes and see "sensibly" amazing things, forms, and shapes; but when you open your eyes again, you don't see anything. No one would consider this "intelligible." No one would believe it unless you put it in an analogy, at which point it would become understandable. What is it like? It is like a person who sees in a dream a hundred thousand things, not one of which it would be possible for him to see while awake.

It is like an architect who envisions a house—its length, its breadth, and its shape—within himself. This would not seem intelligible to anyone else unless the architect drew it on a piece of paper, at which point it would be visible. When he expresses how it is to be, it becomes intelligible. Afterward, having become intelligible, the house can be built and in such a way becomes sensible. Hence, it can be understood that all

---

191 The reference is to the Koranic "Light Verse," 24:35.

unintelligible things become intelligible and sensible through analogies.

Again, it is said that in the other world books will "fly," some to the right hand, some to the left, and that there will be angels, God's Throne, hell-fire and paradise, scales, reckoning and accounting. None of these things is understandable unless said as an analogy. Although there is no parallel to those things in this world, they can be expressed by means of analogy. By analogy, in this world all creatures—cobbler and king, judge and tailor alike—go to sleep at night. While asleep, their thoughts take flight, and no one is left with any thoughts until dawn, when—just as Israfel's blast on the trumpet will revive the particles of all bodies—every man's thoughts return like "flying books" to their owner without mistake: the tailor's thoughts to the tailor, the lawyer's to the lawyer, the ironsmith's to the ironsmith, the tyrant's to the tyrant, and the just man's to the just man. No one goes to sleep at night a tailor and wakes up the next day a shoemaker because, whatever one's occupation is, it is to that occupation that one returns. Thus, you can see how it is in the other world. If one follows this analogy through to its source, one can find traces of all the conditions of the other world here in this one. One must experience a revelation in order to realize that everything is within God's power. Many a bone you see rotted in the grave, enjoying pleasant repose and intoxicated sleep, fully aware of that pleasure and intoxication. Not in vain do they say, "May the earth lie pleasantly upon him." If the earth were not aware of pleasantness, how could they say such a thing?

A hundred years may that moon-like idol remain.
My heart is a quiver for her arrows of grief.
In the dust of her threshold my heart died sweetly.
O Lord, who prayed that her dust be sweet?[192]

---

192 The quatrain is found in Rumi, *Ruba'iyyat*, p. 130; *Divan, ruba'i* 434.

An analogous situation occurs in the world of sensibles. Say there are two people asleep in one bed. One of them dreams that he is in a heavenly garden surrounded by beauties, while the other sees himself among serpents, scorpions, and the myrmidons of hell. If you look you won't see either the one or the other. Why should it be astonishing for the parts of some people to enjoy a pleasant, intoxicated repose in the grave, while others are in torment, pain, and inquisition? You can't see the one or the other. It is thus to be understood that unintelligibles become intelligible through analogies and that analogies are not parallels.

A mystic may call an expansive and pleasant state "spring" and a constrictive and grievous state "autumn," but in what manner of form does pleasure resemble spring or grief autumn? It is just an analogy, without which the mind is not able to imagine or comprehend the concept.

God said, "*The blind and the seeing shall not be held equal; neither darkness and light; nor the cool shade and the scorching wind*" [35:19-21]. By this he likened faith to light and infidelity to darkness, faith to cool shade and infidelity to the merciless blazing sun that broils the brain; but how does the bright grace of faith resemble the light of the other world, or the vile darkness of infidelity the gloom of this world?

If anyone dozes while we are talking, his sleep is not from heedlessness but rather from security. It is like a caravan traveling by dark night over a difficult, frightful road and fearful of bandit attack. As soon as the people in the caravan hear a dog barking or rooster crowing, they know that they have come to a settlement, where their minds can be at ease, where they can stretch out and sleep securely. On a road where there is no noise or barnyard cacophony they are afraid to sleep. In a settlement where their security is guaranteed, they can sleep peacefully and securely despite the barking of dogs and crowing of roosters. Our words also come from a secure settlement, which is the prophets' and saints' report. When spirits become familiar with these words, they are secure. They are released from fear because from these words wafts the odor of good hope.

Say there is someone in a caravan on a dark night. He is so afraid that he constantly imagines bandits to be attacking the caravan. He wants to hear and recognize his fellow travelers' voices. When he does hear them he feels secure.

"Say, 'Recite, O Muhammad,' for your essence is subtle and cannot be reached by sight. But when you speak, men comprehend that you are acquainted with the spirits, and so they feel secure and relax."

> My body is so emaciated
> that it scarcely suffices to indicate that I am a man:
> Were it not for the fact that I address you,
> you would not see me.[193]

In the fields and meadows there is a little animal too small to be seen. It can only be "seen" through its cry when it makes a noise. That is to say, people are sunk in the field of this world, and your essence is too subtle to be seen. Speak so that they can recognize you.

When you desire to go somewhere, your heart goes first, sees the place and finds out what it is like; then it returns and takes the body there. People are all "bodies" in relation to the saints and prophets, who are the world's "heart." First, they come out of their humanity, flesh and skin, and travel to the other world. They observe both the other world and this world high and low and traverse many leagues until they find out how to get there. Then they return and invite the people, saying, "Come to the 'original' world. This world is a ruin, a transitory abode. We have found an agreeable spot and have come to inform you."

It is thus to be understood that the heart is attached to the beloved's retinue in all circumstances. It has no need to traverse leagues, to fear highwaymen, or to suffer the mule's

---

193 The line is quoted from Mutanabbi, *Diwan*, p. 2.

packsaddle. Pity the poor body, which is chained to these things.

> I asked the heart, "Do you know, foolish heart,
> of whose service you are deprived?"
> "You read me wrong," the heart replied.
> "I am constant in service.
> It is you who have gone astray."[194]

Wherever you are, in whatever circumstances you may be, strive to be a lover. When love comes into your possession, you will always be a lover—in the grave, at resurrection, in paradise, ad infinitum. When you plant wheat, assuredly wheat will grow. And that wheat will be the same in the storehouse and in the oven.

Majnun wanted to write a letter to Layla. He took a pen and scribed this verse:

> Your image is in my eye, your name is upon my lips,
> The memory of you is in my heart.
> Where then should I write?[195]

That is, your image dwells in my eyes; your name is never absent from my lips; your memory has its place in the depth of my soul. Since you roam free in these places, where should I address a letter? Majnun broke the pen and ripped up the paper.

Many a person whose heart is full of these words is unable to express them verbally. It is not surprising that such a person is a lover, a seeker after this. Love is not hindered by an inability to express it because love is the principal thing of the heart. An infant loves milk and is nourished by it. Nonetheless, it cannot explain what milk is or define it.

---

194 The quatrain is attributed to Rumi, *Ruba'iyyat*, p. 354; *Divan, ruba'i* 1865.

195 See note 90.

Although its soul is desirous of milk, it is unable to express verbally what pleasure it derives from drinking milk or how it suffers if deprived of it. An adult may explain and describe milk in a thousand different ways, but he derives no pleasure or joy from it.

## FORTY-FIVE

"What is that young man's name?"

"Sayfuddin (Sword of Religion)."

The sword is in its scabbard. It cannot be seen. The "sword of religion" is that which wages war for the sake of religion and which endeavors utterly for God. It discerns the right way from the wrong and the true from the false. However, one should wage war first with the self and discipline the character of the self. "Begin with yourself."[196] All good counsel must be made with the self.

After all, you are human. You have hands and feet, ears, sense, eyes, and a mouth. The saints and prophets, who had good fortune and reached the goal, were also human. They had ears, reason, tongues, hands, and feet like me. How is it that doors were opened for them and not for me? You should box your ears and wage war night and day with the self and ask yourself: "What have you done? What act have you committed to be unacceptable?" Do this to be a "sword of God" or a "tongue of the truth."

For example, there are ten people who want to go inside a house. Nine of them are admitted, and one is denied entry and left outside. Naturally this one person will fret and wail and say: "What have I done not to be let in? What faux pas have I committed?" He must of necessity lay the blame on himself and realize his own shortcomings. He mustn't say: "God is doing this to me. What can I do about it? It is His will. Had He so willed, He would have let me in." This amounts to

---

196 The prophetic hadith *(ibda' bi-nafsika)* is given in al-Suyuti, *al-Jami' al-saghir,* I, 4.

cursing God and wielding a sword against Him, and that would be a "sword *against* God," not a "sword *of* God."

God transcends equals and relatives. *He begetteth not, neither is He begotten* [112:3]. No one gains admittance to Him except through servitude. *God wanteth nothing, but ye are needy* [47:38]. It is not possible to say of a person who is granted admission to God that he is more closely related to God or better acquainted than you are. His access is easier only because of his servitude.

God is the Absolute Giver. He filled the lap of the sea with pearls; He garbed the thorn in the raiment of the rose; He bestowed life and spirit upon a handful of dust without ulterior motive and without precedent. All parts of the world have a share of Him.

When someone hears that in a certain city there is a generous person who engages in extreme liberality, he will certainly go there in hopes of gaining a share in that generosity. Since God's munificence is so well known, since all the world is aware of His grace and kindness, why don't you ask Him for a robe of honor and a purse? Instead you sit like a dunce and think that if He wants, He will give you something. You make no entreaty, while a dog, which has neither rational intelligence nor understanding, will come to you when it is hungry and wag its tail as if to say: "Give me something to eat. I have nothing to eat, but you do." This much discernment it has. You are not less than a dog which would not be content to sit in a dust heap and say, "If he wants, he will give me something to eat." No, a dog will beg and wag its tail. You too "wag your tail" and beg God, for before such a donor begging is what is required. If you are not blessed with good fortune, seek your fortune from him who is not stingy and who is possessed of wealth. God is extremely close to you. Whatever idea or conceptualization of Him you may have, He is something like that because it is He who brings that concept or idea of yours into being and holds it up for you to see. However, He is too close for you to see Him. Why should this seem strange? In your every act your mind is not only with you but is the initiator of that act; yet you can't see your mind. Although you can see it through its effects, you can never see its essence.

For example, when a man goes to the bathhouse, he gets warm. Everywhere he goes in the bath the fire is with him; although he is warmed by the effect of the fire's heat, he cannot see it. When he comes out and actually sees the fire, he realizes that he was warmed by the fire, that the heat of the bathhouse was from the fire. Man's being is a marvelous "bathhouse." In him is the "heat" of the mind, the spirit, and the soul. Only when you come out of this bathhouse and go to the other world will you actually see the essence of the mind. You will witness the essence of the soul and the essence of the spirit. You will realize that your cleverness was due to the "heat" of the mind, that temptations and deceits were due to the lower soul, and that your vitality was due to the spirit. You will see plainly the essence of each one. So long as you remain inside the "bathhouse," however, you cannot see the "fire" sensibly, only through its effect. It would be like taking someone who has never seen running water and throwing him blindfolded into water. He feels something wet and soft against his body, but he doesn't know what it is. When the blindfold is taken off, he realizes that it is water. Before, he knew it through its effect, but now he sees its essence. Therefore, beg of God and make your request of Him that it not be all in vain. God says, *Call upon Me, and I will hear you* [40:60].

*

We were in Samarqand, and the Khwarazmshah, having laid siege to the city, was waging war with his ranks drawn. In our quarter there was an extremely beautiful lady, who had no equal in that town. I kept hearing her say: "O Lord, how could you let me fall into the hands of the tyrants? I know you will never permit such a thing. I put my trust in you." When the city was plundered and the people were being carried off, that lady's maids were taken prisoner, but no harm befell her. Despite her great beauty, no one even looked at her.

Thus you should realize that whoever entrusts himself to God will be safe from all harm. At His court no one's petition goes in vain.

A dervish had taught his son to ask God for everything he wanted. Whenever the child cried and asked God for something, the parents would bring it to him. This went on for several years. One day the child was alone in the house and wanted some porridge. As usual, he said, "I want porridge." Suddenly a bowl of porridge appeared from the unseen realm, and the child ate his fill. When the father and mother returned and asked if he wanted something to eat, he said, "I asked for porridge and ate it."

"Praise be to God," said the father, "that you have attained this station and that your trust and reliance on God have grown so strong!"

*

When Mary was born, her mother made a vow to God to give her over to the service of the temple. So she relinquished custody of the child and placed her in a corner of the temple. Because Zaccharias and many others too wanted to be her guardian, an argument ensued. To settle disputes in those times it was the custom for each person to cast a stick into water. The person whose stick remained on the surface was the winner. As it happened, Zaccharias cast the winning lot, so they said that it was his right to be Mary's guardian. Every day when he brought food to her corner of the temple, he found the likes of it already there.

"Mary," he said, "after all, I am your guardian. Where do you get this from?"

She answered, "When I am in need of food, God sends me what I want. His generosity and mercy are without limit. Whoever relies upon Him will never go astray."

"O Lord," said Zaccharias, "since you grant all requests, I too have a desire. Give me a son who will be a friend to You. Let him be familiar with You without my having to urge him, and let him concern himself with acts of obedience to You." And God did bring John into being after his father had become weak and bent with age and after his mother too, who had not given birth in her youth, experienced menstruation and became pregnant.

You may thus realize that all that is a pretext in the face of God's power, that everything is from Him and that He is the absolute decreer of things. A believer knows Who behind this wall is informed of our every condition and Who sees us even though we do not see Him. This much is certain to a believer, in contrast to one who does not believe and says, "No, this is all a fable." The day will come when his ears will be boxed; he will regret and say, "Oh, I was wrong to say that. I was mistaken. Everything was He, but I denied it."

For example, you know that I am behind the wall while you are playing the rebeck. Assuredly if you are a rebeck player, you will keep on playing without stopping. Prayer does not mean that you should be standing, bowing, and prostrating yourself all day long; the object is that the state that manifests itself during prayer should remain with you constantly, whether asleep or awake, whether writing or reading. In no state should you be void of the remembrance of God. You should be one of those *who carefully observe their prayers* [70:23].

Hence, all speaking, keeping silent, eating, sleeping, wrath, and forbearance, all these qualities are the turning of a millstone. Its turning is of course by means of water because if it has tried itself without water it knows it cannot turn without it. So if the millstone thinks its turning is of itself, it is sheer ignorance and stupidity. There is a narrow sphere for that turning because such are the conditions of this world. Cry out to God: "O Lord, other than this traveling and turning of mine, give me another, spiritual turning since all needs are met by you and your generosity and mercy are common to all existing things." Petition Him every moment for your needs and be not without remembrance of Him, for the remembrance of Him is strength; it is a wing to the bird of the spirit. If that goal is fully attained, it will be *light upon light* [24:35]. If you are mindful of God, little by little your interior will be illuminated and you will attain release from the world. If a bird tries to fly to heaven, it may never reach it but it still gets farther from the earth every moment and flies higher than other birds.

If you have musk in a container with a narrow neck, you put your finger into it. You can't get the musk out, but your finger is perfumed nonetheless and your sense of smell is gratified. Being mindful of God is like this. Although you cannot reach His essence, remembrance of Him has many effects, and many great benefits accrue.

## FORTY-SIX

Shaykh Ibrahim is a mighty dervish. When we see him we are reminded of our friends. Mawlana Shamsuddin held him in great favor and always used to call him "our Shaykh 'Brahim," thereby establishing a connection with him.

Divine favor is one thing, and personal endeavor is another. The prophets did not reach the stage of prophecy through personal endeavor. They got that gift through divine favor, but anyone who attains that station conducts his life and career through endeavor and rectitude. This goes for the common people too so that they will rely on the prophets and what they say. The common people cannot see the interior; they only see the exterior. If they follow the exterior, through it they will find their way to the interior.

Pharaoh also made great personal endeavor to be beneficent and distribute good things, but since he did not have divine favor, his acts of obedience, personal endeavor, and beneficence lacked splendor and were clouded over.

A commander is beneficent and kind to the people of a fortress when his design is to rebel against the king. But such beneficence as his, of course, has no worth or splendor.

Even if one cannot deny divine favor to Pharaoh altogether—since God may have held him in surreptitious favor—He did reject him outwardly for some good purpose because a king must command both severity and clemency, both robes of honor and prisons. The "people of the heart" do not deny Pharaoh divine favor altogether, but the people of externals consider him totally rejected, which is proper for the maintenance of externals.

When a king sentences someone to the gallows, he is hung high in public, although he could just as well be hung from a low peg in a room away from the people. However, since it is necessary for the people to see and for an example to be set, the king's order and command are carried out publicly. Not all gallows are made of wood: official positions, exalted rank, and worldly success are also very high gallows. When God wishes to catch someone, He gives him a great position or a large kingdom in the world, such as Pharaoh, Nimrod, and their likes. All that is like a gallows on which God puts them so that all the people may be aware. God says, "I was a hidden treasure, and I wanted to be known"[197]—that is, I created the whole world and the end of it all was our manifestation, sometimes through kindness and sometimes through wrath. He is not a king whose kingdom could be made known by one thing. If all the atoms of the universe were to proclaim Him, they would fall short. So, all creatures, day and night, make manifestation of God. Some of them know what they are doing and are aware of their manifesting, while others are unaware. However it may be, God's manifestation is confirmed. It is like a prince who orders someone beaten as a chastisement. The man sentenced will yell and scream, but everyone knows that both the beater and the beaten are subject to the prince's orders. By means of these two the prince's order is "manifested."

One who affirms God's existence always manifests God, but one who denies God's existence is also a manifestor because affirmation is something that cannot be imagined without denial. It is flavorless and flat without it. For example, when a debater makes a proposition in a gathering, if there is no one to contest him, how can he prove it? What delight can his point have? Proof of affirmation is pleasant only in the face

---

197 See note 125.

of denial. This world is a gathering for manifesting God: without both affirmer and denier the gathering would be dull, for both are manifestors of God.

A group of friends went to the Mir-i-Akdishan. He grew angry at them and asked, "What do you want here?"

"We are not gathered in such numbers to wrong anyone," they said, "but in order to assist each other in forbearance and patience."

When people gather for a funeral, it is not in order to contest death but to console the bereaved and drive grief from his mind. "The faithful are like one soul."[198] Dervishes act like one body. If one of the members is suffering in pain, the rest of the parts suffer too: the eye ceases to see, the ear to hear, and the tongue to speak, and all concentrate on the one part that is in pain. The rule of friendship is that one must sacrifice oneself for one's friend, one must hurl oneself into the fray on behalf of one's friend because all are facing the same thing, all are drowned in the same ocean. This is the effect of faith and rule of Islam. What is a burden borne by the body in comparison with a burden borne by the soul? *It will be no harm unto us; for we shall return unto our Lord* [26:50].

When a believer has sacrificed himself to God, why should he be concerned over catastrophe or danger, or his own physicality? When he is going toward God, what need has he of hands or feet? God gave you hands and feet to use to set out from Him in *this* direction. When you are going back to the Maker of hands and feet, if you lose them and go like Pharaoh's magicians, what cause is there for grief?[199]

> One can sip poison from the hand
> of one's silver-breasted beloved.
> The bitterness of her words

---

198 The prophetic hadith *(al-mu'minûna ka-nafs)* is given in *FAM* 43 #109.

199 When Pharaoh's magicians were defeated by Moses, Pharaoh ordered their hands and feet cut off. See Thackston, *Tales*, p. 229.

can be swallowed like sugar.
Sweet is the beloved. How sweet!
And where there is sweetness
the bitterness of grief can be endured.

And God knows best!

## FORTY-SEVEN

God the Exalted wills both good and evil, but He is only pleased by good. Because He said, "I was a hidden treasure, and I wanted to be known,"[200] there is no doubt that God wills both positive commands and negative injunctions. But a positive command is only valid when the one so enjoined is averse by nature to what he has been enjoined to do. A hungry person does not have to be told to eat sweetmeats and sugar; if he is so told, it cannot be called a command but rather an act of kindness. Also a negative injunction is not valid with regard to a thing man does not desire. It is not a valid injunction to say, "Don't eat rocks," or, "Don't eat thorns." If such a thing is said it cannot be called a negative injunction. So, for a positive command to good and negative injunction against evil to be valid, there must be a soul desirous of evil. To will the existence of such a soul would be willing evil, but God is not pleased by evil. If He were, He would not have enjoined good.

This is like a man who desires to teach. He, therefore, wills that the student be ignorant since it is not possible to teach unless the student is ignorant. To will a thing is to will the concomitants of that thing. The teacher, however, is not pleased that the student should remain ignorant; if he were, he would not teach him. So also does a physician will that people should be ill if he wills to practice medicine because it is impossible for him to display his medical arts unless people are sick. He is not pleased, however, that people should remain ill; if he were, he would not treat them. So also does a baker will

---

200 See note 125.

that people should be hungry in order to make his living; but he is not pleased that they should remain hungry, for, if he were, he would not sell bread. For this same reason generals and cavalry will that their ruler should have opponents and enemies; otherwise, neither could their manliness and love for their ruler be displayed nor would the ruler muster them because there would be no need. On the other hand, they are not content that opposition should remain or otherwise they would not fight. Similarly God wills there to be motivations to do evil in man's soul because He loves a thankful, obedient, and pious servant, and this is not possible without the existence of such motivations in man's soul. To will a thing is to will all that pertains to it, but one need not be pleased with those concomitants because one can strive to eliminate them from one's soul.

Thus it can be realized that God wills evil in one respect but does not will it in another.

An opponent may say that God does not will evil in any respect whatsoever, but it is impossible for Him to will a thing and not will its concomitants. And one of the concomitants of positive commands and negative injunctions is this willful soul, which by its nature desires evil and shuns good. One of the concomitants of this soul is all the evil in the world. Had God not willed this evil, He would not have willed the soul; and if He did not will the soul, He would not will the positive commands and negative injunctions that apply to it. If He were content with the soul, He would not have enjoined upon it to do certain things and not to do others. Thus, evil is willed for other than itself.

Your opponent may say then that if God wills every good and one good is the repulsion of evil, then He wills the repulsion of evil—and evil cannot be repulsed unless it exists. Or he may say that God wills faith, but faith is only possible after infidelity, thereby making infidelity concomitant with faith.

In short, willing evil is heinous when it is willed for its own sake; however, if it is willed for good, then it is not heinous. God said, *"In this law of retaliation ye have life"* [2:179]. There is no doubt that retaliation is an evil and destructive of God's foundation, but this is a partial evil, whereas keeping people from committing murder is a total good. Willing partial evil for the sake of willing total good is not heinous, but partial abandonment of God's will while approving total evil is. An example would be a mother who does not want to punish her child because she views the partial evil, while the father, viewing the total good, is content to punish the child in order to nip trouble in the bud.

God is all-pardoning, all-forgiving, and severe in punishment. Does He will that these epithets be true of Him or not? The answer must be yes, for He cannot be pardoning and forgiving without the existence of sin. To will a thing is to will what is concomitant with it. Thus He has enjoined pardon upon us as He has enjoined upon us reconciliation and restitution, but this injunction has no meaning without the existence of hostility.

Similar to this are the words of Sadru'l-Islam to the effect that God enjoined upon us the earning of our livelihood and acquisition of wealth because He said, *"Contribute out of your substance toward the defense of the religion of God"* [2:195], and wealth cannot be contributed unless there is wealth. So it was an injunction to acquire wealth.

When one man says to another, "Come on, let's pray," he enjoins the performing of ablutions, the obtaining of water, and everything that pertains to prayer.

## FORTY-EIGHT

To express gratitude is to stalk and ensnare good things. When you hear the sound of gratitude, you will be prepared to give more. "When God loves a servant, He afflicts him; if he is patient, He chooses him; if he is thankful, He makes him elect."[201] Some people thank God for His wrath, and some

---

201 Similar hadiths are found in al-Munawi, *al-Ithafat al-saniyya*, pp. 14–16, #9–13.

thank Him for His tenderness—and both are right. Because gratitude is a panacea that turns wrath into tenderness, the perfectly rational man is thankful for harshness both in and out of God's presence. It is such a man God elects. If God's will be the bottom of hell fire, by thanks is His purpose hastened, for outward complaint is a diminution of inner complaint. The Prophet said, "I am the laughing slayer"[202]— that is, when I laugh in the face of a harsh person, I slay him. What he meant by laughter was thanks instead of complaint.

The story is told of a Jew who was a neighbor of one of the Apostle's Companions. The Jew lived in an upper apartment from which dirt, filth, his children's urine, and the wash water all poured down into the Companion's quarters. Nonetheless, the Companion was always grateful to the Jew and ordered his family to be grateful also. After eight years the Muslim died and the Jew came to offer condolences to the family. When he saw the filth in that house and how it came from his apartment, he realized what had been happening all the while. Extremely regretful, he asked the family, "Why didn't you tell me? Why were you always thanking me?"

They replied, "Because he always ordered us to be thankful and admonished us against abandoning gratitude." And the Jew became a believer.

The mention of the good provokes goodness.
Just as the minstrel is a cause for the wine cup.[203]

For this reason God mentioned His prophets and pious servants in the Koran and thanked them for what they had done for Him, the All-Powerful and Forgiving.

Gratitude is to suckle at the breast of good things. Even when the breast is full, its milk will not flow unless you suck.

---

202 See note 158.

203 From Sanai, *Hadiqat*, p. 582, line 16, with some variance. Sanai says, "The deeds of the good. . . ."

Someone asked what causes ingratitude and what keeps people from being grateful. A person who refuses to offer thanks is so possessed by "raw greed" that no matter how much he gets he is greedy for more. His raw greed makes him like that. When he gets less than what he has set his heart on, he refuses to be thankful. He is unaware of his fault: he does not know that the cash he tenders is flawed and spurious. Raw greed is like eating unripe fruit, uncooked bread, or raw meat. Of course it causes the illness of ingratitude. When you realize you have eaten something harmful, you have to vomit. God in His wisdom afflicts a man with ingratitude in order to make him vomit to rid himself of corrupt notions lest that one illness multiply a hundredfold. *And We proved them with prosperity and with adversity, that they might return from their disobedience* [7:168]—that is, we provided their sustenance from a place they would never guess, which is the unseen realm, while their gaze was averse to seeing secondary causes, which are like God's partners.

Bayazid said, "O Lord, I have never associated anything with You."

"O Bayazid," said God, "not even on the 'night of the milk'? One night you said, 'The milk made me sick.' But I am the one who inflicts harm and confers benefit."

Bayazid had looked to the secondary cause, so God reckoned him as having associated something with Himself and said, "I am the one who inflicts harm before and after the milk, but I made the milk as a sin and its harmful effect as a punishment a teacher might administer."

When a teacher says not to eat the fruit and the pupil eats it, the teacher beats him on the soles of his feet; however, it is incorrect for the pupil to say, "I ate the fruit, and it hurt my feet."

On this basis God will undertake to weed out the seedlings of polytheism from the spirit of anyone who restrains his tongue from associating anything with God. A little in God's sight is much.

The difference between praise and gratitude is that gratitude is for good things received. One cannot be thanked for beauty or courage. Praise is the more general term.

## FORTY-NINE

Someone was leading the prayer and recited, *"The Arabs of the desert are more obstinate in their unbelief and hypocrisy"* [9:97]. An Arab chieftain who was present gave the man a harsh slap. In the next *rak'a* the prayer leader recited, *"And of the Arabs of the desert there is who believeth in God, and in the last day"* [9:99]. The Arab said, "That slap taught you a lesson!"[204]

We are constantly being slapped from the unseen realm. Since we are slapped down for everything we undertake, we turn to something else, as is said, "We have no power of our own: it is all 'throwing down' and 'tossing out.'" It is also said, "Cutting the joints is easier than cutting a connection."[205] "Throwing down" here means to descend into this world and to become worldly, and "tossing out" means to fall from favor. When someone eats something that turns sour in the stomach, he spits it up. If that food did not sour and he did not spit it up, it would become part of him.

A disciple fawns and is servile in order to make his way into his master's heart. If—God forbid—the disciple does anything displeasing to the master, he will be cast out of the master's heart in the same way that food is vomited. Exactly as that food would have become part of the man but was vomited and spit out for having soured, so too would that disciple, with the passage of time, have become a master; but he was cast out of the master's heart because of some displeasing action.

---

204 The story is given in a slightly different version in al-Abshihi, *al-Mustatraf*, II, 222.

205 The "connection" *(wisâl)* here that is so difficult to break is presumably the connection to the world, into which one has descended and part of which one has become.

> Love of you so proclaimed itself to the world
> that all hearts were thrown into confusion.
> Then it burned all to ashes
> and cast them to the wind of indifference.[206]

The atoms of the ashes of those hearts dance and cry out in the wind of indifference. If not, then who brings these tidings and renews them every moment? If the hearts do not perceive their life in being burned and cast to the winds, why are they so desirous of being burned? Do you hear a cry or see a gleam in hearts that are burned to ashes in the lusts of this world?

> I have discovered
> —and exaggeration is not in my nature—
> that he who is my sustenance will come to me.
> I run to him, and my quest for him is agony for me.
> Were I to sit still,
> he would come to me without my distress.[207]

I know truly the rule for God's provision, and it is not in my character to run from pillar to post in vain or to suffer needlessly. Truly whatever my daily portion is—of money, food, clothing, or of the fire of lust—if I sit quietly, it will come to me. If I run around in search of my daily bread, the effort exhausts and demeans me. If I am patient and stay in my place, it will come to me without pain and humiliation. My daily bread is seeking me out and drawing me. When it can't draw me, it comes—just as when I can't draw it, I go to it.

The upshot of these words is that you should be so engaged in the affairs of religion that this world will run after you. What is meant by "sitting" here is sitting on the affairs of religion. If a man runs, when he runs for religion he is sitting.

---

206 Not traced.

207 The poetry is by 'Urwa ibn Adhîna, an Umayyad poet; see al-Isbahani, *Kitab al-aghani*, XIX, 300, note 1.

If he is sitting, when he is sitting for this world he is running. The Prophet said, "Whoso makes all his cares a single care, God will spare him all his cares."[208] If a man has ten concerns, let him be concerned with religion: God will see to the other nine without his having to see to them. The prophets were not concerned with fame or bread. Their only concern was to seek God's satisfaction, and they acquired both fame and bread. Whoever seeks God's satisfaction will be with the prophets in this world and the next; he will be a bedfellow with *those unto whom God hath been gracious, of the prophets, and the sincere, and the martyrs* [4:69]. What place is this? He will be rather sitting with God, who said, "I sit next to him who remembers Me."[209] If God were not sitting with him, there would be no desire for God in his heart. Without a rose there is no rose-scent; without musk there is no aroma of musk. There is no end to these words, and even if there were it would not be like the end to other words.

＊

"The night is over, but our story has not yet ended."[210] The night and darkness of this world may pass, but the lights of these words shine brighter every moment. So also did the night of the prophets' lives pass, but the light of their words has not yet ceased—nor will it ever.

People asked what was so strange about Majnun's being in love with Layla. After all, they were children together and

---

208 For the prophetic hadith *(man ja'ala 'l-humûm)* see *FAM* 136. Full text: "Whoso makes his concerns one concern, God will spare him the concern of this world; but whoso allows his concerns to branch out, God will not care in what valley of this world he perishes."

209 The full text of the hadith qudsi *(ana jalîs)* is given by Munawi, *al-Ithafat*, p. 110, #254: "Moses said, 'O Lord, are you close enough for me to whisper in your ear or so distant that I should shout?' And God said, 'I am behind you, before you, at your right and your left. O Moses, I am sitting next to my servant whenever he remembers me, and I am with him when he calls me.' "

210 The line is attributed to Rumi, *Ruba'iyyat*, p. 170.

were in school together. "These people are fools," said Majnun. "What pretty woman is not desirable?" There is no man who is not attracted to a pretty woman. Women are the same. Love, however, is that in which one finds sustenance and joy. Just as one finds pleasure in seeing one's father, mother or brother, in having children, or in lust, all sorts of pleasures are found through love. Majnun thus became a prototype for lovers, just like Zayd and Amr in grammar.[211]

> If you eat sweets and roast meat or drink pure wine,
> you will dream of drinking water.
> But you will awake from your dream thirsty.
> Dream water quenches no thirst.[212]

"This world is like a sleeper's dream."[213] This world and its pleasures are like someone who drinks something in a dream. So also to desire worldly things is like asking for or being given something in a dream. When one awakes one will not have benefited from what one ate or drank while dreaming. One will simply have asked for and been given something in a dream. "The getting is in proportion to the asking."

## FIFTY

Someone said that we have come to know each and every condition of mankind. Not an iota of man's condition and nature or his hot and cold humors has escaped us; yet it has not been ascertained what part of him will abide forever.

If that could be known merely by words, then such effort and exertion would not be necessary and no one would have to go to such pain or toil. For example, someone comes to the seashore. Seeing nothing but turbulent water, crocodiles, and

---

211 Zayd and Amr are the standard examples used in traditional Arabic grammar.

212 Not traced.

213 For the prophetic hadith *(al-dunyâ ka-hulm)* see *FAM* 141.

fish, he says: "Where are the pearls? Perhaps there are no pearls." How is one to obtain a pearl merely by looking at the sea? Even if one measures out the sea cup by cup a hundred times over, the pearls will not be found. One must be a diver in order to discover the pearls; and not every diver will find them, only a fortunate, skillful one.

The sciences and crafts are like measuring the sea in cupfuls; the way to finding pearls is something else. Many a person is adorned with every accomplishment and possessed of wealth and beauty but has nothing of this intrinsic meaning in him; and many a person is a wreck on the outside, with no fairness of feature, elegance or eloquence, but within is found the intrinsic meaning that abides forever. It is that which ennobles and distinguishes humanity. It is because of the intrinsic meaning that human beings have precedence over all creatures. Leopards, crocodiles, lions, and all other animals have skills and particular qualities, but the intrinsic meaning that abides forever is not in them. If man will but find his way to the intrinsic meaning, he will attain his pre-eminence; otherwise, he will remain deprived of pre-eminence. All these arts and accomplishments are like jewels set on the back of a mirror. The face of the mirror is void of them, for it must be clear. Anyone who has an ugly face will desire the back of the mirror because the face tells all. Anyone who has a fair countenance will go to any length for the sake of the face of the mirror because it reflects that person's own beauty.

A friend of Joseph of Egypt came to him from a journey. "What gift have you brought?" asked Joseph.

"What do you not have already? Is there anything you need?" asked the friend. "Nonetheless, because there is nothing more beautiful than you, I have brought you a mirror so that you can see your face reflected every moment."

What does God not have? What does He need? One must take a polished heart to God so that He can see Himself in it.

"God does not look at your forms or at your deeds, but He looks at your hearts."[214]

"The city of your dreams you found lacking nothing save noble men."[215] In a city where you find all the beauties, pleasures, delights and various adornments of nature, you won't find an intelligent man. Would that it were the other way around! That city is the human being. If it has a hundred thousand accomplishments but not the intrinsic meaning, it would be better for it to be in ruins. If it does have the intrinsic meaning, no matter that it have no external embellishments. The *mysterion* must be there for it to flourish. In whatever state man may be, his *mysterion* is concerned with God, and his external preoccupations in no way hinder that inner concern. In whatever state a pregnant woman may be—war or peace, eating or sleeping—the baby is growing, is being strengthened, and is receiving sensations in her womb without her being aware of it. Mankind likewise is "pregnant" with that *mysterion. But man undertook [the faith]: verily he was unjust to himself, and foolish* [33:72], but God does not leave him in his injustice and foolishness. If out of man's apparent burden come companionship, sympathy, and a thousand acquaintances, then consider what marvelous friendships and acquaintances will issue out of the *mysterion* to which man gives birth after death. The *mysterion* is necessary in order for man to flourish. It is like the root of a tree: although it is hidden from view, its effects are apparent on the branches. Even if one or two branches break off, when the root is strong the tree will continue to grow. If, however, the root suffers damage neither branch nor leaf will survive.

God said, "Peace be with you, O Prophet"—that is, peace be with you and with all who are of your species. If this were

---

214 In this form the hadith *(allâhu lâ yanzuru)* also occurs in Ayn al-Qudat, *Tamhidat*, 146. A variant form, "God does not look at your forms or your possessions but at your hearts and deeds," is given in *FAM* 59.

215 The line of poetry is quoted by Rumi, with slight variance, from the *Diwan* of al-Mutanabbi, p. 93.

not so, the Prophet would not have contradicted God and added, "With us *and* with God's righteous servants." If God's peace had been restricted to him, he would not have extended it to include righteous servants, meaning, "That peace you gave me is for me and all righteous servants who are of my species."

While making ablutions the Prophet said, "Prayer is not correct without these ablutions." He did not mean those specific ablutions, for if the conditions for correctness of prayer were the Prophet's own ablutions and no other, then no one's prayer would be correct. What he meant was that prayer without that type of ablution was not correct. It is like saying, "This is a dish of pomegranates." Does that mean that only these are pomegranates? No, it means that these things are of the species pomegranate.

*

A villager who had come to town as a guest of a townsman was given some halva. He ate it with relish and then said: "Townsman, I had learned to eat nothing but carrots. Now that I have tasted halva I have lost my taste for carrots. I won't be able to have halva whenever I want, and what I had no longer appeals to me. What am I to do?" When the villager tasted halva, he was inclined to the town. The townsman had captured his heart, and he had no choice but to follow in pursuit of it.

*

Some people give greetings that smell like smoke; others give greetings that smell like musk. This is understandable to someone who has a sense of smell.

*

One must test a friend in order not to be disappointed later on. This is God's way too. "Begin with yourself."[216] If the self claims to be servile, do not accept this statement without putting it to the test. Before washing, people bring water to their noses and then taste it. They are not content merely to

---

216 See note 196.

look at it because, although it may look all right, its taste and smell may have altered. This is how one tests water for purity; only after such a test does one put the water on one's face. God causes all the good and evil you have hidden in your heart to appear on your exterior; the effect of everything hidden in a tree's roots appears on the branches and leaves. *Their signs are in their faces* [48:29]. And God said, *"We will stigmatize him on the nose"* [68:16]. If everyone is not to know your innermost thoughts, what color are you going to make your face?

### FIFTY-ONE

"You will never find anything until you seek—except this beloved, whom you will not seek until you find."[217] For a human being seeking means to search for something that he has not found, to be looking for it day and night. To have found or attained something and then seek it is strange and inconceivable for man because his search is for new things that have not yet been found. This search, that is, to seek out what has been found, is God's search because God has "found" everything. Everything is within His omnipotence. The One, the Glorious says, *"Be!"* and everything *is* [6:73]. He is the Finder because He has found everything; nonetheless, He is the Seeker, inasmuch as He is known as "the Seeker, the Dominant." This is as if to say, "O man, so long as you are in this search, which is temporal and a human quality, you are far from your goal. When your own search passes away into God's search, when God's search gains dominion over your search, then you will be a seeker through God's seeking."

*

Someone said: "As to who is God's saint or who has achieved union with God we have no categorical proof—not by words, deeds, miracles, or anything else. Words may have been learned, and deeds and miracles are also performed by monks who can read the subconscious mind and who have

---

217 Quoted from Sanai, *Divan*, p. 541, line 10,214.

displayed many miraculous things through magic." And he enumerated several.

"Do you believe in anyone or not?"

"Yes, by God, I do believe in and love someone."

"Is your belief in that person based on reason and deduction, or did you just close your eyes and pick him out?"

"It is certainly not without reason!"

"Then why do you say that there is not rationale in belief? You speak in contradictions."

*

Someone said, "Every saint and great mystic claims that no one else enjoys the nearness and favor that he enjoys with God."

"Who said this? Did a saint say it, or someone other than a saint? If a saint said it, then, since he knows that every saint harbors the same belief with regard to himself, he is not singled out to enjoy such favor. If someone other than a saint said it, then that person is actually God's friend and elect, for this is a mystery God has kept secret from all the saints—but not from that person."

Then the disputer gave a parable. "A king had ten slave girls. The slave girls said, 'We want to know which of us is loved best by the king.' The king said, 'Tomorrow this ring will be in the room of the one I love best.' The next day the king ordered ten duplicates made of his ring, and one was given to each of the slave girls."

"The question still stands," said the Master, "because that was no answer. It was irrelevant to the issue. That story was related either by one of the ten slave girls or by someone other than the ten. If it was one of the ten, then she had no preference and was not loved best because she must have known that she was not the only one to receive a ring and that they all got similar ones. If the story was related by someone other than the ten slave girls, then that person was the king's favorite."

✽

Someone said, "A lover must be abject, humble, and long-suffering." And he enumerated a number of such qualities.

The Master replied, "Must he be like that only when the beloved so desires or not? If it is not according to the will of the beloved, then he is not a lover but a follower of his own will. If it is according to the will of the beloved, how can he be abject and humble when the beloved does not will him to be so? Thus, it is obvious that the lover's states can be known only insofar as how the beloved wishes him to be."

✽

Jesus said, "I am amazed how one living being can eat another." The literalists say that human beings eat the flesh of animals and that both are living beings. This is an error because flesh eaten by humans is not alive but inanimate. When it is killed, its animating spirit departs from it. Perhaps he meant it in the way a master can "devour" his disciple without why or wherefore, and he was amazed at such an exceptional thing.

✽

Someone posed the following dilemma: "Abraham said to Nimrod, 'My God can cause the dead to live and the living to die.'

"Nimrod countered, 'When I dismiss someone, it is as though I have caused him to die; and when I appoint someone to a post, it is as though I have caused him to live.'

"Then Abraham abandoned the argument and embarked on a new line of reasoning by saying, 'My God brings the sun up from the east and sends it down in the west. See if you can do the opposite.' The one seems to be at variance with the other."

God forbid that Abraham should be forced to cede to Nimrod's argument or be unable to answer. No, both are the same—just put in different ways. That is, he was saying that God brings a foetus out of the "east" of the womb and sends it down in the "west" of the grave. Abraham's line of defense was all the same. God recreates man anew every moment and sends ever new things into his mind. The first does not resemble the second, nor the second the third; but man is unaware of this and does not know himself.

*

Sultan Mahmud was given a marvelous horse,[218] an extremely fine animal with a wonderful form. On the festival day he rode it out, and all the citizens were seated on the rooftops to see it. A drunkard who was sitting inside his house had to be dragged out onto the roof. "You come too and see the horse," they said.

"I am busy by myself," he said. "I don't want to see it. I have no desire at all." But in the end he had no choice. As he teetered dead drunk at the edge of the roof, the sultan happened to be passing by. When the drunk saw the sultan on the horse, he said, "What is this horse to me? If right now a minstrel were to sing me a ditty and that horse belonged to me, I'd give it to him!" When the sultan heard this, he grew very angry and ordered the man imprisoned. After a week the man sent a message to the sultan to say: "What did I do wrong? What was my crime? Let the lord of the world say, so that his slave may know." The sultan ordered the man brought before him.

"You insolent tramp," began the sultan, "why did you say what you did? What gall you had!"

"O lord of the world," the man said, "it wasn't I who said it. At that moment a drunken wretch was standing on the roof, and it was he who spoke. He is gone now. I am not he. I am a sober, rational man." The king was so pleased that he ordered the man to be released from prison and given a robe of honor.

Whoever develops an attachment to us and is "drunk on this wine" is with us in actuality, no matter where he may go, no matter with whom he may be, and no matter with what

---

218 Literally "sea horse" *(asp-i bahri)*, a wonderfully rare type of horse that often occurs in Iranian fables and legends.

people he may associate. He mingles with other types because association with "others" is a mirror to the delicacy of one's beloved's company. Mingling with other than one's own type causes affection and friendship with one's own type. "By their opposites are things known."

*

Abu-Bakr the Righteous called sugar "congenitally" sweet. Now people prefer other fruits to sugar and claim, "We have experienced so much bitterness in order to arrive at the stage of sweetness." What do you know of the pleasure of sweetness when you have not experienced the hardship of bitterness?

## FIFTY-TWO

A question was asked concerning the interpretation of this line of poetry: "When desire reaches its end, amity turns to utter hostility."

Compared with the world of amity, the world of hostility is cramped; and people run away from the world of hostility in order to get to the world of amity. Even the world of amity is confining in comparison to the world from which amity and hostility receive their being. Amity and hostility, belief and unbelief, are causes for duality because unbelief is a repudiation, and for a thing to be repudiated there must be someone to repudiate it. Similarly, for a thing to be confessed there must be someone to make the confession. Hence, it is obvious that accord and discord are causes for duality, while the other world is beyond belief and unbelief, amity and hostility. Since amity is a cause for duality, and since a world exists where there is no duality but only pure accord, when one reaches that world one will shed amity and hostility because they do not belong there. When one attains that place, one is parted from duality. Therefore, in comparison with the world to which one has now been transported, one's former world—which was of duality, love, and amity—is low and mean. Consequently, one no longer desires and is averse to it. When Mansur's friendship with God reached its logical end, he became an enemy of himself and annihilated himself. He said, "I am the Real"—that is, I have passed away; only God remains. To say this, that only He exists, is extreme humility and servitude. It is pretentious and prideful to say, "You are the Lord, and I am a servant," for by so saying you will have affirmed your own existence, and duality necessarily follows. When you say, "He is God," there is also duality because the use of the third-person "he" is not possible unless there is a first-person "I." Therefore, since there is no existent thing other than God, only He can say, "I am God." Mansur had passed away, and so his words were God's.

In comparison with the world of concepts and sensibles, the world of mental images is broader because all concepts are born of mental images; but the world of mental images is narrow in relation to the world where mental images are given being. This much can be understood from words, but the reality of the substance is impossible to understand through verbal expression.

"Of what use then is verbal expression?" someone queried.

The usefulness of words is to cause you to seek and to excite you, but the object of your search will not be attained through words. If it were so, there would be no need for strife and self-annihilation. Words are like seeing something moving at a distance: you run toward it in order to see the thing itself, not in order to see it through its movement. Human rational speech is inwardly the same. It excites you to search for the concept, although you cannot see it in actuality.

Someone was saying: "I have studied so many branches of knowledge and mastered so many concepts; yet I still do not know which concept in man will abide forever. I have not discovered it yet."

If it could be known by means of words, there would be no need for the annihilation of individual existence or for so much suffering. You must strive to rid yourself of your own individuation before you can know that thing which will remain.

Someone says: "I have heard that there is a Kaaba, but no matter how much I look I don't see it. Let me go up on the roof and look for it." So he goes on the roof and cranes his neck. Because he doesn't see the Kaaba, he denies its existence. If one cannot see the Kaaba from where one is, it will take more effort than this to see it. In the wintertime you would give your soul for a fur coat. When summer comes you toss the fur coat off and your mind shudders at the thought. Now, you sought the fur coat for the warmth it gave when you were a "lover" of warmth. Because of some hindrance you were not able to find warmth during the winter and so you were in need of the medium of a fur coat. Yet when that hindrance no longer existed, you threw the fur coat away.

*When the heaven shall be rent in sunder* [84:1], and *when the earth shall be shaken by an earthquake* [99:1]. These verses indicate to you that you have seen the pleasure of being joined together, but soon now a day will come when you shall see the pleasure of these parts being separated and when you shall witness the expansiveness of that other world, where you will be released from the confinement of this world. For example, a man has been tied to four pegs. Having forgotten the pleasure of freedom, he thinks he enjoys it. When he is released from the pegs he realizes what torment he was in. Similarly, infants are nurtured and pampered in the cradle even though they are bound and swaddled. If an adult were to be tied down in a cradle it would be torment and imprisonment.

Some people enjoy flowers when the bud opens in full bloom; others take pleasure when the parts of the flower have all scattered and rejoined their origin. Now, some people want there to be no more friendship, love or affection, unbelief or belief so that they can rejoin their origin, for all these things are "walls" that cause constriction and duality, while the other world causes expansiveness and absolute unity.

These words are not so great. They are not so strong. How could they be great? They are just words after all. Really, they themselves are causes for weakness, but they do stimulate and excite people to seek God. The stimulation, however, is not apparent. How is a combination of a couple of letters to cause vitality and excitement? For example, one person comes to see you, and you receive him cordially and bid him welcome. He is pleased by that and it causes affection. Another person you call a couple of bad names. Those two or three words cause anger and pain. Now, what is the connection between a combination of two or three words and an increase in affection and pleasure on the one hand or stirring up anger and hostility on the other? God has made these things as secondary causes and "veils" so that not everyone's gaze falls upon His beauty and perfection—with weak veils appropriate to weak gazes. He then gives dominion to the veils as secondary causes. In actuality, bread is not a cause of life, but God has made it a cause of life and strength. After all, it is inanimate; so, from the point of view that it itself does not possess human vitality, how can it cause an increase in strength? If it did have life it would keep itself alive.

## FIFTY-THREE

A question was asked concerning the meaning of this line of poetry:

O brother, what you really are is a notion;
The rest of you is bones and sinews.[219]

Consider this meaning: "notion" is a reference to that particular notion we have expressed by the word *notion* in its widest sense, but in reality it is not a notion. If it is, it is not what people generally understand by the term. What we mean by the word *notion* is the intrinsic meaning. If anyone wants a lower interpretation for the common people, let him say, "Man is an animal possessed of rational speech." The power of rational speech is a "notion," whether implicit or explicit. Anything other than that is animal. So, it is correct to say that

---

219 This line occurs in Rumi, *Masnavi,* 2:277.

man consists of "notions" and that the rest is just bones and sinews.

Speech is like the sun. All men derive warmth and life from it. The sun is always existent and present, and everyone is always warmed by it. However, because the sun cannot always be seen, people do not know that their warmth and life come from it. When this notion is expressed verbally through some medium, be it thanks or complaint, be it good or evil, the sun comes into view. Although the sun in the sky is constantly shining, it is not visible until its rays strike a wall. Similarly, unless there be the medium of words and sound, the sun of speech cannot be seen. Although it always exists, since the sun is subtle *(latif)—and He is the gracious (latif)* [6:103]—there must be a medium of grossness for it to be seen. Someone once said that the word "God" had no apparent meaning for him and that he was left perplexed and melancholy by the word; but when people said that God did thus and so, commanded thus and so, and prohibited thus and so, the man warmed up and saw. Thus, although God's subtlety existed and "shone" on him, he could not see it until they explained it to him through the medium of commandments and prohibitions or creation and omnipotence.

There are some people who are too feeble to tolerate honey. They can eat it, however, through a medium such as rice pudding or halva until they grow strong enough to eat it without a medium. We realize then that although rational speech is a subtle sun that shines without cease, you need some gross medium in order to see the sun's rays and enjoy them. When you have grown accustomed to seeing the subtlety of the rays without a gross medium, then you will grow bold in looking at them and derive strength. In the essence of that sea of subtlety you will see amazing colors and spectacles. And why should this be strange, seeing that this power of rational speech is always within you, whether you actually speak or not? Even though you are not even thinking of speaking, we say that it is always there, as is said, "A human is an animal possessed of rational speech." This animality exists in you as long as you are alive; so it follows that the power of rational speech is also always in you. Chewing is a means to manifest animality, not a prerequisite. So also is the power of rational speech a means for talking and chattering, not a prerequisite.

Man has three states. The first is not to focus on God but to adore and serve anyone and anything—woman, man, wealth, children, stones, land. Next, when he acquires a certain knowledge and awareness, he does not serve other than God. Finally, when he progresses in this state, he falls silent: he says neither, "I do not serve God," nor, "I do serve God"—that is, he leaves both states. In their world no sound comes from such people.

Although God is neither present or absent, He is the creator of both presence and absence. He must then be other than both of these because, if He were present, then there must be no such thing as absence. But absence does exist. It is not present either, although it does exist in the presence of presence. He cannot, therefore, be qualified by presence or absence, for it would necessarily follow that an opposite proceed from an opposite in that it would be necessary in the state of absence for Him to be the creator of presence, and presence is the opposite of absence. So also in the state of absence. Opposite cannot be said to proceed from opposite, and God cannot be said to create His like because He says, "He has no like." If it were possible for like to create like, then a state would exist without there being a cause and a thing would have created itself. Both propositions are untenable.

When you have come this far, stop and apply yourself no more. Reason has no further sway: when it has reached the edge of the sea, let it halt.

All words, all knowledge, all crafts, and all professions have the taste and flavor of this speech. If it were not so, no job or profession would have any delight. The "end of the chapter" is not known, but knowing is not a prerequisite for reading. It is like the man who sought the hand of a rich lady who owned flocks of sheep, horses, and so forth. The man looks after the sheep and horses and waters the orchards.

Although he keeps himself occupied doing these things, the delight in doing them is derived from the existence of the lady. If she were no longer in the picture, he would not take delight in his chores. They would seem distasteful and dull. So also are all the world's professions, sciences, and so forth: the liveliness, pleasure, and joy come from the reflection of the mystic's delight. Were it not for his delight, were people to take no pleasure or delight in his existence, everything would seem empty.

## FIFTY-FOUR

When I first began to compose poetry, there was a strong impetus that caused me to compose. At that time it was very effective. Even now, when the impetus has flagged and is "setting," it still is effective. It is God's way to nurture things while they are "rising," when great effects and much wisdom are produced. Even in setting that nurture stands. The epithet *Lord of the east and west* [26:28] means that He nourishes both rising and setting motivations.

*

The Mu'tazilites say that man is the creator of his own actions, that man "creates" each and every action that issues from him. This cannot be so because every action that issues from man is either by means of an instrument he possesses—such as intellect, spirit, strength, or body—or without means. It is not right to say that man is the creator of his actions by means of these things because he is not in control of the totality of them. Therefore, since the instrument is not subject to him, he is not the creator of his actions by means of an instrument. He cannot be the creator of his actions without instrument either because it is impossible to imagine an action coming from him without instrument. Therefore, we realize absolutely that the creator of actions is God, not man. Every action, be it good or evil, that issues from man is done for a specific purpose; but the wisdom behind the action may not be conceivable to him. The meaning, wisdom, and benefit that man sees in an action are in proportion to his instrumentality in the creation of the action; only God knows what total benefits will result from any given action. For example, you pray with the intention of gaining reward in the next life and good repute and security in this world; yet the benefit of your prayer is not limited to that. It will yield thousands of benefits you cannot imagine. God, who keeps man to his deeds, knows those benefits.

Man is like a bow in God's omnipotent grasp, and God uses him to do many things. In reality the agent is God, not the bow. The bow is just a tool, a means; but for the sake of the stability of the world it is unaware of God's agency. Oh, what a great bow it is that knows in whose hand it lies! What am I to say of a world whose props and mainstays are heedlessness? Don't you see that when someone is waked from the "sleep of heedlessness" he is disinterested in and cold to the world? He pines away to nothingness. From infancy, when he begins to grow, man exists in heedlessness; otherwise he would never grow at all. Then, when he has reached full maturity in heedlessness, God imposes pain and strife upon him by means of determination and free will in order to wipe clean that heedlessness and make him pure. After that he can become acquainted with the other world.

Man's being is like a garbage dump or a pile of manure. If there is anything precious about this pile of manure, it is because the king's seal is upon it.

Man's being is like a sack of grain. The king calls out, "Where are you going with that sack? My cup is in it."[220] Man, being totally absorbed in the grain, is unaware of the cup. If he knew the cup was there, what interest would he have in the grain? Now, every "notion" that attracts you to the sublime

---

220 A reference to the Koranic version of the Joseph story. In order to detain his brother Benjamin in Egypt, Joseph had a cup concealed in one of the sacks of grain he had sold to his brothers. On the pretext that Benjamin had stolen the cup Joseph held him hostage to insure the return of the other brothers. See Kor. 12:70ff. and Thackston, *Tales*, p. 184.

world and makes you cold and indifferent to the lower world
is a reflection cast by that "cup." Man is inclined to the other
world. When he inclines the opposite way, to the lower world,
it is a sign that the "cup" has become hidden behind a veil.

## FIFTY-FIVE

Someone said, "Qadi Izzuddin sends his greetings and
always speaks highly of you."

May the good memory of anyone who speaks well of us
remain long in the world.

If you speak well of another, the good will return to you.
The good and praise you speak of another you speak in reality
of yourself. A parallel would be when someone plants a garden
and herb bed around his house. Every time he looks out he
sees flowers and herbs. If you accustom yourself to speak well
of others, you are always in a "paradise." When you do a good
deed for someone else you become a friend to him, and
whenever he thinks of you he will think of you as a friend—
and thinking of a friend is as restful as a flower garden. When
you speak ill of someone else, you become detestable in his
sight so that whenever he thinks of you he will imagine a
snake or a scorpion, or thorns and thistles. Now, if you can
look at the flowers in a garden day and night, why would you
wander in a briar patch or a snake pit? Love everybody so that
you may always stay among the flowers of the garden. If you
hate everybody and imagine enemies everywhere, it would be
like wandering day and night in a briar patch or snake pit.

The saints love everybody and see everything as good, not
for anyone else's sake but for their own, lest a hateful,
detestable image come into their view. Since there is no choice
in this world but to think of people, the saints have striven to
think of everybody as a friend so that hatred may not mar
their way.

So, everything you do with regard to people and every
mention you make of them, good or evil, will all return to
you. Hence God says, *"He who doth right, doth it to the
advantage of his own soul; and he who doth evil, doth it against*

*the same"* [41:46], and *"Whoever shall have wrought evil of the weight of an ant, shall behold the same"* [99:8].

*

The following question was posed: When God said, *"I am going to place a substitute on earth,"* the angels said, *"Wilt Thou place there one who will do evil therein, and shed blood? But we celebrate Thy praise, and sanctify Thee"* [2:30]. Adam had not yet come to be, so how could the angels judge that man would do evil and shed blood?

There are two aspects here: one is "received" and the other "reasoned." Here is the "received": the angels had read on the Preserved Tablet[221] that there would be a race with such characteristics. Therefore they were merely relating what they had read.

As for the "reasoned" aspect, the angels had deduced by logical reasoning that the race would be of the earth. They must necessarily then be animals, and such acts would of course proceed from animals. Although they would have the intrinsic meaning and would be possessed of the power of rational speech, nonetheless, because of their animality, they would have to wreak corruption and commit bloodshed, which are concomitants of humanity.

Other people give a different reasoning. They say that the angels, being pure intellect and unadulterated good, have no free will in anything. For instance, when you do something in a dream, you are not a free agent; and so no recrimination can be taken against you for your dream, no matter whether you speak infidelity or monotheism or whether you commit adultery. The angels are like this while awake. Humans are just the opposite: they have free will as well as desire and cupidity. They want everything for themselves and are willing to murder to get it. This is an animal characteristic. So, the angelic state is opposite to the human condition.

---

221 In Islamic cosmogony the Preserved Tablet *(al-lawh al-mahfûz)* is the tablet upon which was inscribed at the dawn of creation all that would ever come to be.

It is thus permissible to relate that the angels spoke in this fashion, although not vocally or orally. It would be like supposing that those two mutually exclusive states were to speak and tell about themselves. It is as though a poet were to say, "The pool said, 'I am full.'"[222] Now, since a pool cannot speak, what this means is that if the pool could speak, that is what it would say in such a state.

Every angel has within itself a tablet, from which, in proportion to its rank, it reads off the conditions of the world and what will come to be. When what it has read and ascertained does come to be, its belief, love, and "intoxication" for the Creator increase and it marvels at God's majesty and ability to know the unseen. The increase in love and belief and the unverbalized, unexpressed marvelling are its glorification. It is like a master builder who tells his apprentice that a building they are going to build will need so much wood, so many bricks, so much stone, and so much straw. When the building is finished and exactly that amount of material has gone into it, no more and no less, the apprentice's belief increases. The case of the angels is like this.

*

Someone asked the Master, "Although he had such greatness that God said, 'Were it not for you I would not have created the heavens,'[223] the Prophet nonetheless said, 'Would that Muhammad's Lord had not created Muhammad!'[224] How can this be?"

It will become clear by an analogy. Let me tell it so you may understand. In a village a man fell in love with a woman.

---

222 The reference (in Persian) is to an anonymous line of Arabic poetry quoted in the major Arabic dictionaries, *Sihah al-lugha* by al-Jawhari, al-Zabidi's *Taj al-arus,* and Ibn Manzur's *Lisan al-arab,* s.v. QTT. The line is: "The pool was filled and said, 'Take it easy. You have filled my bowels.' "

223 See note 92.

224 This saying attributed to the Prophet *(yâ layta rabba Muhammadin lam yakhluq Muhammadan)* has not been located in hadith collections. It is also quoted in Ayn al-Qudat, *Tamhidat,* p. 194 and 199.

The two had their houses and barns near each other and lived happily in each other's company, growing fat and thriving on each other. Their lives were inextricably entwined, like a fish and water. And this continued for years on end. Suddenly God made them rich and gave them many sheep, cattle, horses, property, money, slaves, and servants. Now they were so well-to-do and prosperous that they moved to the city, and each bought a huge, regal mansion and took up residence with great pomp and circumstance, one at one end of the city and the other at the other end. When things reached this point, they were unable to enjoy their former union, and they slowly pined away and lamented in secret, unable to stifle their inner cries. When this pining became unbearable, they were completely enveloped in the flames of separation. When this conflagration reached its limit, their cries were heard by God. Their sheep and horses began to grow fewer, and gradually they returned to their former condition. After a long time they were reunited in their old village and once again embraced in pleasure and union. When they remembered the bitterness of separation, the cry went up, "Would that Muhammad's Lord had not created Muhammad!"

As long as Muhammad's soul was incorporeal in the world of holiness and enjoyed union with God, it swam like a fish in the sea of mercy. Although in *this* world it held the station of prophecy and leadership of creation and enjoyed greatness, regality, renown, and companionship, when it returned to that former enjoyment, it said, "Would that I were not a prophet and had not come to this world, for in relation to absolute union it is all burdensome, painful, and torturing."

In relation to the merit and might of the Creator all this knowledge, striving, and servitude is like someone who bows his head, performs a service, and departs. If you bow for all the earth in service to God, it is like touching your head once to the ground, since God's merit and grace precede your existence and service. From where did He bring you into being and enable you to serve that you should pride yourself on being a servant? These acts of servitude and this knowledge are as though you make little mannikins out of wood and felt and then say in God's presence: "I like these mannikins. I made them, but giving them life is your job. If you would give them life you would quicken my deeds. If you don't, it's up to you."

*

Abraham said, "God is He who *giveth life, and killeth.*"

Nimrod answered, *"I give life, and I kill"* [2:258]. (Since God had given him dominion, he considered himself omnipotent and attributed nothing to God.) He said that he too caused life and death and that what he desired of his dominion was knowledge. Since God has bestowed upon man knowledge, cleverness, and skill, man attributes these things to himself, saying, "Through this act and deed I give life to all actions and obtain enjoyment thereby." Abraham said, "No, *He* gives life and kills."

Someone posed the following to our great master: "Abraham said to Nimrod that his God was He who brought the sun up from the east and sent it down in the west, in accordance with the Koranic verse, *Verily God bringeth the sun from the east* [2:258]. 'Now you,' Abraham continued, 'claim godhood, so do the reverse.' Hence it follows logically that Nimrod had forced Abraham to cede the first argument, and Abraham, unable to respond, had begun another line of reasoning."

As others have spoken nonsense, now you are speaking nonsense too. This is one argument put two different ways. You are mistaken and so have others been. There are many meanings here, one of which is that God forms you out of the seclusion of non-existence in your mother's womb: your "east" is your mother's womb, from which you "rise," and you go down into the "west" of the grave. This is the first argument put in another way—that is, *He giveth life, and killeth* [2:258]. If you are omnipotent, bring forth something from the "west" of the grave and put it back into the "east" of the womb. Another meaning would be to say that since the gnostic finds illumination, intoxication, rest, and repose through acts of obedience, endeavor, and splendid deeds, and since that pleasure "sets" like the sun when he abandons those acts of obedience and endeavor, then the two states of obedience and disobedience are his "east" and "west." If you are capable of giving life during the state of apparent setting, which is corruption, ungodliness, and disobedience, then now, in the state of setting, bring forth that illumination and repose that arose from obedience. This is not an act for man to do; man would never be able to do it. Only God can do such a thing, for if He wills He can make the sun rise in the west and if He wills He can make it set in the east, since *it is He who giveth life, and causeth to die* [40:68].

*

Both unbelievers and believers glorify God. God has said that whoever follows the right road, exercises righteousness and adheres to the divine law and way of the prophets and saints will have great joy, illumination, and life. He has also said that whoever does the opposite will find darkness, fear, the pits of hell and calamity. Since both believer and unbeliever practice accordingly, and since God's promise comes true, neither more nor less, then both are glorifiers of God, one in one "language" and the other in another. But what a difference between the one glorifier and the other! For example, a thief steals and is hanged for his crime. He is a "preacher" to Muslims—that is, he "says," "Whoever steals will wind up like this." Another person is rewarded by the king for his righteousness and trustworthiness. He is also a "preacher" to Muslims. The thief preaches in one "language" and the trustworthy man in another, but see what a difference there is between the two!

## FIFTY-SIX

Your mind is at ease. How is that? Because the mind is a precious thing. It is like a net, and a net must be in good repair to catch prey. If your mind is disturbed, then the net is torn and is of no use. Therefore, neither love nor enmity for anyone should be overdone because in either case the net will be torn. Moderation is necessary. Now, the love that should not be carried to excess I say applies only to other than God; with regard to the Creator, however, no extreme is conceivable. The more love, the better. When your love for someone other than God becomes excessive, you wish him constant good fortune, a manifest impossibility because all people are subject to the constantly turning wheel of fortune. Since the conditions of men are constantly in flux and you wish constant good fortune for someone, your mind becomes disturbed. When your enmity for someone becomes excessive, you wish him constant ill fortune and bad luck; yet the wheel of fortune turns on and so do his conditions change, sometimes favorable, sometimes unfavorable. Since it is not possible for it to be unfavorable all the time, your mind becomes disturbed. On the other hand, love for the Creator is inherent in the whole world and in all people—Zoroastrians, Jews, Christians—all creatures. How could anyone not love his Maker? Although such love is inherent, certain barriers keep it behind the veil. If those barriers are removed, that love will surface.

Why speak only of existent things? Non-entities also foment in expectation of coming into being. Non-entities are like four people standing before the king, each one hoping and expecting that the king will grant him a post. Each one is ashamed before the others because the fulfillment of his expectation would exclude the others. Since non-entities stand in line in expectation of God's giving them being and in hopes that each one's existence will precede the others, they are ashamed in each other's presence. Now, if non-entities are like that, how do you think existing things must be? It comes as no surprise that *there is not anything which doth not celebrate His praise* [17:44], although it is surprising that there is not any "no-thing" which doth not celebrate His praise.

Both unbelief and belief are seeking Thee,

216

Saying, "Alone is He, no partner hath He."[225]

*

The foundation of this house is heedlessness. The mainstay of this world, as well as of all bodies, is heedlessness. Even this body has grown through heedlessness. Heedlessness is unbelief; and religion, being the abandonment of unbelief, is not possible without the existence of unbelief. Therefore, a state of unbelief must exist before it can be abandoned. Since the one cannot exist without the other, then both are one thing—they are inseparable. Their creator is also one because if their creator were not one they would be separable: a different creator would have created each one of them and they would be separable. Since the Creator is one, He is alone, without partner.

*

They said, "Sayyid Burhanuddin speaks very well, but he quotes Sanai's poetry too often."

This is like saying the sun is good but it gives too much light. Is it a fault? To quote Sanai's words is to cast light on the discourse. The sun casts light on things, and one can see things in the sunlight. The purpose of the sunlight is to cast light on things. After all, this sun in the sky casts light on things that are of no use. The real sun is that which casts light on things that are of use; the sun in the sky is metaphoric and secondary to the real sun. You too, in proportion to your own partial intellect, have your heart set on the real sun and seek its light of knowledge in order to see something intangible and in order for your knowledge to increase. You have expectations of understanding and comprehending something from every master and every friend. So we realize that the sun is something other than the physical sun: it is something from which revelation of realities and truths comes. We realize too that this partial knowledge in which you take refuge and pleasure is secondary to the great knowledge of which your

---

225 From Sanai, *Hadiqat*, p. 60, line 13.

partial knowledge is but a "ray." This "ray" calls you to the original sun of great knowledge. *These are they who are called unto from a distant place* [41:44]. You try to pull that knowledge toward yourself. It says, "I won't fit there, and it will take you a long time to get here. It is impossible for me to fit there, and it is difficult for you to come here." It may be impossible to do the impossible, but it is not impossible to do the difficult. So, although it is difficult, strive to reach that great knowledge, but do not expect to contain it here, for that is impossible. Similarly, out of their love for God's wealth the rich gather money bit by bit in order to acquire the attribute of wealth through the "ray" of wealth. This "ray" of wealth says, "I am calling to you out of that great wealth. Why are you trying to pull me to where I cannot be contained? Come rather toward this wealth." In short, the principal thing is the end, and may it be praiseworthy. A praiseworthy end is like a tree whose roots are firmly established in the spiritual garden and whose branches and fruit hang over into another place. When the fruit falls, in the end it should be taken back to the garden where its roots are. In the opposite case there is glorification and shouting hallelujah in outward form, but because the roots are in this world all the fruit is carried to this world. If both are in the garden of the other world, then that is *light upon light* [24:35].

## FIFTY-SEVEN

Akmaluddin said, "I love our master and desire to see him. I don't even think of the next world, for I take such comfort in the master's image that I can do without such notions and thoughts. I find peace in his beauty, and I derive much pleasure from the essence of his form or image."

Even though he doesn't think about the next life or God, it is all inherent in this love and is thus remembered.

A beautiful dancing girl was playing the castanets for the caliph who said, "Your art is in your hands."

"No," she replied, "it is in my feet, O Caliph. There is excellence in my hands because the excellence of foot is inherent therein.[226]

Although a disciple may not think of the next life in all its details, his pleasure at seeing his master and his fear of being separated from him comprehend all those details. It is as inherent within him as it is in a person who loves and cherishes his son or brother without thinking about the filial or fraternal relationship, the hope of faithfulness, compassion, kindred affection, the outcome of the relationship, or any of the rest of the benefits one expects of relatives. All these details are as inherent in the degree of encounter and regard as air is in wood, even though the wood may be under the earth or under water.[227] Because air is vital for kindling fire, if air were not inherent in wood, fire would have no effect on it. Don't you see that when you blow on it fire comes alive? Even when wood is beneath the earth or under water, air is inherent in it. If it weren't, it wouldn't float. The words you speak are similar: although many things are concomitant to these words, such as intellect, brain, lips, mouth, palate, tongue, all parts that control the body, the elements, the temperaments, the spheres, and thousands of secondary causes on which the world depends, and so on until you reach the world of attributes and then the essence of being—although none of these is explicit in your words, they are all inherent in what you say, as has been mentioned already.

Five or six times a day man experiences involuntarily disappointment and pain. Absolutely these things do not come from him; therefore, they must come from other than him, and so he is subject to that other. That other supervises him

---

226 Cf. the story told of the grammarian al-Asma'i and a beautiful woman in Ibn Qutayba, *Uyun al-akhbar*, IV, 111.

227 The argument depends upon the ancient scientific notion of the qualities of the Four Elements (fire, water, earth, and air) and their distribution throughout all matter. Air is said to be an element of wood, and fire has an affinity to air; therefore, wood burns.

and gives him pain after a bad deed. If there were no supervisor, how could the pain be inflicted accordingly? Despite all these disappointments man's temperament does not acknowledge with certainty that it is subject to someone else's command. "God created man in his own image."[228] Your divine attribute, which is opposite to the attribute of servitude, is vicarious. Man is often knocked on the head, but he does not let go of that vicarious obstinacy and soon forgets these disappointments. But it is of no benefit to him. Until such time as he makes the vicarious his own possession, he will not escape such hard knocks.

## FIFTY-EIGHT

A mystic said, "I went into the furnace room of a bath in order to relax, for that had been a place of refuge for some of the saints. I saw that the chief stoker had an apprentice who was hard at work. The chief was telling him to do this and do that, and the apprentice was working nimbly. The stoker was pleased by the lad's quickness at obeying orders.

" 'Yes,' he said, 'be nimble. If you are always quick and mind your manners, I'll give you my post and put you in my place.'

"I had to laugh, and my worries were over, for I saw that all bosses in this world act the same with their underlings."

## FIFTY-NINE

The stargazer says, "You claim that something exists outside of the celestial spheres and this earthly orb which I can see. In my opinion there is nothing other than these. If there is, show me where it is."

The question is invalid from the very beginning because you ask to be shown where something is that has no place. Come, tell me where your objection is. It is not anywhere. It is not in your tongue, your mouth, or your breast. Search

---

228 The hadith *(khalaqa 'llâhu âdam)* is given in *FAM* 115, #346.

through all of these. Tear them apart bit by bit. You'll see that your notion of objection won't be found in any of them. Therefore, we realize that your notions have no place. Since you cannot determine the locus of your notions, how are you going to determine the locus of the creator of notions? Many thousands of notions and conditions come upon you, but they are neither in your hand nor subject to your control. If you knew where these things came from, you would be able to increase them. There is a "corridor" for all these to you, but you are unaware of where they come from, where they go and what they will do. Since you are incapable of ascertaining your own conditions, how do you expect to ascertain anything of your creator?

Someone whose sister-in-law is a whore says that God is not in heaven. You dog, how do you know He is not? Have you measured out the heavens span by span and traversed them all so that you can report that He is not there? You don't even know you have a whore in your own house! How are you going to know the heavens? Yes, you've heard of heaven and the names of the stars. And the spheres you call "something." If you knew anything of the heavens or had gone one span toward heaven, you wouldn't be saying such nonsense.

What do we mean by saying that God is not in heaven? We do not mean that He is not in heaven but that heaven cannot encompass Him. He encompasses heaven. He has an ineffable connection with heaven just as He has an ineffable connection with you. Everything is in His omnipotent hands; everything is a manifestation of Him and subject to His control. So, He is not *outside* the heavens and the universe but is not totally *inside* them either, that is, they do not encompass Him but He encompasses them totally.

Someone asked where God was before the earth, skies, and Divine Throne existed. We said that the question was invalid from the outset because God is by definition that which has no place. Now you ask where He was before! After all, everything about you is non-spacial: have you found out where these things are in yourself that you seek? If they are non-spacial, how can you imagine a place for your thoughts and states? Now, the creator of a thought is more subtle than the thought itself. For example, a builder is more subtle than a building he has built because he is capable of building, aside from that one, a hundred other buildings and things that would not resemble each other. Hence, he is more subtle and more precious than the building, but his subtlety cannot be seen except through the medium of a house or some other work that comes into being in the sensible world to display its subtle beauty.

You can see your breath in winter but not in summer. It is not that your breath ceases in summer, but since both summer and breath are subtle it does not show up, as opposed to winter. Likewise, all your attributes and substances are too subtle to be seen except through the medium of action. For example, your quality of clemency exists but cannot be seen. Only when you forgive someone does your clemency become sensible. Your wrath cannot be seen either; but when you exercise wrath against a criminal by striking him, your wrath becomes visible—and so on ad infinitum.

God is too subtle to be seen, so He created the earth and heavens in order that His omnipotence and handicraft might be seen. For this reason He says, *"Do they not look up to the heaven above them, and consider how We have raised it?"* [50:6]

٭

I am not in control of my words, and this pains me because I want to advise my friends; but the words will not be led by me. For this reason I am saddened; but, in view of the fact that my words are higher than me and that I am subject to them, I am glad because wherever words spoken by God reach they give life and have profound effects.

*Thou didst not cast, when thou didst cast; but God cast* [8:17]. An arrow that flies from God's bow will not be stopped by any shield or armor. For this reason I am glad. If all knowledge and no ignorance were in man, he would be burnt up and cease to exist. Therefore, ignorance is desirable from the point of view that continued existence depends upon it. Learning is desirable also inasmuch as it is a means to knowing the Creator. So, although they are opposites, each one helps the other. Although night is the opposite of day, it is an ally of day in that they both do the same thing. If night lasted forever, nothing would get done. If day lasted forever, people's brains would get so addled they would go crazy and malfunction. Thus, people rest asleep at night so that all the "instruments" of the body—the brain, the mind, the hands and feet, vision and hearing—can regain their strength and be expended by day. Thus, although in relation to us opposites seem opposite, in relation to the wise they all do the same thing and are not opposites at all.

Show me what evil in the world does not contain some good and what good does not contain some evil. For example, someone sets out to do murder but is waylaid by fornication so that the murder does not take place. On the one hand, fornication is evil; but on the other hand, since it prevented murder, it is good. Therefore good and evil are one thing, inextricable. Here is where we disagree with the Zoroastrians. They say that there are two gods, one the creator of good and another the creator of evil. Now show us good without evil so that we may confess there to be a god of good and a god of evil. It is impossible because good is not separate from evil: good and evil are not two different things with a clear line of demarcation between them. Two creators are therefore impossible. Do we not force you to cede that it is so?

We have said so little that a suspicion might arise within you as to whether it might not be as they say. Of course, you are not certain that it is so, but how can you be certain that it is not so? Gods says, "Miserable infidel, *do not these think they shall be raised again at the great day?* [83:4-5]. Haven't you suspected that the promises We have made might come true?" According to this, the infidels will be taken to task and asked: "Didn't you have an inkling that you would be punished? Why didn't you take precaution and seek Us?"

## SIXTY

Abu-Bakr was not given preference because of much praying, fasting, and alms-giving. He was revered because of what was in his heart.[229]

What is meant by this is that Abu-Bakr's superiority over others was not on account of his great praying and fasting but on account of the divine favor he enjoyed. And that favor was God's love.

Prayers, fasts, and alms will be brought forward on Resurrection Day and placed in the balance, but when love is brought it will not fit in the scale. So the principal thing is love. Now, when you see love in yourself, make it increase and grow more. When you see in yourself "capital," which is the urge to seek, increase it by seeking, as is said, "Blessing is in work." If you don't increase your capital, you will lose it.

You are no less than the earth which is altered by working it and turning it over with a spade so that it will yield crops, but if left alone it will turn hard. So when you see the urge to seek within yourself, get busy and don't ask what the use of this coming and going is. Just keep going: the use of a man's going to a shop is to say what he needs. God gives daily bread; but if one sits idle at home, it is tantamount to claiming one has no need, in which case one's sustenance will not come. It is amazing that a child can cry and its mother will give it milk. If the child were to wonder what the use of crying was and how it caused the mother to give it milk, it would be deprived of milk altogether. We can see now that it gets milk because of its crying.

Does anyone wonder what the use of kneeling and prostrating in prayer is or why he does it? You bow and scrape and kowtow before a prince or chieftain, and the result is that the prince has compassion on you and tosses you a crust of bread. What causes compassion in the prince is not his flesh and blood. His flesh and blood are just as much there when he

---

229 The hadith *(mâ fuddila abû bakr)* is found in al-Ghazali, *Ihya*, I, 40 *(juz' i, bâb* ii).

is dead as when he is asleep or unconscious, but at any of those times your bowing and scraping would be wasted. So we realize that the compassion in the prince is not visible. Since it is possible for us to serve something in the flesh we do not see, it must also be possible outside the flesh. If that thing which is in the flesh were not concealed, Abu-Jahl and Muhammad would be the same, with no appreciable difference between them. Externally an ear that can hear and a deaf ear look the same. They both have the same shape, but one does not hear. Hearing then is concealed in the ear and cannot be seen.

The principal thing, therefore, is divine favor. Let's say you are a prince and have two slaves. One of them works hard and has served you well on many errands while the other is lazy. Yet we see that you have more affection for the lazy one than for the active one, even though you do not let the active one's talents go to waste. Since it does happen like this, one cannot judge divine favor. The right eye and the left eye look the same outwardly; yet what service has the right eye performed that the left has not? What service has the right hand or right foot performed that the left ones have not? Nonetheless, favor has befallen the right eye. So also Friday is considered superior to the other days of the week. "God has gifts other than those ascribed to Him on the Tablet, and let them be sought on Friday."[230] Now, what service has Friday done that the other days have not? Nonetheless, favor fell to Friday and it was singled out to be ennobled. If a blind man says, "I was born blind. I am not to blame," it really does not help him to say that he is not to blame for being blind. It will not lessen his suffering.

Unbelievers sunk in infidelity suffer the pain of unbelief. When we look closely, we see that their suffering is actually the essence of divine favor. If left in peace, the unbeliever would forget the Maker, but his suffering keeps him mindful. Hell, then, is a place of worship, a mosque for unbelievers where they remember God, just as they do in prison, in time

---

230 The hadith *(inna lillâhi arzâqan)* has not been traced.

of torment, or when they have a toothache. When one has pain, the curtain of heedlessness is torn asunder; one confesses God's presence by crying out, "O Lord! O Merciful! O God!" Yet when one is well, the curtain of heedlessness again falls and one says, "Where is God? I don't see Him. Why should I look for Him?" How is it that when you were in pain you saw Him clearly enough, but now you don't see Him? Since you see Him during pain, pain is given supervision of you to keep you mindful of God. The inhabitant of hell was heedless and unmindful of God while he was at ease. Now, in hell he remembers God night and day.

God created the universe, heavens and earth, the sun and moon and planets, as well as good and evil to remember Him, serve Him and glorify Him. Since the only reason for the creation of all these things is to remember Him, and since unbelievers do not do it when they are at ease, they go to hell to do their recollection. Believers do not need pain; they are not heedless of suffering during times of ease but always have that suffering before them. Similarly, a clever child only need suffer the bastinado once in order never to forget it, while a stupid child forgets and has to undergo it time and time again. A smart horse tastes the spur once and never needs it again. It will carry a man many leagues without forgetting that one sting of the spur. A stupid horse, however, needs to be spurred every minute: it is not worthy to carry people, and so it hauls dung.

## SIXTY-ONE

Hearing something constantly repeated is as good as seeing it. For instance, your mother and father tell you that they produced you. Although you were not an eye witness to the fact, nonetheless, as it is repeated so many times, it becomes a reality to you. If you were told that they had not given you birth, you would not listen. Again, you have heard people talk so much about the existence of Baghdad and Mecca that if they were to swear they did not exist, you would not believe it. So we know that when the ear hears something constantly repeated it is as good as seeing it.

Just as constantly saying something is externally as good as seeing, it is also possible that what a certain person says is equivalent to being repeated not once but thousands of times. That is, when such a person says something once, it is as though it has been said thousands of times. And why should this seem strange? One visible king is as good as a thousand men, even though he's only one. Thousands may say to advance but nothing will happen, yet when the king says it once the army advances. If this is how it is in the external world, how much the more so in the world of spirits!

*

Although you traverse the earth, if you do not do it for God, you will have to traverse it again. *Go through the earth, and behold what hath been the end of those who accused Our prophets of imposture* [6:11], that is, God says, "That traversal of the earth was not for Me but for garlic and onions." If you did not traverse for Him, it must have been for some other purpose; and that other purpose became a veil that kept you from seeing Him.

Similarly, when you look in earnest for a particular person in the bazaar, you don't see anyone else: any others you may see you see as phantoms. When you are looking for a particular matter in a book and your eyes, ears, and concentration are filled with that matter, you turn the pages and do not see anything else. So, whenever you have one particular purpose or goal in mind rather than another, no matter where you go you are too full of that purpose to see the other.

In Umar's time there was a man who was so old that his daughter had to feed him milk and tend him like an infant. Umar said to the girl, "In this age, no child is so dutiful to its parent as you."

"You are right," the girl replied, "but there is a difference between me and my father. Although I am unstinting in my service to him, when he was tending and serving me he used to tremble lest any harm befall me. Now I serve him and pray night and day that God will let him die that I may be relieved of the burden. So I serve my father, but how am I to tremble for him as he did for me?"

"She is more understanding than I am," said Umar, meaning that he had judged externals whereas she had spoken the heart of the matter.

Understanding is he who, informed of the heart of a thing, discovers the reality of the thing. Not, God forbid, that Umar was not aware of the reality and mystery of things, but the way of the Companions was to deprecate themselves and exalt others.

*

There are few who can tolerate God's presence.[231] For most people it is better for Him to be absent. The brightness of day comes from the sun; but if anyone were to spend all day gazing into the orb of the sun, he would be useless and his eyes would be dazzled. It is better for him to occupy himself with something that could be called "absence"—that is, absence of gazing into the sun. Similarly, the mention of good food to a sick man may stimulate his appetite and induce him to get better, but it would be harmful for him to have that same food in his presence. Thus, it is obvious that "trembling" and the urge to search are necessary to seek out God. Anyone who does not have this "trembling" should serve those who do tremble. Fruit grows, not on untrembling tree trunks, but on trembling branches. Nonetheless, the trunk gives strength to the branches and secures itself by means of the fruit against harm from the axe. Since a trembling tree trunk will wind up against the axe, it is better for it not to tremble. It is the proper job of the trunk to remain stable and serve those who do tremble.

---

231 As in Bayazid Bistami's dictum: "God is aware of his friends' hearts. Among them are some who are not capable of bearing cognizance of him at all, so he employs them in pious acts" (Sulami, *Tabaqat*, p. 71).

✤

If one is named Mu'inuddin ("helper of religion"), one cannot become Aynuddin ("essence of religion") by adding the letter *m*.[232] "Adding to perfection is a detraction." The addition of an *m* is a detraction. Although six fingers are more than normal, the addition is a detraction. "One" *(ahad)* is perfection; "the Prophet" *(ahmad)* has still not reached the stage of perfection. When the letter *m* disappears from *ahmad* it becomes total perfection *(ahad)*—that is, God encompasses everything. Any addition you make to Him is a detraction. One is in all numbers[233]. Without it no number is possible.

✤

Sayyid Burhanuddin was giving a learned discourse. A fool broke in and said, "We need words without analogies."

"You who are without analogy," said the Sayyid, "come hear words without analogy."

After all, you are an analogy of yourself. You are not this thing. Your person is only a shadow of you. When someone dies, people say that he has departed. If he were this thing, where has he gone? It is obvious then that the exterior is an analogy of the interior, something from which the interior can be deduced. Everything that can be seen consists of density, just as your breath is not visible when it is warm—whereas, because of density, it can be seen when it is cold. It was incumbent on the Prophet to manifest God's power and to warn people by preaching. It was not incumbent on him to take people to the stage of preparedness to receive God's truth, because that is God's job.

---

232 A play on words involving the Arabic script. *Mu'in* is written *M'YN*, and *'ayn* ("essence") is written *'YN*; when the letter *m* is added to *'ayn* it becomes *mu'in*. Similarly, with the addition of an *m* to *ahad* ("one") it becomes *ahmad* ("most praiseworthy"), an epithet of the Prophet.

233 In medieval reckoning, "one" was not a number but the symbol of unity. The first "number" was two.

＊

God has two attributes: wrath and kindness. The prophets manifest both; believers manifest kindness, and unbelievers wrath. Those who acknowledge God see themselves in the prophets, hear their own voices in them, and perceive their own scent in them.

No one denies himself, for which reason the prophets say to their nations: "We are you, and you are we. There is no alienation between us." When someone says, "This is my hand," no one asks for proof because the hand is an inseparable part. When, however, someone says, "This is my son," proof may be required because a son is a separate part.

## SIXTY-TWO

Some have said that love necessitates servitude, but it is not so. Rather, the beloved's behest is what necessitates servitude. If the beloved wants the lover to be servile, servitude will issue from the lover. If the beloved does not want servitude, the lover will cease being servile. The abandonment of servitude does not nullify love. If the lover does not perform service, the love within him will. Love is the principal thing, and service is secondary to love.

If your sleeve moves, it comes from moving your hand. But conversely it is not necessary for the sleeve to move every time the hand does. For example, it is possible for someone with a huge cloak to roll around inside the cloak without it moving, but it is not possible for the cloak to move without the person inside moving too. Some people have taken the cloak to be the person and considered the sleeve to be the hand and the boot and trousers to be the leg. The hand and foot are one thing, and sleeves and trousers are another kind of hand and leg. People say, "So-and-So is under So-and-So's *hand*," and "So-and-So has a *hand* in many things," and "You have to *hand* it to So-and-So when he speaks." Certainly what is meant here by "hand" is not the physical hand.

The prince came and gathered us together and then left. Similarly, the bee gathers together wax with honey and then flies away. Wax and honey are conditional upon the bee's existence, but they are not conditional upon its continued existence. Our mothers and fathers are like bees in that they unite the seeker with the sought and gather together the lover and beloved. Suddenly they fly away. God makes them a means in uniting wax and honey. They fly away, leaving the wax, honey, and the gardener. They themselves do not leave the garden, for it is not a garden that can be left. One can only go from one corner of the garden to another.

We are like a beehive in which the wax and honey are the love of God. Although the bees, our mothers and fathers, are means, even they are educated by the gardener who builds the hive. God gives these bees another form. When they are laboring here, they have a garb appropriate to that labor. When they go to the other world, they change their garb because there they are put to a different task. The person, however, is the same as it was.

For instance, somebody goes to battle. He puts on battle dress, straps on his arms, and puts a helmet on his head because it is wartime. When the same person comes to a banquet, he takes those clothes off because he is engaged in something else. His person remains the same, although if you had seen him in his former garb, whenever you think of him you will imagine him in that form and in that garb, even though he may have changed his clothes a hundred times.

Somebody loses a ring in a certain spot. Although it may have been taken away, he will keep looking around that spot, as if to say, "I lost it here." Similarly a bereaved person walks around and around a grave not knowing what he is doing. He kisses the earth, as if to say, "I lost it here"—yet how could it have been left there?

God fashioned so much and manifested His omnipotence until out of divine wisdom He combined body with spirit for a day or two. If man were to sit with a body in the tomb for one instant, there would be fear of his going mad. When he escapes the net of form and the trench of shape, how could he stay there in the tomb? God made it a sign in order to frighten the heart over and over again so that a fear would come into the heart from the loneliness of the grave and dark earth—just as the people in a caravan attacked at a certain place will pile a few stones one on top of another as a sign, as if to say, "This is a dangerous place." So are graves palpable signs for a dangerous place. That fear has an effect on people, but it is not necessary that it be acted out. For example, if it is said, "So-and-So is afraid of you," without any action proceeding from him, an affection for him will certainly appear in you. If, on the other hand, you are told that So-and-So is not afraid of you at all and that you inspire no awe in him, by merely hearing this a disaffection for him will develop in you.

This "running" is an effect of fear. The whole world "runs," but each person runs appropriately to his state—for man one sort, for plants another sort, for the spirit another sort. The spirit's "running" is without paces and footprints. See how far the green grape has to "run" to reach the blackness of a mature grape. As soon as it turns sweet, it reaches that stage, but its "running" cannot be seen or felt. Yet once it reaches that stage, it is obvious that it has "run" far to get where it is. It is like someone who goes into the water unseen by somebody else. When all of a sudden he puts his head out of the water, it is obvious that he went into the water to have gotten where he is.

## SIXTY-THREE

Lovers have heartaches that cannot be cured by any medicine, not by sleeping or wandering or by eating but only by seeing the beloved. "Meeting the friend is mending the ailment." If a hypocrite associates with believers, he will immediately be influenced by them to become a believer, as God says, *"When they meet those who believe, they say, We do believe."* [2:14]. If hypocrites can be so influenced, what will the effect be on a believer? Consider how wool is turned into a figured carpet by coming into contact with an intelligent person. See how earth can be turned into a fine palace by coming into contact with an intelligent person. If association with the intelligent has such an effect on inanimate objects, think what effect there will be when one believer associates with another. Inanimate objects are elevated to such a stage through association with the partial soul and intellect. If all this is a shadow of the partial intellect, and if one can deduce a person from his shadow, then deduce what intellect and reason is necessary to produce the heavens, the sun and moon, the seven layers of earth and all that lies between. All these existing things are shadows of the Universal Intellect. Just as the shadow of the partial intellect is proportionate to the shadow of its person, the shadow of the Universal Intellect, which is all existing things, is proportionate to it.

God's saints have witnessed heavens other than these. These heavens are too lowly to enter their gaze. They have put these heavens beneath their feet and passed them by.

There are heavens in the realm of the soul
That rule the heaven of this world.[234]

Why should it be strange for one person out of all humanity to have developed the ability to place his foot on the seventh heaven? Were we not all of the same species as the earth? Nonetheless, God placed within us a power by means of which we were elevated above and given control of our species to do with as we wish.

Sometimes we raise it up, and sometimes we put it down. Sometimes we turn it into buildings, and sometimes we turn it into pots and jugs. Sometimes we lengthen it, and sometimes we shorten it. Although we were at first the very earth and the same species as it, God elevated us through that power. Now,

---

234 In a heading in Rumi's *Masnavi* (1:2035); this hemistich is attributed to "Hakîm" (Sanai), but it has not been located.

why should it be strange if God elevates one of our species, in relation to whom we are like inanimate objects? He has control and is aware of us while we are unaware of Him. When we say "unaware" here, we do not mean absolute unawareness, for an awareness of one thing implies an unawareness of something else. Although it is inanimate, the earth is aware of what God has given it. If it were unaware, how could it be receptive to water, or nurse and nurture every seed accordingly? When someone is diligent and sticks to one thing, his awareness of that task necessitates an unawareness of something else, by which we do not mean absolute heedlessness. Some people wanted to catch a cat but could not. One day the cat, preoccupied with stalking a bird, became heedless and got caught. Thus, one should not be completely preoccupied with worldly affairs. One should take them lightly and not be in bondage to them lest this one and that one suffer. The treasure should not suffer. If these worldly people suffer, that one—the saint—will transform them, but if that one suffers—God forbid!—who will transform him?

If, for example, you have many pieces of cloth of all sorts, which one will you clutch when your boat is going down? Although all are "necessary," still it is certain that of the whole bundle you will grab one precious piece, for of one pearl or one piece of ruby a thousand ornaments can be made.

One sweet fruit appears on a tree. Although that fruit was part of the whole, God selected and elevated it above the whole when He filled it with sweetness and not the rest. By that means the part was preferred over the whole; it became the choicest thing, the final purpose of the tree, as He says, *"Verily they wonder that a preacher from among themselves is come unto them"* [50:2].

*

Someone was saying, "I have a state in which there is room for neither Muhammad nor the cherubim."[235]

It is an amazing state for a servant of God in which there is no room for Muhammad! Muhammad does not have a state in which there is no room for a foul creature like you!

A jester wanted to make the king feel good, and everyone undertook to reward him because the king was in a foul mood. The king walked back and forth angrily along the edge of a brook. The jester walked back and forth on the other side opposite the king, but in no way would the king look at the jester. He just kept gazing at the water. Finally the jester gave up and said, "Your majesty, what do you see in the water you keep staring at?"

"I see a cuckold," he said.

"Your humble servant is not blind either," replied the jester.

It is strange for you to have a state in which there is no room for Muhammad when Muhammad does not have a state in which there is no room for a foul creature like you! After all, the state you have attained is because of him and through his influence. All gifts are first showered down upon him; only then are they distributed through him to others. Such is the custom. God said, "Peace be with you, O Prophet, and God's mercy. We shower you with all gifts." The Prophet added, "*And* upon God's righteous servants."

God's way was extremely terrifying and blocked by snow. Since the Prophet risked his life first to drive his horse forward in order to clear the way, whoever goes this way does so because of his guidance and favor. He first discovered the way, leaving signposts everywhere to say, "Do not go this way!" and, "Do not go that way!" and, "If you go that way, you will

---

235 The prophetic hadith *(lî ma'a 'llâh)* on which this statement is based is: "I have a time with God wherein there is room for neither cherub nor apostle-prophet" (see *FAM* 39, #100).

perish like the people of Ad and Thamud," and, "If you go this way, you will find salvation like the believers."

The whole Koran expresses this one thing: *therein are manifest signs* [3:97]. That is, we have put signposts along these routes. If anyone intends to tear down any of these posts, everyone will set upon him and say: "Why are you ruining our route? Are you trying to get us killed? Are you a highwayman?" Now realize that the leader is Muhammad. Until one reaches Muhammad one does not reach us. It is like when you want to go somewhere. First your mind guides you by telling you that it is in your best interests to go to a certain place. Next your eye takes charge; then your limbs begin to move, in that order, although neither are the limbs aware of the eye nor the eye of the mind.

Even though a man may be heedless, others are not heedless of him. If you are really serious in worldly affairs, you will be heedless of the reality of things. One must seek God's contentment, not people's, because contentment, love, and sympathy are "on loan" in people, placed there by God. If He so desires, He can withhold ease and pleasure and then—despite the existence of the means of enjoyment, food, and luxury— everything becomes trial and tribulation.

All these means are like a pen in God's omnipotent hand. The mover and scrivener is God. Until He so wishes, the pen does not move. Now you look at the pen and say, "This pen needs a hand." You see the pen, but you don't see the hand. You see the pen, and remember the hand. Now what is the relation of what you see to what you say? The saints always see the hand and say that it needs a pen too. They are so intent upon the beauty of the hand that, ignoring the pen, they say that such a hand must not be without a pen. You enjoy contemplating the pen too much to think about the hand. How can they think about the pen when they enjoy the sweetness of contemplating the hand?

Although you like barley bread too much to remember bread made of wheat, how can others think of barley bread when they have bread made of wheat?

If you have been given such enjoyment on earth that you do not desire heaven, which is the true locus of enjoyment and from which the earth derives its life, why should the inhabitants of heaven think of the earth?

Don't consider pleasure and enjoyment as coming from secondary causes. Substances are "on loan" to secondary causes. It is He who causes profit and loss since they are all from Him. Why do you cling to secondary causes?

*

"The best words are those that are few and to the point." The best words are those that are beneficial, not that are many. *Say, God is one God* [112:1]: although these words are few in form, they are preferable to the lengthy chapter *Baqara* by virtue of being to the point.[236] Noah preached for a thousand years, and forty people joined him. It is well known how long the Prophet preached, and yet so many climes believed in him and so many saints arose because of him. Therefore, muchness and littleness are not criteria; the important thing is being to the point. Some people's few words can be more to the point than other people's many words—like an oven. Just as when the fire in an oven gets too hot you can't use it or even get close to it; yet you can use a weak lamp a thousand ways. So it is obvious that the important thing is being to the point. For some people it is more beneficial to see than to hear. If they hear words, it can be detrimental.

A shaykh from India set out to see a great mystic. When he reached the door of the shaykh's cell in Tabriz, a voice came from inside the cell, saying: "Go back. It is beneficial enough for you to have come to the door. If you see the shaykh it will be detrimental to you."

A few words to the point are like a lighted lamp that kisses an unlighted lamp and goes away. That is enough. It has reached its goal.

---

236 Chapter 2 of the Koran, entitled *Baqara*, is the longest chapter with 286 verses.

A prophet is not his form. A prophet's form is his steed. A prophet is love and affection, and that is what remains forever, just as the form of Salih's camel was that of a camel. A prophet is that love and affection that are eternal.

*

Someone asked why God alone is not praised from the minaret, that is, why Muhammad is also mentioned.

After all, praising Muhammad is praising God. It is like when someone says, "May God give long life to the king and to the person who showed me the way to the king, or to the person who told me the king's name and what he was like." Praise of that person is really praise of the king.

*

This prophet says: "Give me something. I am in need. Give me your cloak or some money or your clothes." What is he to do with your cloak or money? He wants to lighten your clothing so that the warmth of the sun can reach you. *Lend unto God an acceptable loan* [73:20]. He does not want a cloak or money. He has given you many things aside from money, such as learning, ideas, knowledge, and vision. He means: "Expend on me a moment of regard and thought, contemplation and intellection. After all, you have acquired wealth by means of these tools I have given you." He wants alms from both bird and snare. If you can go naked into the sun, so much the better, for that sun will turn you not black but white. If you can't, then lighten your garments so that you can at least enjoy the sun. For some time you have grown accustomed to sourness: at least try some sweetness too.

### SIXTY-FOUR

Any knowledge that comes about through instruction and acquisition in this world is knowledge of "bodies." The knowledge that comes about after death is knowledge of "religions." *Knowing* what "I-am-God" is is the knowledge of bodies; *becoming* "I-am-God" is the knowledge of religions. To see the flame and light of a lamp is the knowledge of bodies; to

burn in the flame or light of the lamp is the knowledge of
religions. Everything that is "seeing" is the knowledge of
religions; everything that is "knowing" is the knowledge of
bodies. You say that what is actualized is seeing and sight; all
other knowledge is knowledge of mental images. For example,
an architect thinks up the image of a school building. No
matter how correct that idea may be, it is still just a mental
image. It becomes an actuality only when the school is built.
Now, there are differences between image and image. The
image of Abu-Bakr, Umar, Uthman, or Ali is superior to the
image of the Companions. There is a great difference between
one image and another. An expert architect imagines the
foundation of a house and a non-architect imagines the same
thing, but there is a great difference between the two because
the architect's image is closer to actuality. Similarly, on the
other side, in the world of reality and vision, there is an
infinite difference between one vision and another. So when
they say that there are seven hundred veils of darkness and
seven hundred veils of light, everything that constitutes the
world of mental images is a veil of darkness, and all things that
constitute the world of reality are veils of light. However, one
can make no distinction among or speculate about the veils of
darkness, which are mental images, because of their great
subtlety. Although there is also such a vast, enormous
difference in realities, one cannot fathom that difference either.

## SIXTY-FIVE

The inhabitants of hell are happier in hell than they were
in this world because in hell they are aware of God, while in
this world they were not. There is nothing sweeter than
awareness of God. The reason those in hell long for this world
is so that they may do something to be aware of the
manifestation of grace, not because this world is more pleasant
than hell. Hypocrites are put in the lowest layer of hell
because, although faith was offered to them, on account of
their strong unbelief, they did nothing. Their torment,
however, will be severe enough for them to become aware of

God. The benighted heathen were not offered faith. Because their unbelief is weak, they will become aware with less torment.

It is like a pair of breeches and a carpet that have gotten dusty: one person can give the breeches a shake and they'll come clean, but it takes four people to shake the carpet hard to get the dust out.

When the inhabitants of hell say, *"Pour upon us some water, or of those refreshments which God hath bestowed on you"* [7:50], God forbid they should desire food and drink. What they mean is, "Pour down upon us of what you have and what shines upon you."

The Koran is like a bride. Although you pull aside her veil, she will not show you her face. The reason you have no pleasure or discovery in all your study of it is that it rejects your attempt to pull off its veil. It tricks you and shows itself to you as ugly, as if to say, "I am not that beauty." It is capable of showing any face it wants. If, on the other hand, you do not tug at the veil, but you acquiesce, give water to its sown field, do it service from afar and try to do what pleases it without pulling at its veil, it will show you its face. Seek the people of God, *enter among my servants; and enter my paradise* [89:29-30].

God does not speak to just anyone, as kings in this world do not speak to every weaver. They appoint viziers and deputies through whom people can reach them. So also has God selected a certain servant to the end that whoever seeks God can find Him through that servant. All the prophets have come for the sole reason that they are the way.

## SIXTY-SIX

Sirajuddin said, "I expounded on a problem, but inside I suffered pain."

That is because of a guardian that will not let you speak. Even though you cannot see this guardian tangibly, when you feel longing, compulsion, or pain you know that there is such a thing as a guardian. For example, you go into the water. You feel the softness of the underwater flowers and plants; but when you go to the farther side you are scratched by thorns. So you know—even though you see neither one—that the farther side is where thorns grow, a place of unpleasantness and pain, whereas this side is where flowers grow, a place of comfort. This is called intuition, and it is more apparent than any tangible thing. For example, hunger, thirst, wrath, and happiness—none of these is tangible; yet they are more apparent than tangible things. If you close your eyes, you can no longer see tangibles; however, you cannot dispel hunger from yourself by any ruse. Similarly, heat and cold, sweetness and bitterness in food are not tangible, but they are more apparent than what is tangible.

Why do you have such regard for this body? What connection do you have with it? You subsist without it; you are continually without it. By night you have no care for it; by day you are occupied with other concerns. Since you are not concerned with it for a minute but have concerns elsewhere, why now do you tremble over the body? What is the basis of comparison between you and the body? "You are in a valley and I in another." This body is a great deception: it thinks it is dead. It *is* dead, too. Say, what connection do you have with the body? It is a great sleight-of-hand. When Pharaoh's magicians became one iota's worth aware, they sacrificed their bodies. They saw that they subsisted without this body and that this body had no connection with them. So also, when Abraham, Ishmael, the prophets, and saints became aware, they ceased to care for the body or whether or not it existed.

Hajjaj, having taken a hallucinogen, put his head against the door and cried out: "Don't move the door! If you do, my head will fall off." He thought his head was separated from his body and was being held up by the door. Our state is like that, and so is everybody else's. We all think we have a connection with our bodies or that we are being held up by our bodies.

## SIXTY-SEVEN

"God created Adam in His own image."[237] Everyone is seeking a locus of manifestation. There are many veiled women who uncover their faces in order to test their object of desire, as you might test a razor. A lover says to his beloved, "I have not slept. I have not eaten. I have become thus and so without you." What he means is: "You are seeking to be manifested. I am the locus of manifestation onto which you can impose the quality of being loved." Scholars and learned men are also loci of manifestation. "I was a hidden treasure and desired to be known."[238]

"He created Adam in His own image," that is, in the image of His laws. All of His laws are visible in His creatures because they are all "shadows of God," and a shadow resembles the person who casts it. If you spread your fingers, your shadow will do so too. If you bow down, your shadow will do so too. If you stretch out, your shadow will do so too. Therefore, people who are searching are looking for something to seek, something to love, for they want to be loving and humble before Him, enemies to His enemies and friends to His friends. These are all laws and attributes of God that appear in the shadow.

To sum up this section, the shadow we cast is unaware of us, but we are aware of it. However, in relation to God's knowledge, our awareness counts for no more than unawareness. Not everything in a person is contained in his shadow, only some things. Therefore, not all God's attributes, only some of them, show up in His shadow, which is we. *Ye have no knowledge given unto you, except a little* [17:85].

## SIXTY-EIGHT

Jesus was asked, "O Spirit of God, what is the most tremendous and harshest thing in this world and the next?"

---

237 See note 228.

238 See note 125.

"The wrath of God," he said.

"What can save us from it?" they asked.

"Curb your wrath and suppress your ire," he replied.

The way to do this is to oppose the self and, when it wants to complain about something, render thanks instead. Exaggerate it so much that love is generated within you, for to give false thanks is to seek love from God. Thus does our great master say that to complain of a creature is to complain of the Creator. He has also said that enmity and ire are concealed within you against you, like fire. When you see a spark jump out of this fire, put it out so that it may return to the non-existence whence it came. If you help it along with the match of a reply or word of recrimination, it will find a way to come again out of non-existence and only with difficulty will you be able to send it back. Repel your enemy with something good in order to vanquish him in two ways. Your enemy is not his flesh and bone but his evil thought. When that is repelled from you by means of much thanks, it will be repelled from him also. This occurs naturally, as the saying has it, "Man is a slave to beneficence." The second way is for him to see that what he says or does has no effect on you. When a child calls another a name and the second child calls the first child a name back, the first one is encouraged by seeing that it has had an effect. If instead the first saw no change or effect, it would lose interest. The second case is thus. When this attribute of forbearance is manifested in you, it becomes apparent that your enemy's calumny has missed its mark and that he has not seen right. He has not seen you as you are. It becomes apparent that he is the one demeaned, not you. And nothing humiliates an adversary more than for his lie to be exposed. Therefore, you give him poison by praising him with thanks because, while he is pointing out a deficiency in you, you are manifesting your perfection in being beloved to God like those who *forgive me; for God loveth the beneficent* [3:134]. A person who is beloved of God cannot be deficient. Praise your enemy so much that his friends will begin to wonder to themselves and say, "He must be hypocritical with us if this other person is in such agreement with him."

> Pluck out their beards with kindness
> however rich and powerful they may be.
> Break their necks with firmness
> however strong they be.[239]

May God grant us success in this!

## SIXTY-NINE

Between man and God there are only two veils, health and wealth; and all others arise from these two. A healthy person will say: "Where is God? I don't know where He is. I can't see Him." Yet this very same person, when troubled by pain or sickness, will begin to cry out, "O God! O God!" and will confide his intimate secrets to God. You see thereby that health was veiling that man from God, who was concealed beneath the threshold of pain. So long as a man has wealth and possessions, he can satisfy his wants and occupy himself day and night, but the moment destitution rears its head this same man's soul turns feeble and he turns to God.

> Intoxication and empty-handedness
> brought you to me:
> I am a slave to your intoxication
> and empty-handedness.[240]

God gave Pharaoh four hundred years of life, wealth, kingship, and fulfillment of every desire. They were all veils to keep him away from God's presence. He was not given a single day of deprivation or pain lest he think of God. "Occupy

---

239 The line is from Sanai, *Divan*, p. 98, line 1664.

240 Not traced.

yourself with your own pleasure and think not of Us," said God, "and pleasant dreams!"

> Solomon grew weary of your kingdom,
> but Job was never sated with affliction.[241]

## SEVENTY

They say that in man's soul there lurks an evil that is not found in animals, not because man is worse than the animals but because the bad temperament, evil self, and vileness found in man come from a hidden essence in him, which is obscured by that very ill temper, vileness, and evil. The more precious, magnificent, and noble the essence is, the greater the obfuscation. Vileness, evil, and ill temper are then the secondary causes for the obfuscation of that essence. It is not possible to remove this obfuscation except through great effort, of which there are several kinds. The mightiest endeavor is to mingle with friends who have turned their faces toward God and their backs on this world. There is no greater endeavor than to sit with pious friends, the sight of whom causes the carnal soul to melt and pass away. For this reason it is said that when a snake does not see a human being for forty years it turns into a dragon. That is, it sees no one who would cause its evil and vileness to melt. A big lock indicates that there is something valuable and costly inside. The greater the obfuscation, the better the essence—like a serpent guarding a treasure trove. Don't look at the ugliness of the serpent; look at the value of the treasure.

---

241 The line is from Rumi, *Divan*, II, line 11178.

## SEVENTY-ONE

My beloved asked by what means So-and-So is alive. The difference between the wings of birds and the "wings of aspiration" of the rational is that birds fly on their wings *in* a direction, while the rational fly on wings of aspiration *away from* all directions. Every horse has its stall, every beast of burden its stable, and every bird its nest. And God knows best.

# Works Cited and Reference Works

Abshîhî, Muhammad ibn Ahmad al-. *al-Mustatraf fî kull fann mustazraf.* Cairo: al-Matba'a al-Maymaniyya, A.H.1308/A.D.1891.

Arberry, A.J. *Aspects of Islamic Civilization as Depicted in the Original Texts.* New York: A.S. Barnes, 1954.

'Ârifî, Shams al-Dîn Ahmad al-. *Manâqib al-'ârifîn: Ariflerin Menkibeleri.* Edited by Tahsin Yazïcï. Ankara, 1964. Translated by Clément Huart. *Les saints des derviches tourneurs.* 2 volumes. Paris, 1918–22.

'Ayn al-Qudât al-Hamadhânî, 'Abdullâh ibn Muhammad al-Miyânajî. *Tamhîdât.* Edited by 'Afîf 'Usayrân. Tehran: Dânishgâh, 1341.

Bahâ' al-Dîn Muhammad. *Ma'ârif.* Edited by Badî'uzzamân Furûzânfar. 2 volumes. Tehran: Tahûrî, 1352.

Boyle, J.A., ed. *The Cambridge History of Iran.* Volume 5. Cambridge: Cambridge University Press, 1968.

Burguière, P., and R. Mantran. "Quelques vers grecs du XIIIe siècle en caractères arabes." In *Byzantion* 22 (1952): 63–80.

*FAM* = Furûzânfâr, Badî'uzzamân. *Ahâdîth al-mathnawî.* Tehran: Dânishgâh, 1334.

Farîdûn ibn Ahmad Sipahsâlâr. *Risâla-i Farîdûn ibn-i Ahmad Sipahsâlâr dar ahvâl-i Mawlânâ Jalâluddîn Mawlavî.* Edited by Sa'îd Nafîsî. Tehran: Iqbâl, 1325.

Ghazâlî, Abû-Hâmid Muhammad al-. *Ihyâ' 'ulûm al-dîn.* [Cairo]: Lajnat Nashr al-Thaqâfa al-Islâmiyya, 1356.

Hallâj, al-Husayn ibn Mansûr al-. *Dîwân al-Hallâj.* Edited by Louis Massignon. Paris: Paul Geuthner, 1955. Edited by Kâmil Mustafâ al-Shaybî. Baghdad: al-Ma'ârif, 1394/1974.

Ibn Qutayba. *'Uyûn al-akhbâr.* 4 volumes. Cairo: Dâr al-Kutub al-Misriyya., 1349/1930.

Irâqî, Fakhr al-Dîn Ibrâhîm. *Lama'ât.* In *Kulliyyât.* Edited by Sa'îd Nafîsî. Tehran: Sanâî, 1338.

Isbahânî, Abû'l-Faraj 'Alî ibn al-Husayn al-. *Kitâb al-aghânî.* Volume 19. Edited by 'Abd al-Karîm Ibrâhîm al-'Izbâwî. General Editor, Muhammad Abû'l-Fadl Ibrâhîm. Cairo: Dâr al-Ta'lîf wa'l-Nashr, 1391/1972.

Jalâl al-Dîn Muhammad Rûmî. *Kitâb-i Fîhi mâ fîhi.* Persian text edited by Badî'uzzamân Furûzânfar. Tehran: Majlis, 1330. Reprint: Tehran: Amîr Kabîr, 1362. Turkish translation by Meliha Ülker Tarïkâhya. *Fîhi Mâfîh.* Dünya Edebiyatïndan Tercümeler, Sark Islâm Klâsikleri, 28. Istanbul: Maârif, 1954. Turkish translation by Abdülbâki Gölpïnarlï. *Fîhi Mâ-Fîh.* Istanbul: Remzi Kitabevi, 1959. English translation by A.J. Arberry. *Discourses of Rumi.* New York: Samuel Weiser, 1972. French translation by Eva de Vitrary-Meyerovitch. *Le livre du dedans.* Persian Heritage Series, 25. Tehran & Paris: Edition Sinbad, 1976. German translation by Annemarie Schimmel, *Von allem und von Einen.* Munich: Diederichs, 1988.

_____. *Kulliyyât-i Shams, yâ Dîvân-i kabîr.* Edited by Badî'uzzamân Furûzânfar. 10 volumes. Tehran: Dânishgâh, 1336–46. Selections were translated into English by R. A. Nicholson in *Selected Poems from the Divan-i Shams-i Tabriz.* Cambridge: Cambridge University Press, 1898; reprinted, San Francisco: The Rainbow Bridge, 1973. English translations have also been made by A. J. Arberry, *Mystical Poems of Rumi I,* Persian Heritage Series, 3. Chicago: Chicago University Press, 1968, and *Mystical Poems of Rumi II,* Persian Heritage Series, 23. Boulder, Colorado: Westview Press, 1979. The *Divan* has been translated into Turkish by Abdülbâki Gölpïnarlï, *Divan-i kebir.* 5 volumes. Istanbul: Remzi Kitabevi, 1957–60.

_____. *Maktûbât.* Edited by Ahmed Remzi Akyürek, *Mevlânâ'nïn mektuplarï.* Istanbul: Sebat Basïmevi, 1937. Edited by Yûsuf Jamshîdîpûr and Ghulâm-Husayn Amîn. Tehran: Pâyanda, 1956. Turkish translation and annotation by Abdülbâki Gölpïnarlï. *Mevlânâ'nïn mektuplarï.* Istanbul: Inkïlâp ve Aka Kitabevleri, 1963.

_____. *Majâlis-i sab'a.* Edited by Ahmed Remzi Akyürek and translated into Turkish by M. Hulusi. *Mevlânâ'nïn Yedi Öğüdü.* Anadolu Sekçukileri Gününde Mevlevî Bitikleri, 1. Istanbul: Bozkurt Basïmevi, 1937. Edited by Abdülbâki Gölpïnarlï. *Mecâlis-i Sab'a: Yedi Meclis.* Konya: Yeni Kitap Basïmevi, 1965.

_____. *Masnavî-i ma'navî.* Edited and translated by R.A. Nicholson. 8 volumes. London: Luzac, 1925–40. A one-volume abridged translation was made by E.H. Whinfield, *Masnavi i Ma'navi: Spiritual Couplets.* London: Trübner, 1887, reprinted as *Teachings of Rúmí.* New York: E.P. Dutton, 1975. Book One was translated by J.W. Redhoûse, *The Mesnevi of Mevlana Jelalu 'd-Din, Muhammed, er-Rumi: Book the First.* London: Trübner, 1881. Book Two was translated by C.E. Wilson, *The Masnavi, Book II.* London: Probsthain, 1910. A good many short selections on various topics are given by R.A. Nicholson in his *Rumi: Poet and Mystic,* Ethical and Religious Classic of the East and West, No. 1. London: Geo. Allen & Unwin, 1950. The tales of the *Masnavî* were wrenched from their settings by Muhammad-Ali

# Bibliography

Jamalzada and published as *Bâng-i nây*. Tehran: Anjuman-i Kitâb, 1958. These have been translated into English by A.J. Arberry, *Tales from the Mathnavi*. London: Allen & Unwin, 1961, and *More Tales from the Mathnavi*. London 1963. The *Masnavî* has been translated into virtually every Islamic language from Arabic to Urdu.

——————. *Rubâ'iyyât-i Hazrat-i Mawlânâ*. Istanbul: Akhtar, 1312.

Jâmî, Nûr al-Dîn 'Abd al-Rahmân. *Nafahât al-uns min hazarât al-quds*. Edited by Mahdî Tawhîdîpûr. Tehran: Mahmûdî, 1337.

Khâqânî Shîrvânî, Afzal al-Dîn Badîl. *Dîvân*. Edited by M. Muhammadlûy-'Abbâsî. [Tabriz]: Parvîz, 1336.

Koran. Translated by George Sale. London: Warne, n.d.

Mansuroglu, Mecdut. "Celâleddîn Rûmî's türkische Verse." In *Ungarische Jahrbuch* 24 (1952): 106–115.

——————. "Mevlâna Celâleddin Rûmî'de Türkçe Beyit ve Ibareler." In *Türk Dili Arastïrmalarï Yïlligï, Belleten* (1954): 207–220.

Muhammad ibn al-Munawwar Mêhanî. *Asrâr al-tawhîd fî maqâmât al-shaykh Abî-Sa'îd*. Edited by Ahmad Bahmanyâr. Tehran: Fardîn, 1313.

Munawî, 'Abd al-Ra'ûf al-. *al-Ithâfât al-saniyya bi'l-ahâdîth al-qudsiyya*. Edited by Muhammad 'Afîf al-Zu'bî. Beirut: Mu'assasat al-Risâla, 1974.

——————. *Kunûz al-haqâ'iq fî hadîth khayr al-khalâ'iq*. On margin on Suyûtî, *al-Jâmi' al-saghîr*. Lyallpur: al-Maktaba al-Islâmiyya, 1394.

Mutanabbî, Abû'l-Tayyib al-. *Dîwân Abî'l-Tayyib al-Mutanabbî*. Edited by 'Abd al-Wahhâb 'Azzâm. Cairo: Lajnat al-Ta'lîf, 1363/1944.

Önder, Mehmet, et al. *Mevlana Bibliyografyasï*. Ankara: Is Bankasï, 1973.

Qushayrî, Abû'l-Qâsim 'Abd al-Karîm al-. *al-Risâla al-Qushayriyya*. Edited by 'Abd al-Halîm Mahmûd and Mahmûd Ibn al-Sharîf. Cairo: Dâr al-Ta'lîf, 1385/1966.

Râzî, Najm al-Dîn al-. *Manârat al-sâ'irîn*. MS in Malek Library, Tehran.

Rûmî. See Jalâl al-Dîn Muhammad Rûmî.

Sahlajî, al-. *Risâlat al-nûr min kalimât Abî-Tayfûr*. In 'Abd al-Rahmân al-Badawî. *Shatahât al-sûfiyya*. Cairo: Maktabat al-Nahda al-Misriyya, 1949.

Sajjâdî, Sayyid Ja'far. *Farhang-i lughât u istilâhât u ta'bîrât-i 'irfânî*. Tehran: Tahûrî, 1354.

Sanâ'î al-Ghaznawî, Abû'l-Majd Majdûd al-. *Dîvân-i Hakîm Sanâ'î*. Edited by Mazâhir Musaffâ. Tehran: Amîr Kabîr, 1336.

249

_____. *Hadîqat al-haqîqat wa sharî'at al-tarîqat.* Edited by Mudarris Razavî. Tehran: Sipihr, n.d.

_____. *Sayr al-'ibâd ilâ 'l-ma'âd.* Edited by Husayn Kûhî-Kirmânî. Tehran: Âftâb, 1316.

Sarrâj al-Tûsû, Abû-Nasr 'Abdullâh al-. *Kitâb al-luma' fî'l-tasawwuf.* Edited by R.A. Nicholson. Leiden: E.J. Brill, 1914.

Schimmel, Annemarie. *The Triumphal Sun: A Study of the Works of Jalaloddin Rumi.* Persian Studies Series, 8. London: Fine Books, 1978.

Sulamî, Abû 'Abd al-Rahmân al-. *Tabaqât al-sûfiyya.* Edited by Nûr al-Dîn Shurayba. Cairo: al-Khânajî, 1389/1969.

Sultân Valad, Bahâ' al-Dîn Ahmad. *Valadnâma: Masnavî-i Valad.* Edited by Jalâl Humâ'î. Tehran: Iqbâl, 1315.

Suyûtî, Jalâl al-Dîn 'Abd al-Rahmân al-. *al-Jâmi' al-saghîr fî ahâdîth al-bashîr wa'l-nadhîr.* Lyallpur: al-Maktaba al-Islâmiyya, 1394.

Thackston, W.M. *The Tales of the Prophets of al-Kisa'i.* Boston: Twayne, 1978.

## Chapters and Corresponding Manuscript Pages:

# Glossary of Persons and Terms

Abbas ibn Abd al-Muttalib, uncle of the Prophet Muhammad taken prisoner at the battle of Badr (624). He later had cordial relations with his nephew and was the progenitor of the House of Abbas, which ruled as the Baghdad caliphs from 750 until 1258.

Abu Bakr, one of the first to believe in the Prophet Muhammad, later his father-in-law and first successor to the Prophet as leader of the Muslim community (632–34). He was an exemplar of piety and righteousness to later generations of Muslims.

Abu-Hanifa (d. 767), one of the great jurisconsults of early Islam, eponymous founder of the Hanafite school of legal interpretation, which was to become one of the four recognized schools in Sunni Islam.

Abu-Jahl, one of the Prophet's bitterest early adversaries. In later writings he is often contrasted with Muhammad in the adversary/prophet relationship, as Nimrod/Abraham and Pharaoh/Moses.

Abu-Mansur of Herat, Qadi Abu-Ahmad Mansur ibn Abu-Mansur Muhammad Azdi of Herat (d. 1048), a well-known poet of Arabic.

Ad, the South Arabian tribe to whom the prophet Hud was sent. Because of their wickedness and obduracy in the face of Hud's calling they were destroyed by the Barren Wind.

Akmaluddin, a physician and disciple of Rumi's who attended him in his final illness.

*alast*, the "day of *alast*" is the "day" in pre-eternity when God marshalled forth all the as-yet uncreated souls of mankind and asked them, "Am I not *(a-lastu)* your Lord?" And they answered, "Yea: we do bear

251

witness" (Koran 7:172). In accordance with this "covenant" all human souls are bound to obey God as Lord and will be held accountable at Resurrection for their disobedience.

Ali ibn Abi-Talib, cousin and son-in-law of the Prophet, the fourth caliph of Islam (656–61) and first Imam of the Shia. Ali is the classic exemplar of the melding of manly virtue and spirituality.

Amin, Viceroy = Aminuddin Mikail, who held the post of viceroy in Konya from 1258 until 1277.

*'ârif*, one who knows by cognitive, intuitive knowledge. *'Ârif*, which is often used as synonym for mystic, contrasts with *'âlim*, one who knows by learning.

Atabeg = Majduddin Atabeg, son-in-law of Mu'inuddin Parvana (q.v.) and a disciple of Rumi.

Baha'uddin Muhammad ibn al-Husayn, Mawlana (ca. 1150–1230), known as Baha'uddin Valad and as Sultan al-Ulama ("Sultan of the Learned"), Rumi's father, a noted master mystic of Balkh who migrated to eastern Anatolia with his family around 1220.

Baha'uddin Ahmad, known as Sultan Valad 1226–1312), Rumi's son and successor. It was he who organized the Mevlevi Order of Dervishes.

Bayazid of Bistam (d. 874), an early Sufi whose later legendary renown as an exponent of the God-intoxicated type of mystic almost completely eclipsed the historical personality. He is known for his theopathic utterances and strange locutions.

Burhanuddin Muhaqqiq, Sayyid (d. 1210), known as Sayyid Sirrdan, a disciple of Rumi's father Baha'uddin Valad (q.v.) and Rumi's own teacher and initiator into mysticism.

*dânaq*, Arabized form of the Persian *dâng*, a small coin, one sixth of a *dirhem*.

*faqih,* a jurisconsult, specialist in Islamic jurisprudence.

Farhad, legendary lover of Princess Shirin, who set him the Herculean labor of carving a mountain for her. As the task was completed, a false report of Shirin's death was brought to Farhad, who at once died of grief. The best known versifications of the tale of Farhad and Shirin in Persian are by Nizami of Ganja (d. 1209) and Amir Khusraw of Delhi (d. 1325).

Hallaj, Husayn ibn Mansur, the famed Muslim mystic-martyr put to death in Baghdad in 922. According to Sufi interpretation Hallaj was executed for having "divulged the secret"—that is, for having uttered his famous theopathic saying, *ana 'l-haqq,* "I am Reality," or, "I am God," indicating his total loss of ego-consciousness and the complete absorption of his individuated existence into the collective All of the godhead.

Haman, the evil minister of Ahasuerus in the Book of Esther whose name was transposed in Islamic legend to the wicked vizier of Pharaoh of Egypt.

Hasan, eldest son of Ali ibn Abi-Talib and grandson of the Prophet.

Husamuddin Arzanjani, not traced.

Husayn, second son of Ali ibn Abi-Talib and grandson of the Prophet.

Iblis, the Islamic proper name of Satan. According to general interpretation, Iblis was not originally an angel, in which case he would have been devoid of free will, but was one of the djinn who had been raised to heaven because of his extraordinary devotion. His fall was caused by his refusal to bow down before the newly-created Adam as God commanded. Unable to recognize the spark of divinity that had been breathed into Adam by God, Iblis professed an absolute—though misdirected—monotheism, and in that sense he is seen as a sympathetic character.

Ibn Chavush = Najmuddin ibn Khurram Chavush, a disciple of Rumi.

Ibrahim, Shaykh Qutbuddin, a disciple of Shamsuddin of Tabriz.

Ibrahim ibn Adham (d. ca. 790), an early Khurasani mystic. Legend has made of him a prince of Balkh, who renounced royal pretension in favor of the mendicant life and the practice of asceticism.

Israfel, the archangel whose trumpet blast will initiate Doomsday.

Izzuddin Razi, Qadi Muhammad (killed in 1256 or 1258), vizier who built a mosque for Rumi in Konya.

Jalal of Tabriz, not traced, apparently a disciple of Rumi.

Jamshed, mythical good Persian king equivalent in the Iranian tradition to Solomon. Jamshed is contrasted with the *dev*, or demon, because, like Solomon, he commanded the djinn as well as men.

Jesus son of Mary, known in Arabic as Spirit of God. Jesus is the ascetic par excellence who totally "abstracted" himself from this world while still in it.

Joseph son of Jacob, of Egypt. In Islamic legend, especially in mystical interpretation, Joseph is the human manifestation of divine beauty par excellence.

Junayd, Abu'l-Qasim Muhammad (d. 910), "dean" of the Sufis of Baghdad and leader of the moderate school of Sufism. He is often contrasted with the ecstatics Bayazid and Hallaj (q.v.), although he can never have met Bayazid as in the story Rumi tells in section 39.

Khidr, the strange esoteric prophet-saint who guided Moses on a quest for knowledge (see Koran 18:60ff.). One of the immortals along with Elijah (with whom he shares a number of attributes and from whose legendary persona he may ultimately derive), Khidr roams the earth invisibly and appears from time to time as a deus ex machina.

Khwajagi, a disciple of Baha'uddin Valad's who accompanied him in his emigration from Balkh.

Khwarazmshah. Ala'uddin Muhammad Khwarazmshah ruled Khwarazm from 1200 until 1220 and laid siege to Samarkand in 1207. His successor, Jalaluddin Khwarazmshah (r. 1220–31), spent his reign in heroic but futile attempts to halt the Mongol onslaught into the heartlands of Islam.

Layla, legendary beloved of Majnun (q.v.).

Mahmud of Ghazna (r. 998–1030), sultan of the far-flung Ghaznavid empire. Sultan Mahmud is known for his forays against the infidels in India and is the subject of many anecdotes, mystical and otherwise.

Majnun, Qays of the Bani Amir tribe, who fell passionately in love with Layla at an early age. Because of tribal rivalry they were prevented from marrying, and Qays went mad (*majnun*, hence his epithet) and wandered in the desert, where he sang exquisite love lyrics to his mental image of Layla. Majnun and Layla are the lover and beloved par excellence in Persian poetry; their tale has often been versified, notably by Nizami of Ganja (d. 1209) and Amir Khusraw of Delhi (d. 1325).

Mawlana (Arabic, "our lord"), a title of respect given to Sufi masters. In the text when used without clear reference to a specific person it refers to Rumi.

Mazdean, Zoroastrian.

Mir-i-Akdishan. The *akdish*es seem to have been an administrative or military class in Anatolia, and the *mir-i-akdishan* would have been the chief *akdish*.

Mutanabbi (d. 965), Arabic poet whose poetry is extremely highly regarded. Rumi is said to have been a serious student of his works in his youth.

Mu'tazilite, one who upheld the doctrines of human free will and divine justice against predestinarianism.

Nimrod, the Biblical tyrannical king, adversary to Abraham.

Parvana, Prince Mu'inuddin Sulayman ibn Muhazzibuddin Ali Daylami, powerful vizier of the Seljuqs of Rum executed by the Ilkhanid ruler Abaqa Khan in 1277. He was an admirer of Rumi but perhaps more closely affiliated with Sadruddin of Konya (q.v.).

Paysokhta, Sharif, not traced.

Pharaoh, adversary to Moses. Rumi stresses that although Pharaoh may have enjoyed divine favor cryptically, outwardly he was so deluged by God with worldly success that he was prevented from ever thinking of the hereafter and imagined himself to be God.

*pûl*, a copper coin, the 120th part of a *dirhem*.

Quraysh, tribe of Mecca to which the Prophet Muhammad belonged.

*rak'a*, one cycle of Muslim ritual prayer, consisting of standing, bowing, kneeling and prostrating, along with recitation from the Koran. Each of the five appointed daily prayers consists of from two to five *rak'a*s; more is supererogatory.

Sadru'l-Islam, probably Abu'l-Yusr Muhammad ibn Husayn of Pazda (1030-1100), a great scholar and authority on Hanafite jurisprudence.

Sadruddin Muhammad ibn Ishaq of Konya, Shaykh (d. 1274), a leading exponent of the theosophical thought of Ibn Arabi of Murcia, and a highly influential shaykh in Konya. Although Rumi did not care for Ibn-Arabiesque speculation and Sadruddin did not always approve of Rumi's conduct, they appear to have had rather cordial relations.

Salahuddin Faridun Zarkub (the goldsmith), Shaykh, for ten years after the disappearance of Shamsuddin of Tabriz (q.v.) until his death in 1259, he was the object of Rumi's affection and admiration.

*salawât*, invocations of blessing on the Prophet Muhammad.

Salih, prophet to the South Arabian tribe of Thamud. His miracle was to produce a huge camel from a rock. When the tribesmen slaughtered the camel against Salih's order, Thamud was destroyed.

*samâ'*, a mystical musical session. The *samâ'* of the Mevlevi Order includes the whirling dance inspired by Rumi. The *samâ'* was used to induce ecstasy and as such was highly disapproved by many Sufi masters.

Sana'i, Abu'l-Majd Majdud (d. 1131), Persian mystic and poet. His long didactic spiritual poem, *Hadiqat al-haqiqat*, is thought to have inspired Rumi to compose his *Masnavi-i ma'navi*.

Sarrazi, Shaykh Muhammad, an ascetic of Ghazna mentioned in Baha'uddin Valad's *Ma'arif* and in Rumi's *Masnavi*. There is nothing else known about him.

Sayf of Bukhara, not traced.

Sayfuddin Farrukh, not traced, apparently a Sufi shaykh.

Shaddad ibn Ad, a legendary South Arabian figure renowned for his tyranny and cruelty.

Shafi'ite, an adherent to the Shafi'ite school of jurisprudence, one of the four recognized schools of Sunni Islam (Shafi'ite, Hanafite, Malikite, and Hanbalite). Although the four schools are in general agreement on most matters of legal interpretation, they differ on particulars such as whether a vow is equivalent to an oath.

Shamsuddin of Tabriz, Mawlana, the enigmatic wandering dervish in whom Rumi's personality was completely submerged. Rumi first met Shams in 1244, and, except for a brief interval when Shams wandered away, the two were inseparable until Shams's final disappearance in 1248. It was Shamsuddin who moved Rumi to compose poetry, and Rumi's collected poems are composed in his name, *Divan-i Shams-i Tabriz* (The Divan of the Sun [or, of Shamsuddin] of Tabriz).

Shaykh-i-Mahalla, according to a marginal note in manuscript H, this shaykh is identified as Fakhr of Akhlat.

Sibawayh (d. ca. 793), the grammarian par excellence of Arabic.

Sirajuddin, probably Sirajuddin Masnavikhwan, a disciple of Rumi.

Sunni, by this term Rumi does not mean Sunni in the modern sense as opposed to Shiite: he means an adherent to the *ahl al-sunna wa'l-jamâ'a,* those for whom the revelation of the Koran and precedent of the Prophet *(sunna)* are ultimate authority. "Sunni" here is opposed to "philosopher."

*tahiyyât,* salutation, a form of blessing on the Prophet.

Tajuddin Quba'i, not traced.

*tayyibât,* invocations of blessing upon the Prophet.

Thamud, the South Arabian tribe to whom Salih (q.v.) was sent as prophet.

Turut, a village near Konya.

Umar ibn al-Khattab, second caliph of Islam (634–44) renowned for his sternness, valor, and piety.

Uthman ibn Affan, third caliph of Islam (644–56).

Viceroy = Aminuddin Mikail (q.v.).

*yarghu*, a Turco-Mongolian loan-word meaning law, code, trial, judgment.

Yazden, the Mazdean (Zoroastrian) name for God, equivalent to Ahura-Mazda, the deity, or principle of light and good in Zoroastrianism, as opposed to Ahriman, the principle of darkness and evil.

Yutash Beglärbegi, Shamsuddin (d. 1259), a high-ranking official in the service of the Rum Seljuqs.

Zaccharias, father of John the Baptist and guardian of Mary the mother of Jesus during her period of service in the Temple. According to Islamic legend, Zaccharias, like Abraham, was given a son at a very advanced age.

Zamakhshari (d. 1144), author of the *Kashshaf*, a well-known commentary on the Koran mainly concerned with grammatical exactness and philology.

# CLASSIC SUFI LITERATURE
*available from Shambhala Threshold Books*


RUMI:

*Open Secret, Versions of Rumi*
Translated by John Moyne, Coleman Barks
*Unseen Rain, Quatrains*
Translated by John Moyne, Coleman Barks
*The Rumi Collection*
Edited by Kabir Helminski
*Feeling The Shoulder of the Lion, Poetry & Teaching Stories*
Translated by Coleman Barks
*Rumi Daylight, A Daybook of Spiritual Guidance*
Translated by Camille & Kabir Helminski
*Love is a Stranger, Selected Lyric Poetry*
Translated by Kabir Edmund Helminski


SUFI POETRY:

*The Drop that Became The Sea*, Yunus Emre
Translated by Kabir Helminski, Refik Algan


BOOKS ON SUFISM:

*Forty Days*
Michaela M. Özelsel
*Awakened Dreams, Raji's Journeys with the Mirror Dede*
Ahmet Hilmi, translated by Algan & C. Helminski


*For a complete list, send for our catalogue:*
SHAMBHALA PUBLICATIONS
P.O. Box 308
Boston, MA 02117-0308